A Forgotten Holocaust

Carlos J. Sánchez Sánchez, M.D.

About the Artist

Originally from Norway, Anja Hovland is an internationally known artist who presently lives and works in Bonita, California, where she continues to exhibit her personal work. Anja Hovland has her own studio and accepts commission assignments.

Cover by Anja Hovland

Library of Congress Cataloging-in-Publication Data

Sánchez Sánchez, Carlos J.
The Soul of the Condor
A Forgotten Holocaust
Sánchez Sánchez—1st ed.
p.   cm.
ISBN 0-9652499-0-5
Library of Congress Catalog Number
96-092287

Printed in the United States of America

To the Incas of the great past, to the Indians in bondage during the European conquest and colonization, and to the present-day Native Americans and mestizos who are more in chains than any other race has ever been.

May the forces of history break these oppressive links and may new generations be strong and dignified, their hearts and souls hardened by their past, rising to the glory of good men as effortlessly as a condor's flight.

To Dr. John H. Rowe

May this book help us
To help the people
you know so much
about Dr. Sancha
6/30/99

Contents

Preface

To all my North, Central, and South American brothers—criollos, Indians, mestizos, black and white—to my mother country, Peru, and to my beloved adoptive country, the United States, I offer apologies if in any way or manner I have offended any person, group of persons, or institution, including Brigham Young University, St. Louis University School of Medicine, and the U.S. Navy, with whom in my long journey I have had the privilege to be in contact.

My writing is not so much an abuse of the democratic system and freedom of expression as it is a desire to say what has been repressed and stored throughout my life. My intent is to account how an innocent mestizo boy of humble beginnings got so far as to arrogantly put on paper the thoughts that molded an aging romantic of the past with the unique perception of capturing the vicissitudes of life in others.

I have used the condor analogy mainly to get across the idea that sometimes things are seen more clearly if they are viewed from above. After having experienced years of travels and assimilation into different cultures on a permanent rather than transient basis, I hope my observations are balanced and my conclusions are fair. Unfortunately we are human, and all our endeavors are shaped by what we were to begin with, what we went through, and, eventually, by our spiritual makeup. There is no question that we are a product of the events that mold our lives, the past, the present, and the future. A person aware of history cannot evade the crushing and continuous movements of the tectonic forces of the ancient past that in themselves create a new world.

In exposing my life, I intend to describe my inner self, my inner thoughts, and my turmoil, risking the embarrassment of opening my soul to either the pity or anger of my readers. Nevertheless, the message I want to convey is that we are one people and one planet, and we must try to arrange our future according to the lessons of the past and try to mend the wrongs of one culture or one nation against others. It is not too late; it will never be too late.

Introduction

Why call this book *A Forgotten Holocaust*, a word that denotes widespread annihilation of a people? Other persecuted groups, through continuous exposure, have been able to conquer and overcome their history of cruelty and become so strong as to never have to witness again such a devastating occurrence. Unfortunately, the Indians of the Americas have not arrived at this stage of sophisticated exposition of their own holocaust; they are still in a somber state trying to come to grips with being united and becoming true brothers in order to overcome their past and present bondage and to create a new generation able to confront their present state of affairs and ready to fight injustice, wherever, whenever, and for whomever. For holocaust is everywhere and such practices should be divulged and corrected in every possible way now that we have such an advanced information highway.

Why is it that one feels sad for the Indians of the Andes, or for that matter for all the original inhabitants of the continent? It is not their poverty; it is not their lack of possessions. It has something to do with their spirit, their soul. It seems as if a great war was lost forever, as though their vanquished spirit has never been able to recover from being conquered and subjugated by the Europeans so long ago. Even I, as one of them, feel that faraway defeatism. As I say in this book, no matter how rich, happy, or on top of the world I am, I will always have that longing to return again to the depths of desperation, to the valleys of suffering, even a desire to go down the tortuous, dusty, stony pathways of the past so as not to forget how treacherous was the climb to the top.

When one travels to the untouched regions and sees indigenous Indians in their original costumes, chewing their coca leaves and drinking their hard alcohol, one is seeing a culture that has lost part of its soul. Their faces portray what has happened to them, and there is heaviness in the uplifting of their spirit. One senses that nobody can remove the burden of their past. It is as imprinted in their spirits as when a meteor fell on this world thousands of years ago creating a huge crater—the wound it left remains. People and races of other lands have suffered, have been enslaved, and even now are still enduring the whip of human cruelty. Yet their outlook on life is more optimistic than that of the Indians of the Americas. Africa too was subjugated by the Europeans, but Africans are struggling to get their land and their dignity back. In the process, they have played their drums as loudly as the lions can roar. They have danced and still dance as frenziedly as if they were in a trance. Even the black faces and shining eyes of the dying children of the war-torn places of Africa still portray that hope of the last struggle for survival of dignity.

Thus, as one travels the world, one sees people who somehow have conquered their aberrant history. They have overcome the sad past, and their souls are bathed by the sun rays of optimism.

It is the chains of psychological harm that are the hardest to break, the toughest to get rid of. Sometimes as one walks alone in the cold of the high Andes, where every mountain, every stone, seems a mute and culpable witness to the horrible past, one's soul becomes lonely as if feeling the soft steps of the Indian followed by the arrogant, crushing noise of the hooves of the powerful Arabian horses that once carried the conquistadors who managed to crush the essence of these Inca people. In the obscured faraway distance, one can see only the eternal, huge, white peaks of the Andes: The horizon disappears and one imagines one's journey so full of empty, cumbrous mountains that no men will ever touch them and only a condor can fly to them. That desolate feeling is the entwining of the overpowering nature of the land and the stubborn soul of the native Andean people. The Inca huayno music played on the soft quena flute will play the songs of sadness that will only break one's heart and flatten one's spirit, where not even the singing of a bird will bring happiness to the soul in these unending mountains of hopelessness.

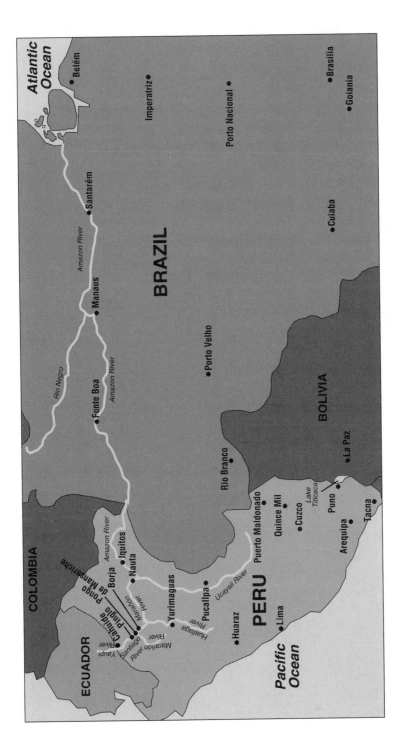

CHAPTER ONE

The Solitude of Nothingness

As the old Inca man who comes down from the high, hidden mountains of Machu Picchu felt, I feel that through the years I have been meditating in my subconscious mind. In my youth I was busy learning the ways of the wise and getting ahead, in my middle years I lived the life of the working man and of the world, and in my older years I long to become a man of wisdom.

What an experience life is. Whoever one is, there is always a sadness in spirit, always a sense of déjà vu when we collide with our past. We are a link in the chain of the millennia connected to the unimaginable beginning of our cosmos. Scientists think of chromosomal continuity in terms of chemical chains of DNA—alas, known only to science. Yet the DNA of our past has not been discovered by the mind of the mighty genius, but rather experienced by the meager intelligence of the ordinary man. As faith may have it, some are given the gift of limited recall of the past (their good fortune), but I, as others, have been given the curse of remembering every plight of inhumanity from its inception. I subtitle this book *A Forgotten Holocaust* because too few people tell, write, or make movies about the injustices suffered by the original people of this old, newly discovered continent. It is possible that long before Columbus appeared on our sun-strewn shores, the natives of the Americas suffered greatly. Of these occurrences I have faint spiritual recollection, but I feel that, as human as we are, there was a profound sense of intrinsic sadness in the souls of my ancestral people.

Chronicles such as *La Crónica del Perú* by Pedro Cieza de León (written around 1550, almost twenty-three years after Francisco Pizarro discovered the empire of the Incas) describe the beginning of the conquest, and the atrocities that were found to have been committed by the original people themselves. But these were of their own free will, and were not imposed on them by the foreign invaders. Although it may have been harsh, this was their way of life. Yet the conquerors took this as an excuse to decimate these people through slavery for pecuniary, moral, and religious reasons.

Perhaps with the pounding of the conqueror's whip, our existential DNA became distorted and imprinted in our souls, a spiritual melancholy that we all carry as if it were our own kind of deformity.

I feel as if this humble book were handwritten by the spirits of my past, as if all my ancestors were pulling, beating, and tormenting me to do something when I already have all the happiness that a terrestrial New World being can attain. Through the telling of my life story, I will try to convey what a torture it is to live with the knowledge that past and present injustices are the mark of the Indian descendants of this continent.

Five hundred years have elapsed, and there is a dying, indigenous culture that has not disappeared. Unlike Atlantis, which vanished without a trace, our ancient culture is still on display; the world can see its decay and forget its greatness. We conjecture that the man of Atlantis was a being of superior culture, but about the natives of the American continent, we assume the opposite. Even what remains of their civilization is assumed by some to be extraterrestrial (like the giant desert Nazca drawings that look like huge outer space landing strips).

As time is forever, maybe these past centuries represent a mere second of our humanity, and perhaps with the coming of the ages the American natives will become known as true wise men, or maybe their descendants are already, since they have endured the painful past.

Somewhere in the depths of my innermost recollection I remember the cloudy mist swirling around the high mountains and peaks with an undisturbed white mass of perpetual ice that carries the prints of many eyes that have gazed upon them from the beginning of time. As the ancient Incas journeyed the vast valleys, they already felt the solitude of nothingness, an irresistible desire in all creatures to fight the disdain of nature. I feel I have walked on the road of infinity, awed by the cascading sounds of the icy river flowing over the same stones that were once stepped on and disturbed by the feet of my ancestors.

Years and events have passed since my childhood. Now I lay moribund, injured in an accident. I am hastily pulled on a stretcher into the operating room, where I have been on many occasions before as a healer. But this time I come as a patient, listening to the crying of all who are close to me. My soul and being disengages from my body, free at last, but still hovering over my remains as gently as a mourning mother reminiscing about who I am or was. It is in this shadow world that I begin to see the child who is me breathe the thin, cold air of the Andes for the first time.

In his eyes there is uncertainty, already trying to overcome the past dominated by the strongest, perhaps not always magnanimous, but at times beastly. There are tears in the eyes of this dark little child's face, who already feels the hardness of his soul. Alas, he looks at the cumbrous mountains and feels the anguish of his existence. As he grows, he walks the tortuous path by the stream, throwing stones into the cold, musical river, and he keeps climbing the high hills of life.

As my unconscious body feels and hears the frantic doctor passing the endotracheal tube, my soul begins to reminisce about this child's past and heritage.

His parents are the continuation of what it was, one bearing more scars of the Indian heritage and the other possessing more Old World blood. A mestizo comes into the world, he is big, and he cries as if he wants to cause an avalanche of the mountains of the past. From the beginning this creature is the product of unpretentious love, just pure instinct of recreation. He is already destined to suffer the imprint of the unconventional. "Condor" will be his name and he will fly the treacherous mountains, and with his solemn face he will transcend the worlds of many people and glide with his big wings for hours, days, and years, all the time looking down and thinking, "Why do I fly so high and far away? What if I get lost in a world unknown to my ancestors?" But he soars to unfamiliar places and learns the ways of his own kind and becomes knowledgeable but timid of the past. He wants to erase the scars of what happened and envision a brighter future, but he is no god, he can only hope that he will be able to fix himself and become a wise man.

Millennia will pass, and all humans will become wiser; of that event humanity is certain, because it is coded into our chromosomes. It is just that some are not patient with the ways of nature and of the infinity of time. What foresight this Condor has! But what can he do? He has learned and experienced too much too fast. It is cumbersome to fly back where he came from; even his seeds have already forgotten the mysteries of his ancestry. He looks up and down, and the eagle eyes of this great bird behold a great future for mankind, but when? Not in this millisecond of his existence.

The sterile operating room is cold, like a tomb, and filled with commotion and anxiety as doctors and nurses hastily don gloves and gowns. The surgeon skillfully rips open my chest, my anesthetized neck is supple, the noises of gasping death are heard through the oxygen hose. They all sweat and an eminent fear can be seen in the eyes of their half-covered faces. Condor's soul still hovers gently as if not knowing what to do as it keeps journeying

back to the faint, long-gone past where he sees little Condor struggling and learning to walk the uphill, narrow, cobblestone Inca
streets of Cuzco.

He recalls the smell of the chuta pan, dark whole-grain
Indian bread, that for centuries has permeated the aroma of
the aldeas, small Indian villages. He remembers his parents—
he is not sure if this is good or not. He sees in his mother's
face the tortuous imprint of the past, its sad contours silently
reflecting the Indian genocide.

The soul of Condor remembers the little town of Andahuaylillas with ladderlike, faint green mountains, clear
skies, and frigid, thin air warmed by a distant sun. He can see
the past in its people, almost as the Spaniards left them.

*Hours have passed. There is quietness in the air, the jagged
monitor tracing of the heart is still intact, like the peaks and valleys of the Andes, with no flat deserts on the EKG screen. He is
still breathing. The surgeon sutures the gap in his heart and rapidly
closes the chest cavity. There is no time to finish with the niceties
of a well-planned surgical procedure. The restless, hovering spirit
waits still a while and remembers that the town has a plaza with
an old church of white yeso, plaster, and old, brown adobes, perhaps made from the dust of the Incas.*

In this small village of his mother's birthplace, Condor sees
Indians for the first time and to him they are like any people,
but for some reason he is not accepted. One Indian asks little
Condor if he would tell his mother to copulate with him. How
would Condor know that this remark was cruel and what it
meant; so he kept it to himself. How old was he? He was very
little, but already old in the ways of human unkindness, and
only his soul can remember this far-distant childhood.

In this little aldea, Condor enjoys himself on the Indian
children's playground, the cemetery. There are many nichos,
where the dead lie, with inscriptions on their headstones; some
are new, some old. He is already aware of the inevitable, but he
continues to play hide-and-seek with the other children.

Andahuaylillas has a plaza with an old church of white yeso, plaster, and old, brown adobes, perhaps made from the dust of the Incas.

He sees his grandfather, tall and slightly humpbacked. He was a poncho weaver in the old, traditional Inca style. Condor's first recollection of him was on the patio of this adobe house in the middle of a sunny, warm day. He was sitting on the floor with a strap around his waist and a half-finished poncho attached to a big, old eucalyptus tree at the far end. The colors of the yarns were bright red, purple, and yellow. Swiftly and skillfully he would move his bone tools on the vertical strings of llama wool while passing another horizontal yarn. Then he would go back with a yellowish-white, worn-out bone spatula and stretch the strings of yarn as if it were a harp. He looked old and experienced compared to other Indians and smelled faintly of coca, virgin coca leaf chewed by many Indians, and agua ardiente, strong sugar cane alcohol, almost as if he wanted to hide it. His grand-father spoke two languages, Spanish and Quechua, and told tales of his past, recalling the people whose graves the children stepped on in the cemetery while playing. He would remember stories about Spaniards, and he knew that he carried more of their blood than others, but he was still an Indian. He wore a felt hat, a dark suit vest, and regular tailored pants and leather shoes, unlike most others, who still wore Indian or Inca-like garb, with sandals and a poncho at all times. He wore a poncho only when it was cold and in the evenings or to hide his bottle of hard liquor. Condor loved to listen to him in the cool, empty evenings in the small, old adobe house, sitting on the hard, dusty adobe bench inside the room with visibly rotten, polilla-eaten beams of eucalyptus wood supporting the roof, who knows for how many years.

The grandfather told about how he heard the Indians used to be treated by the caporal, the master. Long before the roosters, like "El Caballero Carmelo," the name of a rooster in the story by Peruvian writer Abram Lopez Valdelomar,

My grandfather's old adobe house with visibly rotten, polilla-eaten beams of eucalyptus wood supporting the roof, who knows for how many years.

would sing, the Indians were already awake and up. He does not remember if the Indians were chained, but for sure they were whipped in the early chilly morning of this town, and one could hear the stampede of crusted, scaly, bare feet running to the field, with no breakfast but already with a bolus of coca on one side of the mouth as if it were a giant chewing gum but with a fetid odor, showing the purity of their white, hardened teeth. Yes, they worked the hard earth of the climbing mountain. Their companions were the wheezing of the cold wind and the faint warmth of the sun; their occasional rest was to see the white clouds against the blue sky and the infinity of the mountains. They pushed the plowlike llacta with their bare feet, all the time moving large chunks of brown earth from which stones had been removed by their ancestors, but they would still find rocks and throw them off to the side to strengthen the stairs of the andenes, small plots of land, in the steep, hard-to-climb mountain field. Condors flying above have seen this sight from the time both Indian and work were created.

Condor gets to see the monotony of the Indian's existence, just as his grandfather did. He is saddened that some are below and others are above, and many people use others for the benefit of the few.

The nurses rush all around. Everyone is quiet. The doctors, somewhat doubtfully, place the last stitches in a coarse and rapid manner. They remove the cold, blue, sterile paper linen. Now his body is all exposed, as limp as a dead Jesus, but his soul is still around and now waits to see what will happen.

In his netherworld, the Condor's soul goes back to this five-year-old child, who goes to school for the first time with his Indian uncle who wears no shoes. His feet are like a condor's garras, claws—dark, strong, and hard. He will step on pointed stones and feel no pain. Condor, who wears shoes, asks him, "Why don't you feel pain when you walk on sharp stones?" He answers, "Don't look at the stones and keep on walking." Indifference is already a mark of these people; it is as if this is their fate, just as we are indifferent to death.

In the long process of surgery, with his mind in the beyond but his senses in this world, some odors of the operating room bring back faint olfactory memories of a long bygone early morning breakfast.

They had a cup of rich natural cacao made with fresh milk cooked in a clay pot over a small fogón, a rustic adobe oven, in an open kitchen using the soft flame of cow manure. Condor's eyes and body celebrate the faint warmth of the natural fire, his eyes shining in the early morning light. The sun is barely up and the sweet smell of the chuta bread is as if the dust of the Inca people impregnated the soil where the wheat was grown. It is a simple but mystical breakfast, reminding one of the renewal of the spirit and the continuation of life.

The name of his half-uncle Braulio, who is five years older than Condor, will be Jilgero—the name of the beautiful red-chested Andean bird that always sings—because he is always talking. He teaches Condor the ways of the Indians, because he has more Indian blood and knows more of their customs. They are both happy to go to school. They gather something to eat rapidly because they know the morning is getting warmer and this means time is going fast. They have no watches, almost nobody does, and they count the hours by listening to the antique bells of the three-hundred-year-old cathedral. The food—mote, boiled kernels of corn, and fresh, white cheese—is rapidly placed in their chullos, warm, llama-wool hats. Condor puts on this filled headgear and feels the cold water running down his temples from the wet corn. Together they run to school. They pass through their house door that still has the Inca portal stone with two carved llama heads. The street is of dirt and pointed stones. There is a small, open channel made of fine stones in the middle of the road—it is the Inca system for water and drainage. They see Indians and mestizos coming, already with bottles of agua ardiente and chewing coca, some of whom are herding their cows and sheep to the grassy mountains. They arrive at the square, where there is a large, old corrugated tree with red flowers that fall gently on the soil, covering it like a red carpet. Condor picks one up and opens its bright red upper petal and then the little yellow lower portion that looks like a parrot's beak, then throws it away after satisfying his curiosity. They arrive late to school, and Jilgero is fined ten cents that he does not have. He receives two whips on the buttocks with a piece of flat wood.

Condor is not castigated. He wears shoes, he is a lighter mestizo, he is a visitor, and he is welcomed by the teachers and students who have short, straight black hair, slanted bright eyes, beautiful large white teeth, and smiling Inca faces. Classes in the small, adobe dirt-floor classroom begin and his thoughts drift off through the nothingness of time.

At break time, they remove their chullos and place the hat filled with corn in their palms, eating their boiled mote with cheese, which is their noon meal. School is over at the time the sun makes no shadow, then all the Indian children have to go to work in the fields, or worse, go home and find their parents already drunk and the floor full of coca spit. The smell of chicha, fermented corn alcoholic drink, and coca permeates the air. Nobody is doing anything; they are all mesmerized by the alcohol. Tears and complaints come from the voices of the female Indians. Their souls are numb, the unforgettable suffering past is epitomized in their faces.

Condor is welcomed by these distressed, old-looking, young people who accept him as if he were the future. They feel he is a different bird, although a child, for in their eyes he is mature. They think he is more of the Old World and they call him "niñucha," a spoiled, middle-class child, because he wears short pants, suspenders, socks and shoes, and he is lighter and speaks only Spanish. He is happy to be with them and in his heart there is a light of optimism, whereas in the others' hearts there is a darkness of pessimism. To anesthetize their sorrows they dance, drink, and finally fight and beat their wives and children. Condor has seen, in his long voyages, how the English drink, but this is different. Here there is no control; the Indians portray their sorrows openly, and they become remorseful of the past. Condor looks, thinks, and feels that there is another world to escape to; that is why he has large wings. He can always fly to distant places unknown to his ancestors. Condor has been everywhere and now he can write about it. When he tells about what he has experienced, he will not hide his feelings. He can see from far away and he knows the ways of man.

Surgery finished, they place his heavy body, still intubated, gently on a black gurney. They are careful not to disturb the innumerable plastic tubes that keep him barely alive. His soul still journeys through the past, and for the first time he remembers his parents.

His father is wearing a vintage U.S. Army–like officer's uniform. He is mestizo, but has less Indian blood; his mother is plump and wears lipstick, and she has more Indian blood. She is now a young miss or señorita of the Andahuaylillas town. There are few ravens in Peru, but Don Jose, his father, is the embodiment of that beautiful black bird, arrogant and mischievous. He was born in Arequipa and lost his mother when he was young and was raised by aunts. In his teens he escaped and joined the army, as a recruit, with a third-grade education. Condor's mother, Dora, is a regular hen, subservient to Raven, happy with her child but not her lot. She was born in Andahuaylillas, and her mother also died when she was a child. Thereafter she was raised by a drunken father in many different houses, where she probably was abused and was never sent to school. Her destitute situation and motherless status made a German couple feel sorry for her, and they adopted her in Cuzco. But when World War II started, they had to return to Germany. They were going to take Condor's mother with them, but her father opposed the idea.

Maybe if she had gone to that war-torn continent she would have died there, a victim in a strange land.

Unconscious and unaware of what happened, his mind wanders out in space and goes back to the past where he is reincarnated as a bird.

Condor flies and sees the mountains forever vast, always a witness of the time since it began. He moves his neck and his white collar is visible and ruffles in the air as he glides through the blue sky, zooming like a comet. Oh, how he wished he was that bird!

As he lies on the gurney, he is pushed through the cold, empty halls of the hospital, barely hearing the screeching wheels rusty with old blood. He senses the opening of the doors, entering the elevator that he has used when making hospital rounds and where he saw others being wheeled around. His soul is still following closely, and his first faint recollection of Cuzco is that of a house up in the hills overlooking the city.

He remembers one night when he is awakened by his mother's cries in the middle of his sleep at midnight. She has seen a bulto, a ghostly, large, supernatural mass in the entrance of their dirt-floor single room. It was so real to her! Raven picks up his lantern and goes after this bulto in the cold night. He comes back, shaken and mystified at finding nothing. Little Condor sees this incident from his bed. Are there unnatural things in this world? He pulls the covers over his head and, trembling, looks at the door. Is that bulto coming again? What is it that his mother saw? And why?

It is known that long before the conquistadors arrived in Peru in 1532—and only God knows for how long—the Incas used to bury their people, especially their masters, in sad and pompous ceremonies. They would open large holes in the pure earth and place the dead there with all their wealth, food, and chicha, enough to last them through the next journey, just as the Egyptians did. But along with all their belongings, they also buried alive their most beautiful wives, and some of their favorite servants, who apparently made no objection and were actually glad to accompany their loved one to the hereafter. This huge sacrificial orifice was covered with earth, forming a small mound. Then the survivors would mark the area with a large stone bulto or waka, a marker for a burial plot, and for days, weeks, and months, the people would return to the site to mourn their dead. That is how the Spaniards found out and knew where the gold was buried, and there were many wakas or communal graves all over Peru. The conquerors simply had to dig to find what they had come for.

As the elevator slowly ascends, the strong feeling of pulling against gravity causes his agonized body to have a sense of being drawn back to Earth as if to be reclaimed for good. His soul, oblivious to his earthly feelings, remembers when Condor was sent to a Salesian school in Cuzco.

He recalls the tall, red-faced men dressed in black sotanas, robes, and hard, white collars.

They are dignified and they care for children. He remembers being placed in a corner only because he caused a problem. The school is big and close to the Sacsayhuaman Inca fortress overlooking the old Inca city. The claustros, high-ceilinged old classrooms, are large and the air is clean. The priests, mostly white and foreigners, are strong, sturdy, and domineering, and Condor learns the ways of the Old World through them.

One day while on a break at the enclosed school, a sudden fear overwhelms him. He climbs the old, rusty steel gates, sensing that his parents are leaving him, and he runs away from school. Walking fast through the empty streets in the heavy rain, he arrives home wet, worried, and desperate. He sees his mother and father packing the suitcases. They ask him, "Why are you here?" He begs them, "Don't leave me," and they let him stay home. No! they will not leave him because he is theirs, and forever they will be traveling to distant and desolate regions of the Peruvian landscape, always on short notice and with few belongings.

As his mangled body is cared for by the nurses, they carefully take him to the intensive care unit where he seems to be coming around. But still his mind is far away, lost in his primordial distant past as a child in the city where he was born. Condor's soul has seen many things in Cuzco.

He remembers the old Santo Domingo church built by the conquistadors on the remains and foundations of the old Inca ruins of a main temple, Koricancha, which was used to worship their sun god. The temple was destroyed and desecrated after the Spaniards managed to subdue and humiliate these vanquished inhabitants. He has played soccer with the priests in these corridors surrounded by arches and stone pillars and floors covered with blue and yellow Spanish tiles. The walls were lined with huge, old, dusty, fading oil paintings depicting in their decaying canvas pompous priests and bearded men in armor plate with Indians in the dark background. The silent oratorios are big rooms with an eerie feeling of quietness. They were built with large, grey, laserlike cut stone masonry originally placed by the Incas to worship their gods, but now they are empty, devoid of the glittering ornamentations of their golden past. Oh, those pillars are so old, but only now does he know that; back then it was not known to him!

In a secluded, private room full of medical instruments, he opens his eyes to find more darkness than light. Through his cloudy corneas he sees a priest sitting nearby, gently looking at him, trying to do what he has always done, give the last rites. But the priest is uncertain and is not sure if this is the time. Condor listens to distant voices outside the room, recognizing them, and more pain comes to him as he faintly hears their distress. His soul is anxiously pacing and looking at the priest and in reverence he returns to the dying man who as a child goes to church long before his parents wake up.

Come early Sunday he will take a bath in his family's cold, dirt-floor, one-room house. He will boil water outside on the adobe stove with the leftover manure, and fill the tina, a small portable aluminum tub, with freezing and hot water and wash his upper body. In the faintly sunlit room he sees on the adobe wall the faces of Clark Gable and Shirley Temple. They look so distant and different that he feels they are from another world. The pictures are from magazines; they are yellow and faded, but they are nice to look at. He uses more soap and washes his lower body, then he dresses in his short pants and white shirt and goes to church alone, walking on the old cobblestone streets beside which the Inca walls still stand and over which his ancestors probably trudged for centuries before him. He enters the old, colonial church where many elderly kneeling women in Indian clothing are crying and praying in anguish about their misery and begging to the silent, white saints and a crucified God for miracles. To the left of the huge, old, double door with bronze knobs is the Saint of the Temblores, earthquakes, and to the right of the other half-open colossal wooden door is the Virgin Mary. He sees all those inside in reverence and sorrow; and in the resonant quietness of this cave of a cathedral he feels he would rather fly and see the Indians plowing the ground in the quiet faraway mountains.

This town becomes a cosmos of remembrance; everywhere there is untouched history. People there live in houses with foundations laid by the Incas. They walk the winding, narrow, stone streets that climb the hills built by their forefathers. All around there are remnants of what it was—one feels the chains of the past. One smells the humid ground of ancestors, a reminder of what they were and of what happened to them.

In the streets one sees the Indians as if they were left perpetual statues in their thinking, unlike Rome where the white marble remnants of that great culture are a reminder of a glorious past and perhaps not-so-glorious present. It is strange: An Indian, chewing coca, comes walking with his chullo, his poncho, and his ojotas, sandals made out of tires. They are the same. But he is different by just one minute of destiny, so insignificant, yet it makes so much difference. In Cuzco, Condor has learned in his soul and forever that this was the place where

Walking on the old cobblestone streets beside which the Inca walls still stand and over which his ancestors probably trudged for centuries before him.

the greatness and the fall of his people came to pass. This place is the Jerusalem of his ancestry, the Jerusalem of his past.

But nobody fights for this Andean Jerusalem, everything is calm, no one wants to remember what happened. They would all rather forget it, if it were not for the Indian people and ancient buildings that are constant reminders. They would bury the past and let hundreds of years pass, then the new generations would rediscover it and perhaps learn to respect it, like the Jerusalem of the Middle East whose people cling to and revere the last vestiges of an ancient wall.

So is the beginning of flight for this little Condor; he is not sure of the day when he will fly high and strong.

In this town young Condor has encountered little optimism. He has seldom noticed Indian families overtly loving their children, although he has seen instinctive animal-like protection of their young.

He sees discontent in their faces, and so much distrust, and disdain for one another so perverse that it has become a hallmark of this race, just as the Germans are known for their discipline, the English for their past colonialism and present gardening, and the new Americans for their entrepreneurship. Yes, Condor has flown so far and has seen the Rhine of days gone by with many ancient castles and their tales of glorious pasts. The European people are proud and they receive moral sustenance from their history to become wiser, but so universal are the injustices of man that every nation has a past that needs to be mended.

Little Condor has seen harm to the human body, and to the human spirit, but he learns that the past was worse and hopes that the future, as distant as infinity, will become better by the will of the hearts of the people.

As the anesthesia wears off, his sense of the world begins to return slowly. There in a hectic room, amidst the agony of his lifesaving paraphernalia, his soul reunites with him. Now both his body and soul will continue the journey of the past with the uncertain hope of a better understanding of himself, his people, and the world.

CHAPTER TWO

Cumbrous Mountains, Swirling Mist

My father is a young army officer, boisterous, macho, and loose with his drinking. He has not learned the ways of the social climber and he is not trying. He is sent to distant, treacherous, inhospitable, and faraway places in Peru because he has shown the attitude of the daring. This is the first long trip little seven-year-old Condor will take. He has heard that this area is dangerous and that no roads or rivers reach the town, Puerto Maldonado, in the Departamento of Madre de Dios, the state called Mother of God, an ungodly place that borders the impenetrable jungles of Brazil and Bolivia. Perhaps it was given this name to remind the people that this area was as miserable as the pain the Virgin Mary suffered at the death of Jesus. Oh, this growing Condor is happy to go to the jungle, that world glorious in nature but treacherous.

We took an old truck, full of Indians, animals, and stench. The cold was bone-deep, and the passengers liked me, calling me "niñucha." They covered me with their ponchos from the freezing wind. We traveled for days over a road that was like a smashed mud pie that nobody wants to touch.

We stopped many times on the muddy, dangerous, unfinished roads because of mechanical breakdowns, torrential

We took an old truck, full of Indians, animals, and stench.

rains, and blown-out tires. Condor came out and saw the world beyond, the cumbrous, distant sawtooth mountains, the mist of the jungles swirling around, and the air filled with the music of innumerable insects. The land of the Incas was no longer felt here. There was some spiritual happiness, but now the distrust was not of each other, but of nature, because it is cruel and swift.

Condor pissed on the mud and looked at the vastness of infinity up there. I was happy and awed; I saw new undisturbed nature. The yoke of the Spanish conquistadors did not get this far. I recall that this was a virgin land, with only the animals and Indian tribes whose ancestors probably ran away from the domination of their conquerors, Inca and Spanish. Only they know of the trials and tribulations of life in the deep forest.

Days and nights we traveled in this big truck full of human cargo. We had endured enough bad times to add a chapter to *Around the World in 80 Days*, but nobody will write about us; it is the karma of our Indian people to suffer.

We finally arrived at Quince-Mil, a city whose name means "fifteen thousand," probably because of the glittering dusty yellow metal found in the many and unknown rivers of this beginning jungle. That town was the equivalent of the California gold rush mining towns of the 1840s and somewhat worse.

I remember this was the end of the muddy road. From here Condor and his family were to fly for the first time in a small plane to their destination if the stormy weather ever let up. In Quince-Mil, Condor witnessed death and misery of the body, not of the spirit. I saw men dying of snakebites and tropical diseases and observed my mother helping the poor, diseased, and destitute.

She heard of a man left to die in a hut due to a snakebite because he could not go to Cuzco for treatment. She took food to this Indian man of the area, who was known as a selvatico, a man of the jungle. I saw my mother feed this man in the misery of his hut, his right leg swollen, blistering, and smelling of putrefying flesh. She applied a red medicine to it, mercurochrome. We returned to the muddy, one-street town, busy with all the selling of gear and supplies for those who go to the deep jungle to look for gold, rubber, or death. Time went by unnoticed. We used to go to the Marcapata River, a tributary of the larger Inambary River, and enjoy its furious current from the shore and barely dare to touch it, as if it were fire, but I played alone and waded in some distant, safe water hole while my mother washed our clothes in the river.

We returned to the town with our clean, wet clothes. We noticed people gathering around a truck. We went to find out what was happening, and we saw the man with the snakebite injury and bad right leg being taken to Cuzco. I only remember the feet dangling from the stretcher made out of branches and small tree trunks. Three days later we heard that he died on the muddy road and his body was buried in the wet mud. I can only imagine the corpse now, washed by the savage rain and consumed by the many scavenging animals and insects.

Condor was playing with other jungle kids in the makeshift football stadium, and they all raised their eyes and saw an airplane in the blue sky rapidly approaching where they were playing. The little grasshopper plane looked big to me. Oh! that invention of the future, the airplane, landed precariously on this patch of dirt. A tall man came out of the cockpit; he was white, maybe a bush pilot, a gringo! He was different. He said that he would be leaving in fifteen minutes while the sun was still unobstructed by the dark stormy clouds and asked someone to get Sub-Teniente, 1st Lieutenant, Sánchez immediately.

That is the airplane we were waiting months for. We picked up all our wet clothes, which were drying on the porch of the only hotel, placed them along with our meager belongings in a small suitcase, and rushed to the dusty stadium.

First time! The inside was made of materials and instruments I had never seen before. We barely fit in this tiny airplane, a Cessna. We take off. The flight of a condor is smooth and effortless but this was a "flying cow." The sensations of falling were so vivid, my mother was crying from fear all the way. My father was shy; the pilot was indifferent, silent, and looked worried. Only he knew how dangerous this flight could be and has been. Oh, those jungles, those rivers, that great green infinity gave Condor his first sight of the world from above; he admired it and he would never forget it.

Puerto Maldonado is a dirt-street town in Amazonia with sidewalks paved with the ends of empty beer bottles, because they could only be brought in by plane, at great expense, but not taken back. The smell of the whole city was of rotting mango and other unknown fruits. The aroma was so sweet, it became almost unbearable in the hot, humid weather.

Condor saw and heard stories of the not-so-faraway deep jungle. I enjoyed it and also feared it. I saw my first boalike shuchupe snake, caught by a drunk selvatico who showed it to the town as proof of his machismo. All the people—men, women, and children—came to see this man in the euphoria of his alcohol and the searing heat of midday holding with his bare hands the head of this beautiful, huge, half-dead snake. The schuchupe, with its white belly and dark back covered with shiny scales, was being dangled and hit against the dusty street as if it were a giant rope. And all the time the man was telling the onlookers in a loud, stuporous voice how he caught this large animal and how tricky they were and how the snake had been about to kill him. We followed him for blocks as if it were the main event of the day, which it was.

As we lived for some time in this town, I learned to walk alone on the narrow path of the jungle to see the Franciscan priests, who ran a mission church with the only medical post in the town. The priests cured my pus-ridden eyes with algirol, a silver nitrate solution used then against infection. The mission was not far from the city, hidden in the forest by the shores of the Madre de Dios River. I heard and saw the ways of the red-bearded missionaries. They were good people who years ago came to civilize and Christianize the tribes, perhaps unknowingly and even altruistically changing and destroying the ways of the aboriginal people as their forebears did centuries ago when they first came to these virgin jungles, suffering and dying for a questionably noble cause. I could not stay too long at the mission, because darkness descends on the jungle while the sun still shines in the middle of the day. The noise of the insects and the cries of the half-eaten animals create a panic. I walked quickly and imagined that behind me was that big shuchupe snake following me, because that was what I heard they do. I touched my bottom and it was still there. I ran and did not want to look back or sideways. I saw only the path in front of me—red, sandy, leafless ground—and I knew it was dirt and nothing was hidden underneath. I had my shirt in my hands in case I had to throw it to the snake. People there say that is how one can gain distance—while the snake smells the clothing thrown down.

Oh, how can I describe the sweetness of that jungle? It felt like a holiday, with musical streams filled with flocks of beautiful birds and large, tall, green trees. One walked alone, but felt no loneliness as in the frigid, thin air of the Andes.

This town, as Condor remembered it, was like a paradise. Maybe I was too small to know that people were also suffering here. Disease was rampant and death was as common as the falling of the brown leaves from the trees. But as alive as the jungle is, rejuvenation was all around.

The Madre de Dios River was big, brown, fast, and full of remolinos, whirlpools. Nobody dared to swim, but one could see green all over. The white steps down to the riverboats made it look like the fanciest of yacht clubs, where the navy kept a beautiful old iron boat, a steamer just like those used in the U.S. Civil War.

Sometimes I would walk in the rainy forest to the army fort to see my father. For the first time, I observed soldiers who had fully shaved heads and pure Indian faces—some were aborigines. Among themselves they talked roughly and they were harsh to each other, but when their superiors appeared, they were as docile as dogs with their tails under their bellies. Condor observed this behavior frequently everywhere, because there was so much contrast between racial and social classes in this country.

The most important task for those soldiers was to learn to read and write. Their day-to-day language was so intermingled with Spanish, Quechua, and other native dialects that they would learn to spell one word in Spanish and repeat the same word in their language. For doing that, they were hit with the heavy boots of their superiors until they got it right.

When noontime came, my father would take me to eat lunch served in the fort. The soup was made of snake that tasted and looked like chicken, and it was good. So time went by, and now I can only reminisce about those days with a faint memory and recollect sweet odors that my olfactory senses can remember.

The day finally came when we were to leave Puerto Maldonado. It was 4 A.M., warm, humid, and noisy from the cheering of multiple insects. All the townspeople were at the river to see the big airplane coming to pick up passengers. This big bird landed in the Madre de Dios River. It was majestic, beautiful, full bellied, and powerful. It was a Catalina hydroplane built where I live now in San Diego.

In the 1930s Consolidated Aircraft, owned by Reuben H. Fleet, came to San Diego and started building navy seaplanes, with plans to build amphibian civilian aircraft. But World War II came and San Diego emerged as a major producer of PBY Catalina seaplanes and B-24 liberator bombers. Who would have imagined that one day, while I was a lieutenant in the U.S. Navy Medical Corps, my headquarters, the Marine Corps Recruit Depot, would be just beside the huge airplane factory? Now this plant is closing down, and with it the history of these great planes will be gone, but I was lucky enough to have begun my countless flying trips with these gracious watercraft.

I took my second flight. I was already getting used to flying in times when traveling by plane was not common. The amphibian plane took off with its deafening propellers roaring against the rapids of the river. The windows were clouded with brown water. As the glass cleared, I could see the river becoming smaller, and the town looked like a mole in the big, green, giant jungle. All the river tributaries were like snakes and seemed to loop toward an end that did not exist. This trip lingers in my mind as a faraway time and is now somewhat obscure in my memory, but with time I would fly in bigger airplanes to distant places where I would also see in-justices.

It is 1995, and I am a member of the Peruvian doctors of PAMS (Peruvian American Medical Society) in the United States, which has started continuous medical missions to Peru to help in different places. I am proud of PAMS' endeavors and am an active member of their humanitarian missions. After going to Trujillo to help with the Peruvian team, I came back to Lima, which was cold and damp. My mother was suffering from arthritis and the weather did not help, so I convinced her to go to the same jungle that we were in fifty years ago, thinking it would be the paradise that we both still remembered. It was difficult to get a plane reservation to go there; the only planes that went there at my specified time, due to my short stay, were owned by a small company.

We arrived at the new airport at four in the morning to leave for Puerto Maldonado via Cuzco. As we crossed the airport field to what looked like a jet standing by, we were rerouted to an iso-lated area where I could see a well-kept, double-propeller plane that was somewhat different from the ones made in the United States. When we got closer, it looked well used; the tires were al-most worn out, and the inscriptions on the fuselage were in Rus-sian. It was a vintage plane from past Soviet-Peruvian political relations. As we were boarding I just said, "Maybe this is it!" Af-ter embarking through the back ramp, we saw that the aged inte-rior had foam seats on bare aluminum, with only two or three round windows. I was lucky to get one, with a partial view onto creaking landing gear, but also with a good view of the landscape, which is what mattered to me the most. The plane took a while to warm up its noisy engines, and memories of the old Catalina pro-pellers came to me. We took off in the mist of Lima and as we ap-proached the high Sierras I saw the most beautiful rising of the golden sun against the jagged peaks of the Andes with their crusted perpetual snow. It was so breathtaking that it is no wonder the In-cas worshiped this bright star. The scenery was so intoxicating that I forgot about the plane, which was comfortable and cozy. As a matter of fact, this was better than flying in a jet because it flew so low that I could see the land just below the wheels of the plane and could savor all those majestic mountains on the way to Cuzco.

From Cuzco we took on some more passengers, this time more Indians and natives, but wearing Westernized clothing and more sure of themselves. As we were to stay in Cuzco for a while, I got out of the plane and was surprised to find a friend and former classmate with whom I had just attended my old military high school meeting the night before. To my delight, he was the pilot! He had been handsome when we were cadets in Arequipa, tall and fair, but now he looked somewhat different because of an airplane crash he had been in. Well, when one is in distant places, one just takes things in stride. What can one do? If it is time to go, there is nothing anyone can do about it. Besides, I have always had confidence in Peruvian pilots—they know their hazardous terrain very well.

We crossed the Andes and entered the beginning of the rain forest, but to my disbelief there was no jungle in sight. Everything was smoky, worse than in Los Angeles or Mexico City. Where were the millions of green trees and endless rivers which were more visible against a green background? Nowhere. I felt maybe it would come. Since this flight was so short, I could not equate it with the long overland trip that we took fifty years ago. To my astonishment, after only forty-five minutes, the flight attendant told us to get ready to land. But I was still looking through the window . . . did I miss the jungle? Did I sleep? Maybe I had not used my oxygen mask properly. But no, this was Puerto Maldonado. Now it had a paved airport. The city that once was green and full of fruit trees was now just like the airport, bare of natural beauty, but full of people. Luckily enough, there were only a few cars, but modified motorcycles were now used as taxis and spewed a lot of smoke. My poor mother—she had come for the hot sun and there was none. The sky was cloudy and appeared smoky, and the streets were dusty. We stayed for three days and went to all the old places. To be fair, Puerto Maldonado is a capital city; if the tourists want to see virgin jungle, they have to go to special parks and reserves. These large forest reserves, like the extensive Tambopata, Heath, and Manú National Parks, are good places to visit and get a feeling of the rain forest, with plants and animals that are still being studied, but I wish it had never come to that.

I immediately went to see the mission, but the first jungle path I walked as a child was gone. The army fort was in the same area but had no more of those huge castaña, or chestnut, trees. Amazingly, what I thought was far away was close to where we had lived, but now that the forest was destroyed, the distances seemed shorter. The mission was still there, but it was more modern. The Franciscan father who took care of my eyes had died, and people still remembered him. My mother and I went to the fort, but it was not the same. Feeling sad, we went back to the hotel in this now chilly town with no mosquitoes or fruits in the trees. How can people alter nature so? I could not believe it, even though we hear about deforestation and loss of habitat for animals in the media almost daily. Seeing it with one's own eyes is a powerful experience. It is not a trivial matter. The earth is changing, and for the worse. It is much more serious than what one hears about.

We went to the shore and found that it, too, was changed. The riverbanks were full of lumber mills with smokestacks burning the remains of beautiful, old, green trees. In our efforts to find virgin nature and get away from the city, we took a day trip by canoe up the Tambopata River, coming from Puno, which empties into the Madre de Dios River. It took some time to finally see the large, green trees, but still there were no mosquitoes. This was the jungle, but what had happened? Maybe the smoke decimated them. In my younger days in this same area, one was constantly flipping one's hands to kill the many insects. In the course of the day I saw only two macaws flying rapidly across the river, probably in search of greener forests. Those brown waters did not appear threatening anymore, no caimans and fewer fish. The landscape had changed drastically, and I was awestruck.

After three days there, we finally took a cycle-taxi to the airport, and my mother stopped to buy some gold, which had been plentiful in those days, and she also inquired about snake grease for her arthritis. I almost got into an argument with her about that, but the market was full of such potions made from animal derivatives for various ailments. In spite of my pleas, she bought it; it was white and rancid just like lard. Poor snakes; I hoped it was just pork lard (who would know the difference?), and I am sure it was. It is not surprising that she tells me her bones still ache!

We climbed back into the same Russian plane for our return trip to Lima. This time it was clear enough that I could see almost all of the diminished jungle. In places there were a few trees standing by themselves. The whole area looked like a cemetery with the corpses of the trees lying down waiting to be picked up—and ending up being used to make furniture. As we approached Cuzco, the mountains and the city were shrouded in a typical, smoky, brown hue, no longer that infinite blue sky with no end except in one's mind. We made a stopover in Cuzco, then went on to Lima in the same airplane. At the lower altitudes I could see the great works of the Incas in the impenetrable Andes, with the remaining andenes still used by the true descendants of those regions. I am glad I took this trip in a low-flying plane; a lot is lost when flying at higher altitudes and the perspective of the area is missed. I am relating my impressions, not to be critical, but in the hopes of making my readers aware that an area that once was deep, thick jungle teeming with life is now becoming a barren wasteland. The forest is ravaged by the new people who came to desecrate this virgin nature in the name of progress.

CHAPTER THREE

The Ways of the River

Time has passed and Condor finds himself between Lima and Arequipa. His father has been sent to the farthest of all jungles, and will be sent even farther—to where there are no roads, no railroads, only small planes and rapid rivers to take us there. Condor hears that there is a big conflict, World War II, in a faraway continent. He cannot imagine the atrocities committed there, but he will learn that such things are universal and perhaps even galactic. Who knows, maybe for some, if not all, the fact of human existence is already an injustice in itself.

Somehow, in my recollection of trips to uneventful cities, I find myself in Yurimaguas, a town that at that time could be reached only by air. Here again it was hot and humid, and all the action took place by the Huallaga River, a main tributary of the mighty Amazon. Big trunks of freshly cut trees floated in the river; large, heavy, oval blocks of black rubber were carried by malnourished natives; and the stench of rapidly decomposing food was everywhere.

Condor, an only son, now had a brother, his uncle Jilgero, as a companion. My mother, who is his sister, adopted him. Our new family of four would spend months traveling up the Huallaga and Marañon Rivers, finally arriving in Iquitos.

Iquitos is the capital of the Peruvian Amazon jungle, or Amazonia, in the Loreto Department. It is a city that looks much different from others in the Andes; for all practical purposes it is another nation, more like a Brazilian town with Portuguese roots. These inhabitants from the Amazon actually consider the Andean people unusual and call them shishacos, which is the equivalent of an American from the Ozarks. The jungle people are different, for their ancestral suffering is almost nonexistent, and in some cases their misery is not that visible. Maybe the hot, humid, tropical air is a catalyst for the softening of the soul, or perhaps the yugo, oppression, of the Old World never reached this far. Time goes by leisurely in peaceful Iquitos, although the connection with World War II is felt throughout this port city due to the transoceanic traffic of new and necessary raw materials—rubber, wood, quinine, and other products for the killing fields of Europe.

It would seem that the trip to the port of Iquitos would be so effortless, but no, it was not. To begin with, just the knowledge that one had to go to Amazonia in the early 1940s was probably already a sentence as harsh as being sent to Siberia. Death loomed in the jungle as easily as on today's Los Angeles freeways. So constantly hazardous was this journey that even Teddy Roosevelt wrote that his adventurous trip to the Amazon almost broke his spirit, and his stay was only for a short time.

At that time my father was only a low-ranking army officer and his means were modest. There was some question whether my uncle would go to the Amazon with us or have to return to the stale, uneventful city of Andahuaylillas in Cuzco due to our lack of money. The separation from him would have been very painful for me, since I was alone, and I wanted a brother. I remember the crying and arguments in the squalor of the city of Lima, crowded in a small room where one could not hide one's emotions.

Somehow, with the grace of God, I recollect all four of us going to the old airport and bidding farewell to Lima. The feeling of its being the last time was very real. We did not know if or when we would ever see the capital again. Money was so scarce, our knowledge of unknown places even scarcer, and in those days traveling to the jungle required as much preparation as possible. My mother had no knowledge of the jungle or means to take care of us in case my father died or left us in these faraway places. I recall arriving in Yurimaguas, a small jungle city where we stayed in a hotel with its own stream of running water, and walls of a blue Moorish mosaic common in Brazil. I remember getting acquainted with the food and I can still taste those particular flavors so distinctive to jungle food.

For weeks and months we waited for an airplane in this town. My father was to fly to Iquitos alone and we would go by boat later. Time passed without a moment's notice in Yurimaguas. It was like a vacation, and the river alone was a source of enchantment and distraction. Due to the suffocating, hot, humid weather, our daily routine centered around eating, sleeping, and listening for the rare sound of airplanes, which were days or weeks apart.

Luckily one day, just as my father was ready to board a small, amphibian air force craft, the army changed their plans for some reason and told him that he would have to take a riverboat. He had to unpack his few belongings and make different arrangements for the trip. I remember my father was a resourceful man. If he could have controlled his occasional abuse of liquor, which created problems for his advancement and his family, I believe that he would have become a big "jefe," and attained a higher rank more rapidly.

Now we had to wait, not for the airplane, but for the river to swell up with the rains so we could make the trip down the Huallaga tributary to meet the Marañon River and eventually get to Iquitos.

This trip, as I look at the map now, was short, but it seemed so long then. The riverboat we chose was a typical Amazonian river steamer, double-decked with barges on the side for balance and to hold more cargo. The name of the lancha was *San Cristobal*, an old relic that used wood for fuel. We boarded on the spot—the payment and haggling over fares was done right there, and it was as capitalistic as any enterprise could get.

This was another new experience. At first the smell was a mix of oil, food, and virgin rubber: My memories are to a large extent olfactory linked. The trip itself could provide all the intrigue and adventure necessary to write an entire novel.

The lancha was divided into three classes: First class on the upper deck costs more and buys one a small, dark, airless, foul-smelling camarote, or cabin, with four bunks, one on top of the other, to be shared with people one did not know. In second class, on the middle deck, there are posts or hooks to hang one's hammock; and in third class, on the lower decks, one travels with the stench of rotting cargo and the snakes. As I recall, it was the dungeon of the boat; that was where one found the pure Indian of the jungle. That was where I first saw the face of the tribal men with pierced metal or wooden objects in their faces, long or unusually cut hair, and painted bodies. The mothers always had their children stuck to their bare breast. One would look down and see them remain seated almost motionless for hours, days, and months, listening to the cacophony of the old stuttering steam engine and the rush of the river.

My father, mother, and I had a camarote, and my uncle went second class in the open. Oh, if I could describe this trip! I have been on fancy luxury cruises, but none will ever match that first trip down the beginning of the Amazon. Although I was only seven or eight years old, I still remember it vividly.

One could sit and watch the river at arm's length with all of its might and mystique, unlike when cruising on an ocean liner. The brown, muddy waters would always have small and big tree trunks, floating gardens, sometimes with animals hanging onto them for dear life. To see the sights on the shores was a feast for my imagination, not ever having been there. It was somehow forbidding, with tall, majestic, bushy trees, as green as one's eyes could stand, and to hear the deafening noise of the animals and beautiful birds flying everywhere. I am glad that no television, or for that matter any media, was around. I felt nature without knowing it.

The trip took a long time. The river at places got so low, due to lack of rain or the sudden appearance or accumulation of large masses of sediment, that the boat would stall on the sandy bottom for days or weeks. Then the monotony and boredom would become unbearable. On top of that, mosquitoes, suffocating heat, hunger, and the misery of others, especially those on the third deck, were at times intolerable.

To pass the time, we would go to the untouched patches of beach in the middle of the low river where we were varado, stranded, and hunt for turtle eggs, huevos de taricaya as they were called by the natives. The small island was covered with fine brown sand in which one could see the fresh prints of the turtles and the places where they had laid their eggs. We would push hard with the heels of our bare feet in places where there were no turtle traces and hear the popping noise of a broken egg. We would dig fast and happily find a bounty of fresh, small round eggs. They were quite a delicacy, especially when eaten with fariña, mantioca, a small, pelletlike dry staple made from yucca flour.

My father, who had no formal higher education, was well read, always with a book or a magazine in his hand, even though they were so scarce in the jungle. On that trip, he was reading *Quo Vadis*. I never read that voluminous book; I guess I should, just to know what was going through his mind then.

He would stand on the proa, the forward deck, and look forever at the river while smoking a dark Inca, a Peruvian brand of cigarettes. He was a young man, probably thinking of the future and most likely remorseful about his unconventional ways; he was not a social climber. Oh, yes, there are social climbers all over the world, and the poorer the country, the more devious and necessary the social climbing becomes.

After days or sometimes weeks, the boat would slowly begin to float again, and we would come out of this shallow water and then have to spend days waiting on the shores while tribesmen would cut wood for the old steam engines. Worse yet, at times the boat would suddenly slow down or stop, due to low steam pressure or a mechanical breakdown, and repairs would have to be done at places right in the middle of this great river. We often had to wait for parts to arrive.

In this immense solitude, time went on forever, and we wondered whether we would ever get to our destination. There were moments when survival itself seemed to be our main objective.

On the densely forested shores there were many far-apart little villages that survived on the river traffic. We always relished coming to those towns. Although there was nothing to do or buy in these small, squalid, poor outposts, we heard stories of disasters and recent deaths, and we would often pick up sick or injured people. There we would restock with wood and food supplies. We scooped water, which was plentiful though not potable, from the side of the boat with an old tin can or aluminum bucket tied to a rope, and we drank it with no immediate ill effects, probably because we already had all the intestinal parasites and worms there were in those areas.

After months of heavy rains, the unpredictable river, hunger, disease, and near catastrophes, we finally arrived in Iquitos. As I remember, it was a glistening large city with beautiful houses and buildings by the malecón, a riverside walking street adorned with old statues and ornamental railings. In the heyday of rubber, it had been a boom town.

One always thinks of the jungle in terms of the rivers and pristine lakes. Tributaries coming from the Ecuadoran Andes feed the Marañon River, which comes cutting and crossing the high Andes of northern Peru. The enlarged Marañon eventually joins the bigger Ucayali River, which has picked up many southern Peruvian Andean tributaries. They merge in the city of Nauta, where the Amazon humbly begins; it continues to its mighty splendor in the city of Iquitos, where it becomes wider. The colossal and turbulent waters flow to the side of the sunrise, welcoming more wandering rivers on the way to Brazil. Larger rivers like the Rio Negro and others will make the Amazon as gigantic as an ocean as it traverses an area almost as wide as the United States. I will never forget this big mass of brown, fast water, and in unwelcome moments of sadness, my thoughts go to this great, majestic natural wonder.

When Alexander von Humboldt traveled from the Caribe to the Andes exploring the origins of the great Orinoco in 1799, he already noticed the change in spirit of the men. The Andean people were more reserved, distrustful, and difficult to approach, but the native people of the Amazon and the coastal areas were open, happy, and easy to get along with.

In these tropics, one is in another world; the yoke of the Indian is not felt in the spirit of the people. Life is more festive, and philosophical thinking is not a way of life. In Iquitos, Condor tried to live like a child without a past. He attended school for a while, and every day he crossed the plaza where he saw a beautiful monument with bronze portrayals of battles fought in Peruvian oceans against its southern neighboring country.

Although they are in the middle of the Peruvian Amazon, many people in Iquitos feel very distant from and are unaware of the virgin jungle. Most have never ventured more than a few miles from the town. It was a bustling city in the

1940s, and with the war going on, the people were more connected with the United States than with Lima or Cuzco.

As I write this book, my olfactory memory reminds me of Camel cigarettes. I would pick up from the ground the discarded, empty, platinum-colored cellophane packaging. I would smell the aromatic scent to help quench the putrid odors of the humid jungle air. These were my first associations with the North American giant, the country that some day would be my adoptive "Uncle Sam." There I would discover the greatness in the hearts of its people, but I would also see the misery of spirit in the subjugated or vanquished North American natives and other racial groups brought there to labor for the prosperous new European Americans.

In Iquitos began my enchantment with this far-off country, Los Estados Unidos. I saw the multicolored posters at the movie theater showing large airplanes with courageous pilots, falling into the ocean in flames. Monstrous celluloid battle scenes gave me glimpses of the war fought on another continent in a world unknown to me. I could only think that it was too different to even imagine.

The Amazon is wide, deep, and fast in Iquitos. Large ships come to this main fluvial port from the Atlantic via the port of Belém in Brazil, the Amazon's mouth, navigating up the great river through Santarem, Manaus, and Leticia.

Sadly, our stay in this city would not last long. My father was in trouble, probably because of his drinking. This time he was going to be sent to a post deeper in the jungle, a place called Borja, a guarnición, an army fort in distant and desolate places, usually border areas. Again, plans were made to travel upstream through the muddy, dangerous, solitary, and seldom-navigated tortuous tributaries of the Amazon, where we would encounter the most feared of passages, the unforgettable Pongo de Manseriche. The Pongo was an abysmal channel of large whirlpools and torrential rapids rushing at roaring speeds through a dark tunnel of huge granite rocks in whose waters countless people have died. This raging, flowing fury was a natural passage of death.

Because of the time it takes to travel up against the rapid Marañon, my father was sent to the Borja guarnición by hydroplane. Once he departed, we were left to our own ingenuity to travel on this large river. There were no agencies or intermediaries selling tickets. One had to go in person and be ready immediately to board a boat and stake one's place, and the sooner the better, because the spot we secured would be where we would spend the next weeks or even months traveling.

My mother, Braulio, and I came down the malecón to the muddy, noisy port where there were many old river craft going to different places. We shouted to shirtless captains, asking where their boats were going. Sometimes we would board a little steamship, set up our hammocks, and hours or days later, be told that travel plans had changed. Eventually we got on a beautiful old lancha whose name I cannot remember, a typical double-decker, with two small side barges for balance and to hold more cargo. Onboard, the noise, the smell, and the meeting of new people was a feast; they all had stories to tell and their reasons for travel. We would always listen to their plight and see that our lot was better.

All navigation in the Amazon or its tributaries is almost the same. The only changes that make a difference are the encounters with large whirlpools, changes in water depth, currents, and tree trunks that could jeopardize the trip. The continuous sound of the old steam engine and the cutting of the rapid river were forever in our minds even in our sleep. We got to know people in this floating concoction as if they were part of our family. Sometimes we got to know their misery, and sorrow would always be our companion on the trip. Some of the passengers were ill, and some even died. We would then make stops at the orilla, river's edge, and bury those unfortunate people.

The vast green shores and the majestic river were treats for our eyes, but day in and day out, also became a desperation, because somehow we knew we were nowhere in this inhospitable jungle. The moments most greatly anticipated were the mealtimes. We would all sit at hard wooden tables with our own silverware and plates. The food would be as monotonous as the flow of the river. We ate mostly dried paiche, the largest freshwater fish in the world, reaching lengths of twelve feet and weighing up to four hundred pounds. We also ate sungaro and any of the innumerable fresh species such as carachama and boquichico that were occasionally bought. These typical staples would be served with fariña, rice, and beans, which always tasted good, because monotony creates an appetite that distracts the mind from the daily routine.

At times we would do our own fishing from the side of the boat with a small hook and short string, catching smaller prey and having the cooks fry it for us. The only foods that resist rotting in the jungle are dry, salty items that are well cured; nothing fresh would last even a few hours. Because we had no refrigerators, our only source of fresh meat was live turtles that were carried onboard. The cooks would painstakingly cut the hard plate of the abdomen with an ax and remove the live turtle and place it in hot water, where I could see the heart still beating until the temperature became too unbearable for it to palpitate any more. The tribal Indians in third class had to cook and feed themselves with whatever they had. I remember we would take leftovers to the decks below to some of these less fortunate passengers.

It is incredible how accustomed I became to the ways of the river. At times, and in this jungle that meant often, if not hourly, the rains came down, torrential as the rapid waters, accompanied by the most frightening thunder and lightning. I have never seen this climatic fury in any other country. The river would swell beneath us, and the drops of rainfall were so heavy that we could not see the people around us, or for that matter, we could not hear the person we were talking to. That deluge was as close as one can get to the heart of nature, and we would learn to respect it and become humble to the ways of Mother Earth.

Catastrophes were always on the minds of the passengers and crew. The pilot, when confronted with sudden obstacles, would always express fear in his face. It was as if one could read the impending events of disaster in his twisting movements when he frantically and swiftly moved the steering wheel. Due to the powerful downstream flow of the treacherous river, at times there was no noticeable advance in our course. Whenever the heavy downpour finally stopped, the guacamayos, large colorful parrots, and loros, ordinary green parrots, would fly all over as if telling the world that the day was beautiful again and there was no need for fear.

Such was the romance of this boat traveling in the tributaries of the Amazon; as I get older, I can recall it with the mind of my youth, and it pleases my soul.

Days, weeks, and possibly months went by. After passing many ports, we arrived in Barranca, where we rejoined my father. This guarnición was a bigger fort, and my father was temporarily stationed there awaiting further traveling and post assignments. Barranca was a civilized place where large boats would arrive without many problems. From here my father was sent to Borja, a smaller, more distant guarnición, with less river traffic and people. In both those locations my father was a junior officer and followed orders accordingly. Eventually he was sent to Pinglo, a small guarnición of thirty soldiers, where he served as commander.

To get to Pinglo we went by trocha, jungle path, because we could not navigate the Pongo de Manseriche going upstream. It can only be crossed coming down. So we hiked the rising virgin jungle overlooking the high green mountains on one side and on the other the distant, white, snowy cordilleras of the Andes, a beautiful and unforgettable view.

This was a memorable trip. I had seen so many Tarzan movies in Iquitos that my conception of the jungle was more like that of the Hollywood pictures than the real jungle I was living in. The preparations for this trip took days, and we were assigned guides and soldiers to protect us. It was like a caravan. The mission also included taking messages and supplies. I prepared myself as if for a safari, including a casco, jungle helmet, and a knife that I had sharpened, thinking that I would meet the fighting tigers of Johnny Weissmuller.

We began our foot journey early in the morning by entering a narrow path of thick, untouched jungle that had to be cleared at times with machetes. The quietness was awesome, broken only by the occasional sounds of brush disturbed by animals. The trees were so big and moist and all embracing as to create darkness in the midst of sun. Water was everywhere; little rivers were filled with beautiful fish, and if we stayed long enough we would see more aquatic animals like nutria (sea otter–like animals), turtles, and snakes peacefully traveling to their destinations. Sometimes there were deep canyons that had to be crossed on fallen rotting trees that served as bridges. Often these connections consisted of one thin tree. In our fear of falling, or of being unable to keep our balance, we would crawl like lizards clinging tightly to the tree; and in that way we made it across.

We would tire easily due to heat, humidity, fear, and the weight of our packs. Frequent stops were necessary, usually on our feet. We dared not sit anywhere, because there was no suitable place to rest. Everything was wet and possibly infested with tarantulas, snakes, and big curbinses, ants. Most of the trip was spent imagining the dangers and always being worried that the worst would happen. For some reason the trip was more on our minds than on our feet, because of the horrible stories we heard from people when traveling in the jungle. We arrived late at night at the guarnición intact and happy that nothing bad had happened.

This jungle fort, Pinglo, lingers as a peaceful place in the life of my memories; there was nothing but the green forest, the river, the rain, and the stability of human emotions. The Inca Indians and the Andes were so far away that they were never heard of in those areas. This place, called Teniente Pinglo after a lieutenant who possibly discovered it and eventually died there, was a natural paradise. Although death was always on the horizon, it still was a pleasant place to live, as long as one was in good health.

The fort had three or four wooden and palm structures: a large barracks for the soldiers, a storage compound, a smaller structure for the officer's quarters, and the kitchen. The most advanced makeshift structure was the telegraph hut, with its big antenna in a bare tree, where a soldier would receive or relay messages via Morse code.

Our living quarters were above ground, as are all typical jungle houses, built on high wooden poles because of the frequent and sudden rising of the river. This was probably the most beautiful house I have ever lived in. It had open windows with no glass, which allowed the warm breeze to flow through, always welcome in the perpetually debilitating heat. All sleeping rooms had mosquiteros, gauzy tents over the beds, to keep away mosquitoes, bugs, and bats. I remember (as when one gets up in the morning and does things that are pleasant to wake up to), I used to pick up the bats that managed to get in my tent, all full bellied with the blood of my still-bleeding legs. I would stretch their wings and look at their mysterious claws and faces. What a toy! When I finished playing with them, I would let them fly and watch how they attached themselves to the roof and hung by their claws, upside down, to sleep. Such was the way of the jungle. No one harms these animals, even though they are pests. They are too numerous and killing a few of them would not eradicate them. Besides, in this place our friends were the many animals, including three guacamayos; añujes, possumlike animals; monkeys; a tigrillo, small tiger; and a pack of hunting dogs.

When we ate, the dogs would be by us, because they hunted the wild and dangerous game. One dog named Bobby, a mixed breed, comes to my memory. He was big and strong and the leader of the hunting pack because he could fight and track any animal. One day my father and the soldiers went mitaya, a tribal word meaning a long hunting trip, and we heard how Bobby fought and held onto an anteater whose powerful claws dug right through his back. Poor Bobby, he came back to the fort bleeding, and even though we all cared for him, he died a few days later. When living in the jungle, the death of a dog is very sentimental, because they are part of one's survival and they are the friends who will protect their owners until the end of their lives.

From our house the view was beautiful. We could see the river all the time, forever changing in speed, width, and height. How I loved those mornings, eating preserved canned hash with inguire, large, salty bananas, followed by fresh, sweet-smelling oranges picked right outside the window.

In this fort there were no schools, but there were children, the sons and daughters of tribal people such as the Ahuarunas and Huambisas, who came to visit and trade and who were our friends and neighbors. My father was a fanatic for learning. He requested that a sergeant who could read and write be our teacher. His instructions were that we had to learn, even if it took blood to learn whatever he taught.

Our classroom was a hut made out of pona wood, with palm leaves for the roof, and typical windows, which are basically large openings in the wooden walls to let light in and wind pass through. There was no glass or fine wire mesh to protect us from mosquitoes. The tribal children were very playful, and their hair was meticulously cut as if a bowl had been placed on their heads and their hair trimmed precisely around the lower edges.

These children, I think, were smarter than Braulio and I, or else they were more eager to learn, because the sergeant would continually punish us by rubbing our ears with his two hands, sometimes to the point of bleeding, but he would spare our tribal classmates.

We had classes only in the morning, maybe for two hours, mainly because of the hot weather, or perhaps the sergeant got tired of punishing us or ran out of things to teach. We scarcely had books, paper, or pencils. By noon we were free to roam the compound and go to the river, or better, go to a stream of transparent water in the deep, nearby forest, where we swam and caught large shrimp or crawdads

This stream was beautiful and full of surprises. One could see all around how deep and impenetrable the jungle was, and one could only imagine what it was like farther in. The continuous singing of the birds and the noises of the animals were eerie at times. The main threats were snakes that some-times would swim unknowingly to where we were. Often we would see deer and other larger animals approach the stream to drink. It is amazing now to recall that we were at the end of the world, and yet we had our own cook, a sort of butler, and all the help we needed because the soldiers performed some domestic duties.

Once, on my first trip to the jungle of Puerto Maldonado in Madre de Dios, the day after our arrival, the orderly was told to bring some fruit. He went to the nearby forest and brought back a large sackful of different types of fruits that we did not even know how to eat. It was the first time I had seen a papaya, and we actually ate the seeds thinking that was the edible part. To our astonishment, they were bitter.

Time went by, over a year. Then my father was sent up north to guarnición Cahuide to replace a young lieutenant who had died. This fort was the farthest in the upper Santi-ago River bordering Ecuador, and it was the most dreaded place to be sent to. The story went that the dead lieutenant, a young, single officer, had gotten drunk and taken a canoe by himself down the river to the next town where there was more civilization and, possibly, women. He never returned to his post. Two weeks later they found his boot with his tibia and some flesh still inside it. I guess the piranhas finished him off. But as time went on, the soldiers told stories of how the young commander of this distant and isolated guarnición was a tyrant. He used to punish his men severely. Because he was hated by his subordinates, it was assumed that he may have been killed. It was not an uncommon story. Although my father got along well with his troops, in such remote places he still was cautious with soldiers of unknown backgrounds and motives, especially since we were so close to another country with which we had just been at war.

Such was the fate of those who were sent deeper into the jungles of Peru. This trip would be the most perilous of all. The river farther up was more rapid and shallow, and there were big whirlpools that could swallow a large boat. Because of the strong currents, the canoes had to be large and propelled by an outboard motor.

This trip will always be in my mind and in my heart, because it molded my soul to the philosophy of the emptiness of life, the ethereal existence that we have on earth: here was true, naked nature where man was just an intruder. Canoeing up the Santiago to the guarnición of Cahuide lasted an eternity; this is where my recollection of the jungle is most vivid. Later on, I was able to read about von Humboldt's exploration of the Orinoco, which lasted almost five years and probably covered a shorter distance than we did. As I mentioned earlier, Teddy Roosevelt had also spent time traveling on the rapids of the South American jungle and encountered pervasive natural disasters and disease, making him realize that he was at the end of his youth and he could not dominate the jungle as he did other parts of the world in his powerful younger days.

Our preparation for the trip was long and arduous. To go to Cahuide one basically had to say good-bye to the world. One's chances of coming back were slim, and, what is more, one did not take a family to those places. But such was the loyalty of my mother that she followed my father and brought Braulio and me along too.

My father made sure that we had the best and safest trip possible, for he was a man who could adapt to anything, and he almost became a jungle man. He chose the best soldiers for the rowing and hired an Indian guide. Such guides were necessary, for they knew those rivers like the palm of their hand and usually worked in return for items such as a machete, rifle, or clothes. To handle the outboard motor, we needed a mechanically experienced person. For this we had the memorable Lt. Guillen, an older officer who actually was going to Cahuide to fix the refrigerator, check the telegraph, and repair other mechanical things, including rifles. We were taking all the provisions with us: dried fish, fariña, canned food (mainly hash with American labels), salt, and other preserved foods.

On a thundering, rainy day so long forgotten, we said good-bye to guarnición Pinglo—to the soldiers, to the tribal children, and, most of all, to the animals who had been our pets. Pantaleon, the guacamayo, was the hardest for Braulio to leave. The dogs were running up and down the river's shore barking, as if sensing that this was good-bye forever.

Young Condor was already getting used to the sadness and emptiness of leaving places, people, and animals he had come to care for. This would eventually cause him to experience an eternal state of melancholy that would tamper with his beautiful flight on this Earth.

The river was warm and brown, like mud, and looked menacingly dangerous. It was like a liquid coffin that could send one to the next world in no time at all.

The vessel that we would travel in was a fifteen-to-twenty-foot, dark wooden boat carved out of a giant green tree. There were no seams; the ax marks were visible from the time they opened the heart of this majestic, huge, old tree that could easily become our final resting place.

In the middle of the canoe was a cover or hut made out of branches and palm leaves to protect us from the elements. This was the domestic area and was to be our house for days to come. We all had positions to take. Lt. Guillen was at the helm of the outboard motor, the proa. The second man was at the front of the boat, the popa, with a tangana, a large stick, which was used to measure the depth of and protect us from objects floating in the river. His paddle was ready to maneuver the canoe if a big trunk, a whirlpool, or other obstructions were sighted, and he would actually shout in a loud voice at the same time. He was extremely experienced at that; he had to be fast and watchful all the time, for our lives depended on him. The tanganero, as he was called, was usually a tribesman who knew the waters well. Tanganeros were the specialists, the so-called guides, and we knew that we were dependent on them. Then we had two soldiers, one at each side, to row as needed, sometimes to save gasoline or to add more power or to get us out of a tight spot when in trouble. At times when the currents were strong, we all had to paddle, even Braulio and I, just youngsters but able to help when needed.

The trip was monotonous, sad, and long. We passed the time thinking about the vastness of life, our solitude, and the insignificance of our existence. Always aware and waiting for that fatal moment, we canoed by paddle, motor, or both, and always stayed close to the shore. The jungle was like a mantle of loosened threads that one could not even pass one's finger through, and the noise of the many different insects and birds was persistent and never ending, like the sound of a million crickets all in one place.

The days passed with the weather continuously changing. At times it would be indescribably clear, with bright blue skies and calm waters, an unforgiving sun, and an intolerable humidity. Then we would have sudden storms and rough waters, the likes of which I had never seen, and I have traveled extensively.

The rain would pour down like giant buckets of water, becoming part of the river before falling, and it would swell the occasionally low and slow-flowing waters into torrents. The shore was carved away by the rapids, and the rising tide tore apart the ground and the trees in its path.

The storm's fury would leave us soaked, scared, and hungry. The thunder rumbled and the lightning flashed so close to us that it seemed at any moment we would see the end of the world. At times the lightning would spark fires in the faraway jungle and we were happy because we thought maybe they were the fires of a village and people would be there.

By afternoon we would be looking for a place to camp. This was the most difficult thing to find, because usually there was not a single area on the shore that was flat, devoid of vegetation, or safe to be in, and if such an area were found, it was always full of snakes, insects, and animals such as jaguars, looking for prey. Usually the best resting spot was a sandy beach in the middle of the river when the waters were low; but that was seldom found.

Of all the times that I think I have been close to death, there is one episode I will never forget. It was so ethereal and so mystical that thereafter life has probably been on loan to me.

It happened on an afternoon of pounding rain; we all were exhausted from the days of travel, dysentery, shortage of food, and lack of movement. We were mesmerized by the monotonous noises of the jungle, the running river, the rain, and the motor. I was sleeping on my mother's lap when suddenly she burst into a frantic squeal and exclaimed, "Dios mio!" (my God!). My father stood up, alarmed, and shouted, "Mira, mira!" (look, look!) and I quickly woke up and saw the Indian guide, the tanganero, up front, his dark, almost-

naked sweating body performing useless, awkward movements with the paddle, his face full of final agony. The
helmsman, Lt. Guillen, hurriedly stood up and pushed the
stick of the outboard motor all the way to the right almost to
the point of breaking it, while staring in terror and shaking
at what was just beside us. There it was!

Just passing by us, with our canoe at its rim, the tip of the
boat was pointing at the depth of a huge, brown-water, black
hole. It was the biggest remolino, a whirlpool, imaginable,
like an upside-down Texas tornado of water, as deep as a
huge cave, whistling and whirling at such a speed that it
muffled the sound of the motor. It was so wide that the other
side of the funnel seemed like a shore, as it passed by—without us—fast and arrogant! We could see our boat and our
lives being sucked into its depth, and I knew I was dead already. There are times when one sees one's life slipping by
and there is nothing one can do about it. Suddenly everybody froze, and the river carried our unshaken canoe on
downstream. The men were petrified, and everything came
to a standstill, mainly because we had made it—survived the
impossible, we were alive! I think we all cried in silence. We
timidly coasted to the shore and stayed for days. The fear of
the river was in all of us; thereafter, the trip was much slower
and more cautious, and time was of no consequence. After
that episode, I think nobody cared whether we arrived at our
destination.

I remember another event on this treacherous trip that
also brought us close to death. We stopped overnight at an
abandoned house right in the middle of nowhere. It was raining and for a change we were going to camp in a house. But
bats had made this place their mansion, and the trees and
branches had overtaken every corner. The place was more of
a threat to life than a place to feel safe, but a house it was,
and we decided to stay there. After such a long time in
cramped quarters, we were finally able to hang our ham-

mocks and stretch out. Our food supplies were almost gone, but we still had some of the empty cans of hash that we had saved to trade with the different tribes.

Since there was still some meat in the inner rims of the cans, we decided to boil them all together to get some flavor or grease from these mildewed, greying containers; we called it sopa de latas, or soup of cans. The thin, oily, yellowish liquid actually tasted good, especially on such a rainy day, and we finished it all. Then we went to look for fruit and found the most unusual guayaba-like fruit that I or the others had seen. It was called taperibá, and the inside seed was spiny, but it was sweet and juicy, so we ate plenty of them.

By nightfall, Lt. Guillen had primed his trusty Coleman gasoline lamp, and we could see that the place was full of mosquitoes and bats. The open entrance had posts on which we hung our hammocks and, bravely, we all turned in. Lt. Guillen had a stick with him and would continuously move his hammock with it, even while he was in deep sleep, to avoid the mosquitoes and stir a breeze. Everybody was aware of the dangers of the night. We were concerned about tribal Indians, and wondered what had happened to the people who had lived in this house and why they had abandoned it. Around midnight, I heard one of the soldiers run to the shore in a hurry, and he came back moaning. Next, it was Lt. Guillen who raced to the river. Almost running, I soon followed, along with my parents and Braulio. We all came down with dysentery, and I will never forget how sick we were. Even the guide was ill, and being a tribesman he was very sturdy and nearly immune to such problems. We stayed in the house for about a week, all of us in pain, prostrated with fever, running back and forth to the shore just as soon as we got into our hammocks. There was no food and there was no desire to eat; we could only drink mate de yerbaluiza, a tea made from a boiled leaf that tasted like mint and was used by the tribes for stomach ailments. While we lay weak and helpless, the torrential rain crashed down mercilessly. We were in a state of delirium, already feeling as one with nature, enjoying at times the quietness of the absence of rain and thunder. As a doctor I can now only conjecture about what must have been the cause of our illness: the putrefied leftover meat in the cans contained more than simple amoebas or other protozoa. This was a far more toxic bacteria. In any event, we survived a second time on this trip; but this infection could have been a slow and painful death. Had we been swept away by the remolino, we would have met with a swifter, but kinder, fate. We did not have a choice, but we made it.

Again we were upstream on the Rio Santiago, and now we were going to farther-up places where the tribes were more visible and ever present. They were friendly people— Ahuarunas, Huambisas, and the occasional Jivaros, who used to be known for shrinking human heads, who lived deeper in the forest. It was always a delight to come to their posts by the river. Their villages were oases in the jungle, round patches of red, sandy ground cleared of entwined trees and vines, with huts built in a circle. Women, men, and children of all ages, almost naked, were going about their domestic duties calmly, and they were always curious.

Here we could eat to our heart's content. There was plenty of dried fish and yucca, plus we could also have meat such as monkey, turtle, snake, paujil, a large, red-crested, black bird, sajino, jungle pig, and the cowlike sachavaca. We would stay for a day or two and almost become part of the tribe, as our bodies and our spirits were replenished.

The women and children would chew yucca and spit it into a big canoelike container. This white doughlike mass would eventually become fermented because of the chemical properties of the saliva and would turn into a strong drink called masato. This whitish concoction was always offered at all the tribal villages as a gesture of welcoming and could not be refused. I think this was my first introduction to alcohol, and I remember that it tasted sweet, and was thick like a milkshake. I suppose that nobody cared about the saliva since it was chewed only by younger women and children.

In these villages, we would trade trinkets and exchange valuable information on the status of the river, the unfriendly tribes, and the dangers of the upstream trip. We would get a good supply of smoked paiche and other fish, as well as meat, yucca, and other dry foods such as fariña.

On and on we traveled for days on end in thundering torrential rains and rapid currents. We could now frequently stop in villages and rest more often. As the river got farther away from the Marañon and Amazon, it was clearer and more peaceful in some stretches. Eventually we got closer to the guarnición Cahuide, the place where we would live for four years without any knowledge of the outside world.

As we were approaching this sparse army post on a clear day, from the distance we could see a tall round structure made out of balsa wood and pona, a strong, dark grey wood. It was a copy of one of the watchtowers of the Inca fortresses of Sacsayhuaman in Cuzco, especially similar to the taller one where the last Indian warrior, Cahuide, fought bravely in 1536 against the Spaniards. At the top of the wooden tower, facing north toward Ecuador, was the statue of Cahuide carved out of balsa, showing him in all his attire, including head feathers and a brilliant red mantle, and menacingly holding his macana, a weapon made of a wooden stick with a stone ball at one end.

In 1536, as Pizarro conquered northern Peru, he encountered resistance in the south, in Cuzco, where the Incas were still finding ways to take back their empire. Pizarro had three brothers who helped him maintain order, especially to control his own Spanish countrymen, who were always hatching schemes to get more land, gold, and power. The most difficult Spanish adversary was the well-known and avaricious Diego de Almagro, Pizarro's original partner in the conquest of Peru.

After executing the Inca king Atahualpa, Pizarro replaced him with Manco, a puppet Inca monarch, so the Spaniards could continue their conquest with the backing of an Inca ruler. However, this newly appointed leader accepted his position with premeditated ideas of creating an uprising and taking over his reign, so he started to organize the Indians while the Spaniards were exploiting their newly acquired lands. Some of his own people who were loyal to the Spaniards told Juan Pizarro of Manco's plans, and he was captured. Somehow Manco, with promises of more gold, convinced another Pizarro brother, Hernando, to free him, and again he went to gather his troops, while pretending to fetch more treasures. Hernando then sent his brother Juan to recapture him. By that time, Manco had thousands of warriors and led them in battle with Juan for two days. The Spaniards barely held out and thus Juan, Gonzalo, and Hernando Pizarro found themselves hostages in Cuzco with fewer than two hundred men.

Overlooking Cuzco were small mountains surrounding the city, and in one of them was the notable Fortaleza, the fortress of Sacsayhuaman; this grandiose structure still exists. To one side of Cuzco was a great wall, twelve hundred feet long and very thick; to the other side were two more walls built in a ladderlike arrangement of the same length. These walls were made of stones forty feet long, ten feet wide, six feet thick, and an incredible weight in tonnage, which were placed perfectly. These huge boulders had been brought from twelve miles away and placed between two massive, high stone towers.

This fortress was the domain of the Incas and gave them an advantage over the city below. The only way for the Spaniards to get out of the surrounded city of Cuzco was to take over this vantage point. This was their last and only hope, for they were dying of starvation. In a last-ditch effort, they sent three detachments under the command of Gonzalo Pizarro to take over the garrison. The fight was furious, many soldiers died, and the remaining horse-mounted Spaniards had to retreat. Due to severe famine inside the besieged city, another attempt to take over the Fortaleza was carried out by Juan Pizarro, a well-known fighting conquistador.

He and his men left Cuzco at sunset as if they were going to graze the horses, and without being noticed in the darkness by the Indians, they rushed to Sacsayhuaman. The fortress was closed off with two huge stones. They opened them quietly and with great difficulty. Once they entered, they were between two huge walls, at which time hundreds of Indian warriors almost overtook them. Juan left half of his troops there to continue the fighting, opened the second stone door, and entered the second wall. Now the Indians had to take refuge in the two towers, and the Spaniards needed to overtake these last two dangerous defenses. Juan Pizarro attempted the first tower and was injured in the jaw. Unable to strap on his iron helmet, he fought without it, and eventually an Indian with his accurate honda threw the stone that broke his skull. As he lay dying, Juan still inspired his men to keep fighting, but eventually this hero died in Cuzco from his wounds. Thus the Incas still had control of the fortress.

Hernando went to attempt to reconquer this garrison, leaving Gonzalo to take care of the city. The Spaniards took over the first tower in a furious attack with new troops, but the second tower was the stronger and more difficult. Among the Indian defenders of this second tower was a huge and intrepid Indian named Cahuide, who awed the Spaniards by throwing them over the stairs as the conquistadors were climbing to take over the tower. So great was his valor and the conquistadors' admiration for him that Hernando Pizarro gave strict orders not to maim or injure Cahuide. They would have to subjugate him but not kill him. So the Spaniards propped many ladders along the towers, and they simultaneously attacked this last Indian warrior. Meanwhile, Hernando Pizarro, in a loud voice, was trying to intimidate Cahuide into surrendering, promising that his life would be spared. But that brown Hercules, knowing all was lost, picked up some dirt from the floor and placed it on his face and in his mouth, covered his head with his mantle, and threw himself from the tower's highest point down to his instant death. It was at the moment of his self-inflicted sacrifice that the fortress was finally taken and the conquest secured for good.

Thus, the guarnición put up a statue of Cahuide looking defiantly toward the north, which bordered Ecuador. In the 1940s these two countries were at war, and this area became a place of confrontation where soldiers of both sides died.

Our canoe finally came to the Yaupi River, a tributary coming from Ecuador, which also feeds into the beginning of the larger Rio Santiago. It was the clearest water, and I could see all the fish swimming peacefully. Whenever I think of paradise in the next life, this is the river that I wish for in my heart. Finally our ordeals were over, and, exhausted and frail, we were received by the soldiers of the fort. As we climbed up the hill by the tower, the sentinel walked toward us and saluted my father. He was the new commander of the post, replacing the previous officer who died.

This small military village had large wooden buildings, the first of which was our house, built on top of long posts because of the frequent rising waters. Next was the animal coop, then the large dining room and the kitchen. Close by were the soldiers' quarters for about thirty men, then farther away was the telegraph post, with a big bare tree where the antenna was placed. In this place there was no electricity, no running or potable water, no doctors, no schools, and no radio. All we had was just plain virgin jungle and the river. However, this guarnición was better than those at Vargas Guerra and Gueppi, which were considered more dangerous because they were more inaccessible and isolated.

Although we lived in the farthest part of the Amazon jungle, we again had the privilege of being served by all the people around us. We had a cook, a sanitario or male nurse, who was a sergeant, and a guard or guide at all times. The dining room was pleasant, full of hanging plants, and we were surrounded by ravines, bushes, and trees with birds of all colors flying all over in the open—something that many fancy hotels try to imitate to give a festive ambience. The most luxurious item was an old methane or gas refrigerator. It did not work and its repair was the assignment of Lt. Guillen. He tried, but to no avail, for the refrigerator was corroded to the core by the humid weather. Nothing lasts in the jungle, only nature, and even that only for a while and in the prime of its youth.

Lt. Guillen was a jack-of-all-trades; he fixed all the items that needed to be repaired. He inspected all the rifles and machine guns as well as the telegraph. He spent days or months taking care of things; sometimes he had to wait weeks for parts that were brought to him in a P-47–like supply plane that landed in the river.

Finally the day came when Lt. Guillen had to depart with the crew that brought us in. It was sad because we had gone through so much together and we had become almost like family, but down the peaceful river he went, and our eyes filled with tears to see the last vestige of civilization leave this place. He had been kind to me, and was always instructing me like a grandfather; he knew everything. For days we talked about him, and we would marvel at the things he had repaired. He left my father a cigarette lighter that he had made out of rudimentary leftover metal. More than likely, he had saved our lives with his knowledge of the jungle and the rivers.

Now my father was the man to whom everybody would come, even for tribal justice. The days, months, and years went by, and soon my shoes were eaten by the big, aggressive curbinses, ants, that form armies and create micropaths of destruction, and by the moldy, humid weather. Clothing was almost nonessential here. The description of one's daily routine could describe all the years we lived there. The only disruptions of one's routine were natural catastrophe, death, and disease.

We became a central trading post for all the tribes around, including the notorious, aggressive Jivaros who would come to trade and visit. My father had to be alert to the whereabouts of these people. Although some were Ecuadoran and others Peruvian, they were not aware of national boundaries, but the soldiers of both sides were, and their duty was to keep their borders intact.

In those days the limits between the jungles of Peru, Ecuador, Colombia, Brazil, and Bolivia were determined by how much forest was cleared and how much each military post advanced. Gaining one foot of jungle was an unforgiving task that required effort and invited danger to anyone. Most of the soldiers were tribesmen, sometimes recruited for particular abilities, such as their hunting skills or expertise at infiltration; there were even spies from both sides of the border.

Supplies were a constant problem. Our biggest holidays were when a small boat would arrive selling all kinds of survival items, including gunpowder, rifles, salt, clothes, nails, and canned foods. Browsing in this small river craft was like going to the fanciest store in town. It was our only touch of civilization.

Once we were out of supplies for six months due to the loss of a regular delivery boat in the rapids. The item that we needed most was salt, for in this area salt was like gold and silver because it was so rare, and could be traded as such in some parts of the jungle. The lack of salt in the sweltering hot weather can be felt almost overnight. Our organic need for this chemical was so essential that we would have eaten it straight from the soil had we found any in this land covered with thousands of years of leafy ground.

The soldiers used to go to a far and hidden place where a stream of mineral water was available, but the salt content was too low and the water was bulky to carry. The solution was to powder dry fish scales and pour it over the food as a salt substitute. We lived like that for months until some supplies were dropped from an airplane, Oh, those rocks of salt were like candy. We could lick these virgin salty bars for hours and never satisfy ourselves.

In Cahuide I was again introduced to the rudimentaries of tropical medicine. Infections of the eyes, ears, and skin were ever-present. Our favorite pastime was to go to the Yaupi River and swim as often as possible during the day. In the night I would wake up with the most severe earache, and it worsened with the roar of thunder. There were no doctors and no medicines. My mother was told by the curanderos, healers, to place rotten urine in my ears; that was the only cure available. I remember pus coming out of my ears, and somehow the nights were worse than the days.

One constant problem was eye infections. My eyes would be full of pus, with mosquitoes having a feast in this soup of yellow debris. There were no antibiotics, and we even ran out of eyedrops, which I thought was iodine—it looked and smelled like it—but which I later learned was silver nitrate. The final treatment was the one I will always remember. Two or three soldiers would hold my arms and my legs, and my mother would place in each eye two or three drops of lemon juice squeezed right out of one of those acidic jungle tree fruits that were so abundant. This mode of cure would eventually eradicate the infection in the eyes, but the burning was so terrible that it could easily be considered torture. I guess those folk medicines did cure many minor ailments; however, I do not think it is a coincidence that today I am deaf in my right ear.

Another common infestation prevalent in the jungle was that of intestinal organisms. We had all the parasites and worms that are ever-present in these areas. Once a month we used to swallow tiro seguro, or sure shot, early in the morning, a deworming medicine taken by mouth on an empty stomach that had an awful, bitter, acid taste. After fasting all day, by evening our stools were like spaghetti; incredible numbers of all varieties of worms were visible. I am sure we suffered from chronic amoebiasis and other microscopic organisms that we did not know even existed.

Since there was no milk in these areas, we used to take intravenous calcium weekly. The sanitario, after many trials, would place a huge, worn-out needle in our veins, and slowly inject the clear calcium solution while looking at our reactions; his guideline of when to slow or stop the delivery of the large ampule's contents was when we almost passed out. I mean, we became red faced, dizzy, and sometimes lost consciousness. It is a miracle no one had cardiac irregularities, as one of calcium's effects is slowing of the heartbeat and hypotension, even to the point of cardiac arrest. However, this dangerous therapy apparently helped my teeth since I still have all of them and they are strong. I could go on and on about all the varieties of ailments. Suffice it to say, we made it, maybe because we were immune or resistant.

At times we had to evacuate injured soldiers, usually on a P-47 warplane that could land on the river. Many of them suffered from snakebites, broken bones, and acute illnesses. In this area, men would often be lost to disease and desertion. The arrival of those beautiful U.S.-built World War II planes was a treat for everyone at the fort. We would all go down to the river to admire these aircraft. The pilots would never come out of the cockpit; they seemed so detached and they looked at us as if we were some kind of savage or something below them. The sick men would be accommodated like pieces of cargo in the rear seat, and the plane would then roar off down the tranquil river, causing chaos among all the birds and other animals in the surrounding jungle.

The neighboring tribes were always full of intrigue, and their people never seemed to die of natural causes. They often attributed a death to sorcery, and consequently the tribesmen were continuously fighting and avenging the deaths of their relatives.

One time there were orders to capture a tribal man, possibly a Jivaro, who had been hunted for a long time and was feared by everyone because he was thought to have killed many people and he was on the run. Eventually he was apprehended in the deep jungle by the soldiers and brought to the guarnición. He was a big, dark brown man with thick, straight, flattened, shiny black hair, a disfigured face, and legs swollen and full of blisters and nodes. Everyone ran away from him because he had leprosy. He was kept tied to a tree. My mother and I would bring him food and water, and we also poured mercurochrome onto his legs and rubbed them with some foul-smelling cream used by the locals. He was humble and thankful for our kindness. My father contacted Iquitos for a transfer of this fugitive to justice. The response, I remember very well, came by Morse code while we were having supper in the noisy, half-lit jungle evening. The soldier read the ticker tape, which in a few coded words explained that the Indian should be shot right away since he was accused of so many crimes and thus a high risk for escape. My mother was crying and nobody finished what we were eating. My father was very sad and, unable to overrule the order, carried on more correspondence via telegraph, but still the order was to shoot the prisoner somewhere in Cahuide. These were upper-echelon orders and had to be carried out.

I remember the day was assigned, and still nobody could change the sentence. It was a clear, early morning with no clouds or rain. Three soldiers came to get the accused man with the pretext of taking him to the next guarnición. After a meager breakfast, provided by the soldiers since we could not approach him due to our inability to control our sorrow, the prisoner was taken to the monte, deep jungle, with his hands tied behind his back. The soldiers later reported that after a short distance they shot him from behind, in the back, three times, then threw his body into the river. That day ended like any other, but I believe my soul was hardened by the event. Such was the justice of the jungle in those days.

Across the Yaupi River was the Ecuadoran border, with no post or soldiers, and we could cross it anytime. My mother, Braulio, and I would go with a few soldiers to place crosses on and clear away vegetation from the graves of those fallen soldiers of the 1940 conflict who were buried there, and who were probably Peruvian and Ecuadoran. There were no religious symbols or names, just patches of loose ground covering skeletons whose flesh was probably eaten by the different scavenging animals.

Time went by, and my father became a hunter and a trader. He collected large numbers of different hides such as nutria, jaguar, and caiman. Eventually this valuable merchandise filled three rooms. He used to go hunting for days with soldiers, guides, and dogs. Sometimes we were worried he might have been killed because they were gone so long, but then he would return with fresh meat and hides. Often he would bring us baby animals that were taken from the parents that had been shot. I would care for them, but they never made good pets; they usually died of hunger (refusing to eat) or loneliness. I remember an añuje that was given to me by a Huambisa tribesman. This beautiful, orphaned animal was so wild and difficult that the Indians gave me all kinds of advice on how to tame him. One day I was finally able to hold him and pet his soft hair. I was so happy that I would have a friend, but he suddenly died in my arms. He never became docile; he just gave up and decided to die and fight no more.

The tribal families would come often to visit us and trade. When we talked to them, they would always spit on the floor after finishing a sentence, to signify that they were saying the truth. The mothers would bring their children, some of them nursing all the time. They would pick lice and scabs off their children and eat them like monkeys do. We used to have a frog that was always around the house—she was big and we named her Maricacha. One day, as usual, she came out of her hiding place. An Indian mother looked down at the frog and immediately jumped up, picked it up, and tossed it into her basket. Poor Maricacha, she was going to be eaten for dinner. We tried to retrieve the frog but they would not let her go.

So many things happened in the jungle, but now with so much television and the dwindling of the rain forest, there are hardly any more stories; I tell mine because they happened to me; I was there. These experiences molded me into what I am now. And most importantly, they gave me a great leap between cultural backgrounds.

As all things must come to an end, eventually we had to depart from Cahuide. The trip back would be down the Yaupi, Santiago, and Marañon Rivers to meet the Huallaga and continue to Nauta where the Ucayali and Marañon join to form the great Amazon on its way to Iquitos. We had acquired so many hides that the only safe and possible way to travel and transport them was by balsa, a river raft made out of light, floating balsa wood and built to look like a house. This meant another trek down the treacherous rivers, with more adventures and stories to tell, but by now we were more selvatico than we had been four years before and we were more accustomed to the ways of the jungle and river.

CHAPTER FOUR

A World Left Behind

My father oversaw the construction of the big river craft made out of balsa wood, which is so abundant in the jungle. The round, straight trunks were tied together with strong natural string, and no nails or man-made materials were used. The balsa was big, and it had three large paddles, two in front and one in the back, all anchored in heavy wooden bases. They were used more for steering than for rowing. A bungalow-like house on the balsa was made of dry palm leaves with small divisions for sleeping quarters, a cooking area, and space for the three soldier guides, the crew who were going to take us downriver.

Once again, at my tender age, came the anguish of separation. We had lived in Cahuide so long that everything there, even its dangers, was part of my life. All we were taking with us were dead things and our memories. I had a dog, with white and black spots, a mutt whose name was Etico. I guess in everyone's life there has to be a dog, and because its life is so short we all have memories of departure from these animals. Well, mine was coming.

All the hides and rifles were packed. Our personal belongings fit into one suitcase. We had almost no clothes, and my shoes were slippers made out of wood and leather. The only important thing I was taking was Etico, my dog. He was squirmy and playful and he probably had all the diseases of the jungle, but he was a happy animal and I was overjoyed that he was coming with us. Down the Yaupi we went—a river that is clean and tranquil. But my heart was heavy with profound sadness. How can one describe leaving a place that one lived in for so long, knowing that one will never come back? The high tower with its statue of the Inca Cahuide holding his macana was getting smaller as the balsa was carried away by the slow current. My thoughts switched to the excitement of the trip, the way I imagine Huckleberry Finn must have felt in his Mississippi River adventures. But we also knew there were dangers ahead, and anything could happen. Little did we know that farther down the river, on more treacherous waters like the Pongo of Manseriche, this balsa would be as fragile as a matchbox.

After weeks of travel we arrived at the Rabarosa farm, a family-owned huge tract of jungle in the middle of nowhere. We spent two days in its large, pleasant house. My father had to attend to the remains of a soldier who was killed by some tribesman at a nearby post. The Rabarosas had buried the body along with all his military equipment. My father was responsible for those items, so the cadaver had to be disinterred and all the military items removed and accounted for. Our destination was Iquitos, but we had to stop at as many places as before, like Pinglo and Borja. This time we had to navigate that most dreadful of all passages, the Pongo of Manseriche, between these two cities, in order to avoid a long, arduous trip by foot in the high mountain. This natural channel was described more than a hundred years ago by the well-known German explorer Baron Alexander von Humboldt. He wrote, and I translate:

> In the celebrated strait of the Pongo of Manseriche, between Santiago and San Borja, a big mountainous depth exists, where at some points there is so little

daylight due to the mixing of high cliffs, rocks, and hanging trees that form like a roof. In these rapids the large tree trunks that are floating become pulverized and disappear.

This passage was also described well by Mario Vargas Llosa in his beautiful and heartening novel *La Casa Verde*.

Mr. Rabarosa told us all about the catastrophes and deaths of people who went through these dangerous waters. The Indian tribes say that this strait is the sanctuary of a big snake that is the mother of the Ayawaska, a potent hallucinogenic drink. We were told so many stories and our fear was getting worse, but the only way to avoid the Pongo was to walk through the high, mountainous jungles for days and face the danger of its narrow and tortuous jungle pathway, or trocha. But my father had a lot of precious cargo to transport, and the trip by foot would have been impossible.

We were devastated by the stories we had heard and by the death of the soldier; the ominous feeling that our lives were hanging by a thread grew. The next day, early in the morning, we got ready to cross the Pongo. We were told to keep completely quiet and to stay secured to the poles during the crossing, in order not to awaken this giant snake or be thrown out of the balsa. Mr. Rabarosa lent us one Indian tribesman, an Ahuaruna who knew this stretch of waters very well and who would serve as our guide. It was decided that I should leave my dog Etico behind as thanks for Mr. Rabarosa's hospitality. The news came to me so hard that I felt my heart break into pieces, like when the high, rapid river tears the earth and trees from the shores; my tears could not reveal my suffering and my anguish at the loss of my companion and the possibility of death. It was more than a child could withstand. Braulio was also heartbroken. Even now my soul shrinks at the thought of that day. So it goes with the love for an animal, and I am sure many who care for animals will sympathize with this memory.

As we embarked, Etico was howling and running along the shore; I think he knew he would be left behind. As the balsa slowly flowed downstream, I could still hear his barking, and from a distance I could see the fading black dots of his disappearing, spindly body. At this point, the Pongo could have swallowed me, and I would not have cared. Oh, poor dog, you were also breaking inside! Years have passed, and I still remember him. Moments like this are what mold our spirits, and mine was all the time being hammered with the vicissitudes of life.

Well, the forces of nature can bring us to our senses. Before long we started to see more stones and rocks in the water, the river became faster, and at the shore we could see caimans coming or running away. Everything on board was tightened and secured, and preparations were made in case the balsa broke down. All we could think about was whether there would be life after this trip. Only God and the river knew the answer.

As the soldiers and the Indian guide were maneuvering the balsa, an oar broke and the soldier handling it fell into the deep water. We thought he had drowned because it took so long for him to come up, but eventually he surfaced, barely breathing, holding the half-broken end of the long paddle. The other soldiers plucked him out quickly. This man was lucky, because the oar broke not in the Pongo, but near the entrance where the river was not quite so treacherous. We pulled into the middle of the river where there was a stretch of soft sand.

We stayed there overnight. I think we were all afraid, and the soldier was shaken after his accident. My mother cooked tacacho, a salty banana dish with wild pig, and we went looking for taricaya eggs. As the night and silence came, in the distance we could hear the river slamming into the narrow stretch of the Pongo (about five miles long and very narrow, only eighty-five feet wide at places). Our imagination was as turbulent as those waters; I do not think we slept at all.

Morning came and I could think only of Etico. But now the moment of truth had arrived, and we all pushed and boarded the balsa. The craft slowly gained speed, and we could see that the low jungle was now rising into the heavens, intermingling with the dark clouds and rocky mountains as if it were in union with the end of the world and beyond. The waters were faster and noisier. We could hear only thunderous slamming water sounds, no more birds or monkeys, just a pure avalanche of deadly fury. Rapidly we were pulled into this dark, forbidding place bordered by huge, solid granite cliffs with long strings of falling crystalline water and beautiful, dark green moss hanging all over. We could look up or toward the cliffs—both views were awesome—but the river itself was fearsome. The men were fighting and struggling against the rapids, the rocks, and the whirlpools, all the way through the narrow passageway. Nobody could talk, it was taboo. We followed the legends and instructions of the natives, because they knew best. The balsa was thrown all over and shook as if it were ready to break. Sometimes it would be going around and around in a circle and we would see the same place over and over. The men were pushing with the long oars against the rocks and cliffs and paddling with the big oars as their sweat mingled with the spill and foam of muddy water, and our ears were muffled by the torrential noise. We were looking for the "giant snake mother of the Ayawaska stream." It all ended in a flash. It was all a dream that lasted for what seemed an eternity, but then the sun rays started to appear through the moving, menacing, grey clouds. The men calmed down, holding their paddles in the air. The brown water had lazy, large, flat whirlpools and was as silent as a breeze. The jungle started to come down to earth, the sky was no longer part of the green forest, and now the balsa was quiet, its splintered logs no longer creaking. We all looked at each other, still mute with fear of talking. My mother had tears all over her face and was still on her knees praying. We had passed through this incredible Pongo and for this I will always be a man; nothing will ever be insurmountable. I have been baptized by nature and I think now I could also be a phoenix. But then in the calmness of the river, my heart ached for my dog. Throughout my life, sadness and melancholy is something that I will never be able to overcome; it will always be my nemesis.

So we arrived in Borja and other towns whose jungle people had not been upstream and who were curious to know how we fared in the Pongo. We were like local heroes; anywhere we stayed, the tales of the crossing could pay for a good meal and a secure place to sleep. Now, the balsa was king of these waters and the ride down the river was the poetry of nature to my heart. Oh, those faraway jungles on the passing shores! The green hope of those oceans of trees will always stay with me, and in my days of solitude I will always find a refuge thinking about the far-gone times, and gain strength from these fading memories.

We passed many towns, and each time we got closer to civilization. I felt strange. I was more selvatico than the people who lived closer to Iquitos, and I was not looking forward to rejoining that world.

We followed the Santiago into the Marañon and, after months of river rafting, eventually we entered the Amazon at Nauta. After a few more weeks downriver, at a distance we could see the large city of Iquitos with its bleached and blue-tiled buildings. A new world was awaiting us, and we were already missing Cahuide, Pinglo, Borja, and Barranca; those days would never return. Good-bye, great jungle. We arrived and moored our old worn-out raft in one of the many outskirt ports of Iquitos alongside other small river craft.

Arriving in this town was like coming to New York in an ox-driven carriage. My father put on his uniform and we waited in the balsa. He went to buy us clothes and shoes. I think he was embarrassed to go shopping with us. We literally wore the last of our clothes on our backs, and even though the town was big, it was still small enough to notice the family of an officer. Although we looked poor, my father had accumulated several years' worth of salary that he had never spent and a cache of beautiful and expensive hides that sold quite rapidly. Now we had to adjust to another new way of life in a town where we were nobody. We had to find an apartment, and they were expensive, dark, and small. Although Iquitos was in Amazonia, it still was a metropolis compared to where we came from. The problem of school came up. Braulio and I had not attended school for nearly five years.

In Cahuide my father had studied for a test in order to rise in rank; he was self-taught and well read. He had his own books, mainly mathematics; he was, or wanted to be, an artillery officer, and mathematics was their main course. I suppose artillerymen had to calculate how their cannons would hit a target. Well, we had studied both algebra and geometry with him in the early mornings in the jungles of Cahuide, because there were no other books and no curriculum. Now, in Iquitos, my father somehow pulled strings so Braulio and I could take an exam and be placed in the appropriate grades, fifth for me and sixth for him. He was behind because he had not gone to school in Andahuaylillas.

The day of the exam came. I had new clothes, shoes, and a haircut. The teachers looked at Condor. They could not figure him out; he was from the Andes and now he was more of a jungle boy than the rest. In Peru, each region—coast, sierra, jungle—is so different from the others that it might as well be another nation or another continent.

The exam was oral and the first question was about the life cycle and ways of the bees. Poor Condor, he remembered when his little Indian tribe friends used to pick wasp larvae eggs and pull them out of their geometrical nests and eat them as if they were candies. That was all he knew about bees or wasps. No answer, just a blank stare at the blackboard. The next question

was about the birth date and the battles of general and liberator Don Simón Bolívar. Who was he? He had never met the
man. Again a stare from the teachers, and heads going from
right to left and left to right. Well, I supposed now they would
ask the most feared questions and this would be the coup de
grâce. An addition and multiplication problem was given to
start with and then they kept going with geometry, algebra,
and so on. These questions I easily answered, and it was
enough to approve my admission to the school in my own
grade as if I had been attending school all those years. Braulio
and I were still at a disadvantage, because we had lost so much
schooling, but eventually we made it in Iquitos.

The ensuing months and years went by with domestic
problems. My father needed to take his exam in Lima, and
had to go by himself. We were left in Iquitos to fend for ourselves. He took all the money he had saved and made from
the hides. I think that once he was in the capital, the stress
and deprivations of the jungle made him realize what a life of
opulence means. He squandered all the money and somehow
forgot us completely. We were receiving barely enough allowance for survival. I even had to pick up bottles from under the muddy houses, wash them, and sell them. Bottles of
any kind in the Amazon were a valuable commodity in those
days. Braulio was selling alcohol laced with perfume to the
boat people in the poor port of Belén on the outskirts of
Iquitos. Even our friends were of dubious character. They
taught us how to steal, and I remember how easy it was to
take a piece of merchandise, hide it in my shirt, and walk
away. We looked so innocent that people did not suspect us.
Oh, how we missed those days of the jungle! The people in
the city were different from those in the inner jungle; the
tribes in the deep forest were untainted by civilization.

Eventually we saved some money to travel to Lima to
join my father. My mother took the cheapest lancha to travel
up the tributaries of the Amazon to Pucallpa. The name of

the boat was the *San Ramon*. This river craft was a classic, just like the famous boat in the movie *Fitzcarraldo*. It was steam driven with worn-out engines, and the bathroom was a hole out of the stern for defecation directly into the running river. As usual, it had two decks and a first, second, and third class. My mother and I traveled in second class, and Braulio went third class. We had a camarote with four bunks, but we shared this small, hot cabin with other people.

This trip was in itself a story. People made new friends and enemies, fell in love, and even passed away on that boat. It was like a soap opera. We got to know everybody as if they were our family, and we all had the same problems: lack of food, perpetual hunger, disease, mosquitoes, boredom, and fear of any catastrophe on this river. From Iquitos we were bringing our meager belongings and two birds, a toucan and a parrot called Aurora. After days of waiting for the boat to fill with passengers, the *San Ramon* finally left the crowded port of Iquitos. Its noisy engines made little headway against the mighty Amazon, spitting black smoke and whistling its tired, old, rusty steam whistle. In the commotion of people rushing to find a place to hang their hammocks, I could see that a world was left behind me and uncertainties were on the horizon. Pretty soon the city disappeared, and we began the routine of taking care of ourselves in a boat with few amenities.

We stopped after a few days in Nauta, where the Marañon joins the Ucayali to form the Amazon River. From Nauta we would be traveling on one of the main tributaries of the Amazon, the Ucayali River, which comes from the south of Peru. On its course we stopped in Requena, Orellana, Contamaná, and Tirutan, which were medium-size towns by the shore. The point of arrival was to be the large port city of Pucallpa, but this trip felt like an eternity. The boat was so old that we had to stop continually because the steam pressure was low. Sometimes we were delayed for days or weeks waiting for repairs. The *San Ramon* had to load almost half of its cargo capacity just in wood for fuel. We would pick up and leave people in almost every little town we passed. Each loading and departing was a feat in itself. All the people from the small villages would come to see the lancha that was for them a brush with civilization.

It took us about three months to reach Pucallpa. Once more, we had to say good-bye forever to friends and enemies that we had made during the trip. The boat itself had become part of our lives; we were secure in this loyal, little old lancha and we got to know its every angle. We left the *San Ramon* there, in Pucallpa, with heavy fumes belching from its smokestack, as if it were taking the last breath of its life.

The only way to get to Lima from Pucallpa in those days was by airplane. Roads were beginning to open up, but travel by land was hazardous and lengthy. We had no money, so my mother sold her jewelry and some other items. Eventually we had enough for the fare. This time the airplane was a big Douglas DC-3. We boarded and sat down quickly, aware and shy of the people around us. We still felt we were out of place and all the more so on this plane. I had only my toucan with me. I do not remember his name, but he was an awkward yet beautiful bird with a large beak, and a red-and-blue painted face.

The DC-3 took off from the dirt landing strip, and we could see through the window the jungle below looking like a green carpet marked by winding rivers and water all around. We crossed the huge Andes with their eternal and inhospitable glacial cordilleras. The airplane provided oxygen only through tubing that we held against our noses all the time. My toucan and I shared and alternated this contraption. It looked odd and funny—he would open his big beak thinking that he was getting water. He was actually swallowing the rich, cold oxygenated air needed at that high altitude in an unpressurized craft. I am sure he needed this vital element as much as I did, poor little guy. We were friends, and he was my security blanket. He probably was cheaper than the stuffed teddy bears that some rich children had.

The trip on the plane was uneventful. We could only admire the majesty of the jungle and of the Andes, which were both so unforgivable and so impenetrable that it almost made one's body shiver just looking at them. After a few hours we arrived in Lima, a desert landscape from above with sadness in its streets and no greenery. It was humid, cold, and cloudy. The city was strange and unwelcoming. In those days passengers arriving from the jungle were rare and the tales they told were incredible. Only a few people ventured to Iquitos, let alone to Cahuide, the end of the world.

CHAPTER FIVE

Another Kind of Jungle

We were lost in Lima. My father picked us up and took us to a rundown hotel downtown, behind the president's palace, across the Rimac River where the colonial bridge crossed the old city of the viceroys, so well known from the song "La Flor de la Canela." The electric trolley, or tranvia, passed right by the window of our cheap hotel. The noise was constant, and it was no longer the sounds of the monkeys, parrots, crickets, and frogs, but the voices of the small entrepreneurs, fruit vendors, beggars, and shoe shine boys. In itself it was pleasant and it was a jump from the primitive life we had led into the twentieth century, but all I can remember are the conjugal fights. Our memories of domestic tranquility in the Amazon jungle were an oasis for our souls and spirits, and I think that was the only thing that held us together.

My beloved toucan was given to some general, as a bribe, I suppose. I was left only with memories of this funny, beautiful bird with his bright, made-up face. I should never have brought him to Lima. I hope his large beak is in heaven, pecking at the angels. I miss him even now and I regret taking him away from his jungle. But I guess I was too young and we did not realize that such birds belonged in the Amazon; now we know and can only hope that their kind and all animals are more protected and remain in their original environment.

Braulio also loved all animals and had a way with them. In Pinglo he was happy because he had Pantaleon, a large guacamayo that followed him everywhere. However, Pantaleon had been left in Pinglo. But Braulio still had a pet, a talkative parrot named Aurora, who must have been a female. She was smart and could talk forever. One day while traveling up the Ucayali, we were hit hard by such a horrible storm that it almost tossed the *San Ramon* into the depths of the river. As the warm sun thinned the heavy clouds, the boat approached the shore, and there was much commotion coming from a large number of green, noisy parrots, similar to Braulio's. With the call of the wild, Aurora just took off from his hands, and we saw her almost fly, since she had clipped wings, barely making it to the shore and reuniting with her fellow birds. For some reason we were not sad, only worried that she would not survive in the unknown jungle; after all, she was a civilized parrot who had a good command of Spanish.

I wish my toucan had been able to escape. I would be happy now, but he was not so smart. Not to digress, but cruelty to our animals is the last bastion of the worst inhumanity that we are witnessing today. Perhaps thousands of years in the future animals will be able to tell about the atrocities that were committed against them, but certainly many will be mute by their extinction.

With the departure of our pets the last vestiges of the jungle left us, and now we had to deal with the harsh reality of city life, and we were out of touch. Most people in Lima think that they are more civilized than even city dwellers in the rest of the country, let alone people just arriving from the deep Amazon.

We settled into a one-room house, scarcely making ends meet. Life was expensive, and my father had problems that caused him to neglect us. Time passed, and again we were rescued. My father had passed his exams and was transferred to another branch of the armed forces, the Guardia Republicana, with a higher rank and better career prospects. He was sent to Huaraz, a small town north of Lima, in the Department of Ancash, about a one-day trip by bus. The time we spent in Lima brings back few good memories. Like all big cities, it was so removed from nature that its people became hard, almost robotlike. Their daily routine seemed aimless, and even their fight for survival was trivial. Life for an Indian tribesman is more immediately significant; each survivor represents a triumph of life over death. A tribesman earns every day of his very life; nothing is phony about him. He is respected for his skills of survival and admired for his resourcefulness to continue living.

As we were leaving this metropolis by car, the scenery became more beautiful. Leaving the desertlike landscape, climbing up over the mountains, our hearts felt happy, but then a feeling of emptiness set in as the blue-green mountains began to overpower us. Once again, approaching the Andes, we started to see the troubled descendants of the great Incas who had become a social problem that was not being dealt with and still exists. It seemed as if they had been frozen in time, as if the cold of the high altitudes had taken the life out of their spirits.

There was and still is a lack of desire to become again what they once were and surpass it. It seems as if their minds are anesthetized by the fury of the past and by the arrival of a new civilization. Alexander von Humboldt described the difference between the peoples of the coast, the jungle, and the Andes as he was coming from the Caribe down to Ecuador and Peru, observing that the Indians in the Andean regions were more to themselves, closed, distrustful of everybody, and indifferent to their future, unlike those who live in the jungle or close to the oceans, who were more open and confronted life as a happy passage.

We arrived in Huaraz at night. The weather was cold and we wore heavy clothes. The city had its own charm and there was a plaza with palm trees. The cathedral had a large clock, which rang out the time every hour. One of the highest peaks of South America, the nevado Huascaran, its ragged edges perpetually covered with pure white ice, was ever-present and could be seen from all points of the city.

The time we spent in this town was the birth of my good memories, because there was domestic tranquility. Here I learned to play chess with a set that my father had made by hand with the help of some political prisoners who were being guarded at his command. My father went duck hunting in the numerous high, beautiful lakes that surrounded the city, and many times he took me along.

The subtleties of racial discrimination can be described by lingering memories from my childhood. I started to become more aware of the social inequality in my country. While attending a school that had no Indian children in it, I noted that educated, lighter-skinned people who were from families in the government system were not considered Indian or mestizo, but regarded simply as members of a "nondenominational" class. Even direct European descendants

One of the highest peaks of South America, the nevado Huascaran, with its ragged edges perpetually covered with pure white ice.

consider such people as their own kind. But those who were a little darker skinned with more defined Indian features, and who had less education and did not work in the government system, were classified as Indian or mestizo, which was their downfall. They were, and are, ostracized, discriminated against, and exploited by the same people who are their brothers. In North America, England, or Scandinavia, all these classes would be considered virtually the same.

In this school we were all treated as regular children, but one day a full-blooded Indian child made it to our classroom. He actually used to come to school on his horse and wore sandals instead of shoes. He was smart and studious, and we all looked at him and thought of him as a stranger. We followed all his footsteps and were amazed that he could do all the things that we did. Even I was involved and contributed in this social dilemma, although I did not fully realize it at that time.

Huaraz residents lived in perpetual fear, because in 1940 a huge aluvión, avalanche, buried half the city. Since it was situated at the foot of these great snow-peaked mountains where large, high lakes were present, the possibility of natural disaster was always in the minds of the people. The aluvión was described as an avalanche of granite boulders the size of a house, rocks, mud, large chunks of ice, and water coming down the steep slopes of the high cordillera at such furious and devastating speeds that there was no time to run for safety as it buried and destroyed anything in its path. Whole cities could be erased from the land.

One night after the Santa River had swelled due to heavy rains, people were concerned about another aluvión. Sure enough, one ordinary evening the city went to bed, and at about midnight people were running down the streets shouting the dreaded word: Aluvión! Aluvión! We all got up, threw on some clothes, and quickly went running along with all the frightened people to the higher mountains. Once there, in the darkness we could hear the thunder and roaring of the Santa River and we all could imagine the city being buried and razed by those huge boulders. My father left us in a safe place up on higher ground along with thousands of people, and he quickly ran to take care of his men. In the middle of this cold, rainy night we said good-bye to him as if we would never see him again.

That night we slept in the high mountain, and as daylight broke we rejoiced at seeing the cathedral still standing and the city intact. The alarm had come from an overflow of a small lake and had no major consequences. But such was the state of mind of the people in those regions. *The avalanche we feared eventually did happen on May 31, 1970, when approximately sixty-nine thousand people along the Callejon of Huaylas died, and many small cities were buried.*

In spite of the risk of natural disasters, the general tranquility of this town and of our family life there will always be in my heart. Our favorite Sunday pastime was going to the movies. It was there I learned more about the great country to the north where Flash Gordon, Gene Autry, and Roy Rogers lived. It was a place as distant as the moon, and Braulio and I could only perceive the United States in terms of the celluloid fantasy.

After a year we had to leave Huaraz and go back to Lima, where the spirit of the people has always left me in a state of confusion. Again the anguish of leaving friends and memories of majestic mountains increased the perpetual sadness and melancholy in my spirit.

Again, we were lost in the big city. Once more we were nobodies observing the ubiquitous social climbing around us. Here, going along with the latest fashion was of the utmost importance. People gained status by being like everybody else, but the social classes were more distinct. The Indians and mestizos were almost not accepted, especially if they arrived from the interior or the highlands. Then they had to immediately transform themselves into Limeños. Mestizos and Indians had to hide their origin and acquire the customs and the superficiality of the rest as soon as they knew that they were different, because people were so quick to single them out. In Lima everybody pretends to be from Lima. My father even altered my birth certificate, so that I was not from Cuzco, but from the capital. Ipso facto, the respect was felt and the derogatory comments stopped. This attitude is not unusual in Latin America. We all try to appear to be from large cities, when in reality this is not always so; that attitude is a remnant of the colonial mentality.

As a "native" of Lima, I went to school amid the old, smoking cars, heavy traffic, and frequent, petty street theft. We were removed from the treachery of nature, yet we struggled to survive in another kind of jungle.

Again my father was transferred, this time to Puno, located in the southern highlands of Peru, on the Bolivian border. Here was the highest lake in the world, Lake Titicaca, at an elevation of 12,506 feet. The air there was so lacking in oxygen that even the frogs need excess skin to breathe and it makes them ugly, as described by Jacques Cousteau, who found them in the depths of the lake.

On our way to Puno we stayed with my father's family in Arequipa, the beautiful colonial city where he was born. There we picked up two of my cousins, children my age, to help their parents economically. All of us traveled by train to Puno, in what must have been second or third class because chickens and pigs were among the passengers.

The night trip by train up to Puno was arduous, cold, and slow. We were continuously climbing, and the air was getting thinner. The landscape was a vast emptiness of poor or sparse vegetation. At times we saw animals running away from the noise of the steam engine. The view was so serene that we could only think of infinity in those high, desolate mountains, where a multitude of graceful gazellelike vicuñas, llamas, and alpacas were grazing on the horizon.

The train was full of Aymara Indians, who are descendants of the great Tiahuanaco civilization. Actually the great Inca

leaders started here, with the sudden apparition of Manco Capac and Mama Oclla out of Lake Titicaca. These Indians also
chew coca and drink alcohol. They are hard in their spirit and
their future is grim, like a rock that no one can carve.

*They have remained almost the same in all my return trips
during the past forty years. The only visible changes I have seen in
this region were fewer or no vicuñas and more people in similar
circumstances.*

My father was once again sent even farther into higher
altitudes, to a barren, oxygen-poor place called Yunguyo, a
small town bordering Bolivia near Lake Titicaca. The desire
to get closer to nature was always in me. In Yunguyo we went
swimming in the beautiful, inviting, clear lake, but the water
was colder than anyone could stand for long. We searched for
a warmer place to swim. Braulio and I with other youngsters
used to go to an abandoned pool, where we had to clean out
the algae and remove all the frogs before we could swim. Talk
about clean waters! Now I have a private pool. But I still
think we had more fun chasing the frogs out of the water and
swimming in those green, unfiltered waters. Animals were so
much a part of our life that not being around them was like
having a family without children.

Puno brings to mind memories mainly related to the Indians and my growth as a student. We went to the only sec-
ondary school, San Carlos, where the teaching was stern.
The school had the reputation that whoever finished there
did not need to go to college—maybe because there was no
college in town, and the closest one was days away by train.

In this school, there was a music professor who was, as
many others were, feared by all the students, especially by
anyone who was full-blooded Indian or more mestizo. He was
merciless and literally would come into a classroom, identify
an Indian, go to his desk and pull him out by his ears, and
throw him out of the classroom, especially if he could not
sing. In those days, the teachers were supreme dictators and

their aim was to flunk everyone. This particular music teacher, whom we called "perro," or dog, was tall, slender, and as white as milk. He looked like Paganini, the great violinist. Years later, I and many others still remembered him.

In the same school there were other teachers who were kind, but the students were merciless to them. This is where we learned that one had to protect oneself; otherwise, one was taken advantage of. This is probably why some Latin American countries have dictators as presidents. The minute a leader lets down his guard, some wise guy will dethrone him. The students had the same mentality, acquired from centuries of prejudice. Having mixed blood came in handy, and that is why the pure Indian students would always come out the losers.

This was years ago, but I suspect that things have not changed dramatically.

In Puno, Braulio and I were learning to live by ourselves. While we were in school away from distant Yunguyo, we lived in a small room and we had to take care of our own needs, including cooking our meals and washing our clothes. We had no guidance or caretaker and we were becoming independent and responsible.

School was so hard that one time when we had a very difficult subject and exam time was coming, we conveniently became religious. This time we thought studying would not help us much, so we made a half-day pilgrimage to the Virgin of Cancharani (an image of the Virgin Mary left behind after lightning struck a stone). The naturally engraved rock was supposed to make miracles happen. We spent time resting and praying to this Virgin after an arduous trip by foot to the higher mountains without breakfast or lunch. We returned by afternoon to the school to take the test, confident that this Virgin would help us with this difficult exam. One can imagine the results. We flunked miserably. This is the kind of guidance I had, learning by my own wits the hard way. I guess it would have been better to have studied (no offense, dear

Virgin). My faith did not end there, but the next time I just prayed before the exam after studying for the test.

From here, my father was transferred to Tacna, the southernmost city of Peru, a beautiful town close to the ocean, bordering Chile. Again we said good-bye to Puno. I remember no heartbreak at leaving this frigid, barren town that had so few animals close by and so few good memories to say good-bye to.

As I recall, this was the last time I would be in the midst of a pure Indian population. From then on my contacts would be with the so-called upper- or middle-class Peruvians, mainly because I was advanced in school and I was with their children. Indians usually did not make it past primary school.

CHAPTER SIX

Becoming a Man of the World

Tacna was pleasant, and the students were criollos and lighter mestizos with higher status. Usually their families were professionals, government officials, or in the military. If one was borderline or in the limelight, many parents, including mine, excelled in the art of pretending to be more than they were or to have more than they had.

Because of the war with Chile in 1879, I started to be more aware of patriotism, especially in Tacna, which was the area of confrontation. We were also advancing on the social scale, and I was learning to compete. Although we did not have plenty of money, we had an acceptable social status. My father was now higher in rank and respected by this small community. We gradually entered into the mainstream middle class. I was able to have well-to-do friends who even used to hang out at my house, which was above a jail. The place was big and rent-free, since my father was commander of the soldiers taking care of political prisoners.

He used to play tennis, and as I began my teen years, I also started to play this sport of the wealthy. This town was the "cradle" of what I am now. From here on, the middle- and upper-class children looked for the best school to continue their education.

Around that time a new military high school, the Francisco Bolognesi, opened in Arequipa, the second largest city of Peru, whose population had many criollos who knew their position, especially when compared to mestizos. The school was elite—there were only two in the nation and they attracted mostly the sons of the upper and middle classes and very few Indians.

I recall vividly a time in Tacna, when I was sitting alone at the table after dining and my mind went blank, and I felt as if I was living in the States. My knowledge of the United States in those days was all Hollywood fantasy, and my dream was even more remote. Nevertheless, I knew I was going to go there. It gave me an eerie feeling that I had been there at some time in my past, and that going to this military high school would make this dream come closer to reality.

Admission to the school required passing a competitive test. A biology teacher, Dr. Anaya (we called teachers "doctors"), was so kind and always helpful that I discussed the exam with him and told him about the subjects that were on the test. To my surprise, one week later he gave me a typewritten booklet about all the subjects to study.

Also at the school in Tacna we had an English teacher who actually came from England; he was a typical ruddy-faced Englishman with a straw hat and cane. We called him "paparucha" because of his red mustache. For reasons of which I was not fully aware, he disliked a black student in our class, to the point that at times for trivial matters he used to throw him out of the classroom. He would literally pull him by the ears, then, returning to the classroom, he would wipe off his hands as if he were cleaning off dirt, muttering the word "negro" in a despising manner.

In Tacna I first fell in love with a chubby, very fair girl. However, my best friend, Jirón, whom I told of my pain of first love, went after her himself and won her. From then on, he and I were in amicable competition. He was from a wealthy family and we were going to the same military school. We awaited the results of the exam that was taken by the cream of the town's children, and we all passed.

I won a scholarship and went to Arequipa for three years to be interned in the military school. When initially opened, this school was best known for its strict military discipline and its high standards of learning. Competition and excellence were a daily routine there. If one did not do well or if one behaved badly, he could be secluded for months, or worse, thrown out of school.

This school was entirely military, directed by high-ranking active officers and run by young army military academy graduates. In those days, the brightest young minds of Peru were in the armed forces academies. We were cadets with uniforms, real rifles, bands, and parades. We considered

We were cadets with uniforms, real rifles, bands, and parades.

ourselves comparable to cadets at West Point. Our directors tried to imitate this American institution as much as they could; as a matter of fact, some of our officers had trained at the military academies of West Point and Saint-Cyr in France.

I was an above-average student and had a group of friends whose goal was to go to the United States to study. This is where I knew my wishes to come to the United States would come true. We were already learning English. We listened to Glenn Miller's music, especially on Sundays, at the ice cream parlor downtown. Oh, no question about it, the United States was in my blood. Possibilities of such a thing happening in those days were very few and difficult; let's say it was my dream, and it was up to me to find out how to get there.

To describe my three years in this school would take up a whole book. Mario Vargas Llosa, a noted Peruvian writer who also went to a similar military school, Leoncio Prado in Lima, wrote a book about his experiences as a cadet, *La Ciudad y Los Perros* (*The City and the Dogs*), which became well known and won a literary prize. Some of its memories and passages were similar to mine in my military school.

My family was divided; we no longer were together. Braulio did not make it past the third year of high school because of economic reasons and the insensitivity of his teachers. He became a photographer. My father, as usual, shuffled all over. He was sent to Ayqucucho, an Andean town, and I stayed in the military school. I was on my own for three years in Arequipa with only a few distant relatives nearby. Christmas was spent with a few others at school. Most of the cadets went home, but my family was too far up in the mountains for me to go and spend time with them. Besides, Christmas was a children's holiday in Peru, and I was already a teenager.

My pastime was going to the movies, all American pictures, war stories, and even early rock-and-roll movies. My thinking was American, I could feel it, and my role models were actors like Gary Cooper, Jack Palance, Tony Curtis, John Wayne, Roy Rogers, and others.

Finally the time to graduate arrived. All the parents came to see their children at this magnificent military ceremony, but mine, because of distance and military duties, could not attend. I wore my fine uniform for the last time, and bade good-bye to many of my close classmates, who eventually became prominent citizens. Many of the cadets went into the navy, air force, and army. Their careers were cut out for them. Others, like me, had to plan their futures; and mine was in limbo. All I wanted was to go to the United States. But how? And when? I left the military school with sadness, because it had become like my family. This was the only place in my school years where I had lived for three consecutive years without moving or adjusting to new places. Now I would have to go to the epicenter of Peru, the capital, and plan my future from there.

Lima was a desolate place in my soul. We were once more reunited in this big city and we lived in a new, overpopulated housing project. I had no friends, role models, or connections. My father had always molded my mind to become a civil engineer, as most parents there did. This was considered a dignified profession in Peru, and his mind was set on this endeavor. I could not displease him.

Entering engineering school was like trying to get into Harvard or MIT. One had to take an entrance exam that was purposely made difficult to pass. Most students, including myself, had to go to a special preparatory engineering academy on the same campus to prepare for the test. Some students had spent years attempting to enter the engineering school.

The preparatory curriculum, however, was useless as a help to pass the admission test. The teachers, doctors, or engineers in the academy would find the most absurd mathematical problems that only a mathematician could solve. I guess the main aim was to flunk the applicants, who were too many for few positions. I studied day and night—algebra, geometry, arithmetic, physics—but it did not help.

I remember taking the entrance exam and looking at the question, a mathematical puzzle that was half a page long, and just giving up. I sat through the test dreaming about the United States and about how I would go to school there. I did not think it would be easy, but I thought the university entrance exam would be more fair in that country.

I remained in the academy another year at my father's insistence, but by now I started to drift. I did not want to go to those sterile classes. Also, I knew that some students were already chosen and marked to be admitted. Nevertheless, they still had to be smart and work hard, it is just that some of them somehow got into the engineering school.

I was becoming impatient. I wanted to be a doctor. I had seen so much misery in the jungle, and my soul was yearning to be a physician. I was no good in mathematics, anyhow. Then I went to inquire about medical school. The situation there was like that at the engineering school; I did not even attempt to enter or study for admission. Now I became more serious about going to the States, for which I had already done some paperwork the previous year. In the 1950s this was a feat of great doing, requiring extra social and economic resources; even the wealthiest and most able students opted for Spain, Mexico, or Argentina.

I went to the American embassy, my first contact with the United States. I remember the steely blue eyes of the well-dressed U.S. military guard. Light blue pants, dark blue jacket, and a white hat, a picture-perfect marine. Very impressive! Next came the waiting room, with a decor right out of the American movies—leather chairs and pleasant blond secretaries. They made me feel welcome. Oh! If I ever got to the United States, that in itself would be an accomplishment in my life!

Most of my classmates from military school were not attempting to come to the United States. They were more interested in getting into the elite military academies such as the navy and the air force academies. Even if I attempted to get into the air force academy, one look at me and I would have been disqualified due to my short height and probably my looks. The navy—forget it!—required blue eyes, fair skin, and a well-known family name and background. The army was more democratic, but I was disqualified by my father's connection. He never wanted me to be in the military. He knew it was a life of perpetual enslavement for the advancement of rank, with social-climbing servitude.

On my own, I enrolled in a small English academy at night to learn the language and I even started to write to schools in the United States. I took a correspondence course in English from the National School in Los Angeles, which was advertised in the *National Geographic* and *Reader's Digest* magazines. They sent me books and records directly from California.

I was living in a dream world and I became a movie addict. I think I was more American than the Americans. My role models were the actors and not the real, hardworking, poor and lower classes of that country. These people did not exist in my mind or in my little world. My whole energy gravitated on how to get out of Lima. Even if I got into the university or the naval academy, I wanted a different future, a different way of life.

My social upheaval was already determined—it was not for money or position. I just wanted another mentality, a place where I could flourish according to my abilities and desires and not to my class or social standing. I did not want to become part of the system in which I was raised. I wanted to fly far away, which is why I call myself Condor.

I wrote to my friend Ernesto Guerra, a wealthy military school classmate from Puno who lived in Arequipa and who was going to the States. We contacted by mail another ex-cadet friend, Adolfo, who was already in the United States and had been among the most promising and smartest cadets.

He went to Brigham Young University in Utah to study engineering, because he had a sister who married a Mormon. He gave us the address of the school, and I wrote to BYU.

I got a reply from the university coaching me on how to apply to their school. I have never forgotten receiving that letter! The envelope was white, crisp, and clean with the letterhead in the margin, "Brigham Young University, Administration-Admission, Foreign Students Department." After all the paperwork was finished, I was accepted temporarily without an admission test for the time being: no proof of the color of my skin or my social status and no need for someone to speak on my behalf. In fact, my father did not even know I had applied to BYU.

Now the American consulate took me more seriously, giving me more papers to fill out. I was seventeen and had no criminal record, but the consulate was very meticulous about this matter. I had to prove beyond a doubt that I was not a communist and that I did not belong to any political party, especially the APRA, (American Popular Revolutionary Alliance). Since I had not attended the university, I had not joined any party, as was customary among students then. The schools of higher learning were very political, mainly because the youth of any nation are always enthusiastic, altruistic, and eager to fix their country's social ills. Students see injustices and are impatient for reform. The nation then was also in political upheaval, and Peru had a military dictatorship. These young students had the same problems I had, and I empathized with them, but I took the more difficult way of dealing with the situation and that was leaving my country, my family, my jungle, and my past.

All was going well. My English was getting better. I used to look for American tourists to talk to them. I never forgot when the aircraft carrier *Franklin D. Roosevelt* came to the port of Callao. I went to see this huge ship and I made friends with two American sailors and brought them to my house. One was tall and had blue eyes and the other was black and much taller. They were from New York and friendly. I served them beer at home, but I think they were not interested in getting involved with the enthusiasm of a student with ideas of going to the United States.

I also used to go to the wrestling matches, because they always brought in big bullies from other countries. I remember the advance advertisements for a mean-looking, bearded "Russian" wrestler. I went to see him. My friends and I really hated communism after we saw him beat my favorite Peruvian wrestler! After the match I wanted to see him up close and find out who he really was. To my astonishment, he was a nice American guy who needed someone to translate English so he could talk with the fans. So there I was speaking English to this American! Of course, he immediately became my idol. So much for Russian communism!

The days in Lima were becoming unbearable for me. I was so close to going to the United States that I feared that anything could go wrong. The matter of money was beginning to be real. The American consulate wanted to know how I was going to get there and how I was going to support myself. This was a serious problem. Not everybody could afford to go to the United States because the dollar was so strong. At that time I think there were no commercial jets, and flights to the United States took many hours by propeller planes. The airplane fares were also astronomical. Somehow, all these problems were solved.

Finally the day of reckoning came. I was to be interviewed by the American consul and given the OK to travel to the United States. That day was unforgettable. I put on my best suit and tie and got a good haircut. Then I went to the downtown church in Lima to pray for help from Father Urraca, a saint-to-be who had helped many people with miracles. The church wall was full of proof shown by the golden and silver milagros offerings (heart-shaped objects giving testimony for prayers answered), as appreciation or thanks. I prayed, promising him that if he helped me out, I would always be his devotee. *Even now, every time I go to Peru, I visit him first as part of our bargain. I offer a candle and some American money. One time I put in a few soles, Peruvian currency, but this saint looked at me and said, "Dollars, son!" I had no choice; dollars it was, no fooling around with this good, future saint.*

After commending my wishes to the Almighty, I began to walk from Jirón de la Unión, where I could see American tourists in the street as I crossed the Plaza San Martín and entered the American embassy. I was greeted by the marine sentry, and I took the elevator to the consulate offices. There were many people there, including some members of the Kon-Tiki expedition. Finally, I was called to see the consul, a tall, thin, blue-eyed American who looked like Jimmy Stewart. He spoke to me in Spanish, and asked me to sit down. The room was pleasant, with American-made furniture and decoration. Most impressive to me was the picture of President Eisenhower and the American flag. The consul was nonthreatening and sounded more like an adviser. He somehow knew I did not have enough money and told me that once I was there I could get a work permit during the summer and work in the fields. He told me that he had worked baling wheat in Colorado, putting himself through college that way. "Oh, I think that would be great," I answered. He appreciated my enthusiasm. I suppose he figured I was a young man full of aspirations who would not become a problem to his country. He asked me how my English was coming along. I wanted so badly to speak it that I answered in English. Politely he mentioned that it sounded good, but that I needed more practice. He stood up—he was a giant— patted my shoulders and wished me good luck in Utah and told me to "take a lot of warm clothes because it is cold in that Mormon land!" Now I had my visa, passport, the acceptance of the good people of BYU, and Mrs. Muirhead, who sponsored me without even knowing me. My father had to borrow money to pay for the trip. I even think Ernesto, who was going with me, loaned me some dollars.

To save money, the trip was going to be by plane to Mexico City, and from there Ernesto and I would find our way to the States by the cheapest method possible.

I was again separating from my family and country! This time I was off to a far and unknown land. A different culture, a different language; God only knew what was in store for me! The pain of separation was softened by my strong desire to go to the best country in the world, where freedom, justice, and fairness was the motto. This trip was for the best and we all understood that. My poor mother; her only son, the one she had suffered so much for, was leaving. Now I know how kind and humble she was. I remember going with her to the bank to cash a check, and she could not sign her name because she never went to school and did not know how to read or write. She would be so embarrassed, and there was no one else to help her. Now her son would also know the limitations of not knowing how to read or write in another country's language. Eventually she learned to read, but she still cannot write.

At the old Corpac Airport, many people came to see me off; they could not believe what I was doing. They wanted to be part of this trip. We said good-bye and my heart once again was destroyed. My soul was falling apart. I was leaving the people I went through so much with in those bygone days in the jungle. These continuous separations had crippled my soul, a soul that felt like an old man who climbs the mountains of hope knowing that the world of our existence is sometimes hopeless.

Lima! you still look desolate from the air; good-bye. God knows when I will be back. Oh, beloved mother country, your earth gave me the mind and body to witness the existence of all the iniquities that occurred in your land. But Peru, I always loved you with all the powers of existential feelings so that even the faraway past cannot be discarded. The love is so intense that if I had the Herculean means of

Many people came to the old Corpac Airport to see us off, I waving, and Ernesto, smiling at right.

straightening out the bending past, I would ask the gods of the universe to give me the strength to mend all the ills done to my ancestors, creating a new, mixed civilization that will join the pursuit of spiritual philosophy for the love of brotherhood. Someday I hope that all Peruvians will become a content family and that their psychological walls will open as big as the wide oceans and heal their wounds for the benefit of their new generations to come.

The noise of the plane's propellers was deafening. Ernesto and I looked at each other. This was it! We were on our way to the States; nothing could stop us now. We flew for hours, and my thoughts went to the jungles, the beautiful mountains, and the suffering I had seen in Peru. But somehow the desire for the new healed my spirit. I was learning to adjust. I was becoming a man of the world.

CHAPTER SEVEN

A Ladder Full of Loose Steps

Ernesto and I arrived in Mexico City, a modern metropolis; it was much more advanced than any city I had known and the people were more open. It was at once different from and similar to Peru. We made plans to take a bus and a train to the United States. Our destination was Mexicali, the only place where the Mexican train stopped close to the border. We went second or third class. I was a veteran of similar trips; this was a cinch.

After days of traveling with deprivation because of the need to save dollars, we arrived at the Mexican side of the border, and I had only fifty dollars with me. Mexicali was very much like any poor desert town in Peru, with Indians, burros, and beggars, but still to me it seemed somewhat improved.

We crossed the border into the United States at a small town called Calexico. The weather was hot and I was wearing a very big, heavy coat of my father's that he had given to me. The U.S. immigration officers had neat green uniforms with pistols and were very sturdy, all-white gringos. They asked us where we were going and for what purpose while they were looking at our papers. I spoke more English than Ernesto and I said we were going to Brigham Young Univer-

sity in Utah and we were from Peru. They were curious, yet
very cordial to us. Probably they had never seen Peruvians
crossing this part of the border. We entered through the immigration gate on July 17, 1957. To my astonishment, here I
was in North America and I still saw donkeys, poor Mexicans, and dust! My mind went blank. I thought perhaps we
had been tricked by the American government since they
were in a propaganda war with Russia.

We could not believe we were in America. What happened to the tall buildings, the music, the actors, the beautiful people? Was I mistaken? I thought next we would be at a
concentration camp like in the Soviet Union; after all, there
was a cold war going on. Holding my small, leather suitcase,
we walked the dusty, unpaved streets. There were no Americans around, at least no gringos.

Finally we entered a cafeteria, and it looked more like the
life portrayed in the magazines and movies. Clean and air
conditioned, it had piped-in rock-and-roll music, a soda
fountain, and ice cream inside an antiseptic aluminum case.

I saw my first lemon meringue pie inside a cold glass case.
I wanted that fresh white and yellow pastry, but the price was
too high—about twenty-five cents. We just asked for water instead, which was given to us in a clean glass with ice. It tasted
good. Now it began to feel like what I imagined America
would be like. We walked across the street where the taxis
were and asked a gringo in a yellow cab to take us to Los Angeles. We thought it was around the corner. He laughed politely and told us it was too far and expensive, and he
recommended that we take the bus. I chatted with the taxi driver a while. I think he had never seen Peruvians before, and
he found us somewhat unusual. I thanked him for his help and
offered him ten cents, which was a lot of money in my country, about five or ten soles. He laughed and returned my dime.
Taxi drivers were nicer in those days, or maybe my attitude was
different, since I was new to the country.

I remember reading the Spanish version of *Reader's Digest* when I was almost dying of typhoid fever in Huaraz. I had a dream during my febrile delirium that I was traveling in a beautiful blue bus in the United States, just like the pictures advertised in the *Digest*. Then I woke up drenched in sweat and paddling in my watery stools. When I went to the Greyhound station, I saw the same bus—big, sleek, clean, and beautiful. They did not have buses like this where I came from at that time; besides, I had always traveled in trucks with my Indian brothers and their flocks. The blue-uniformed driver said our bus would leave at 2 P.M. We had hours to kill in Calexico. While waiting, I walked into an office where people apparently were giving legal aid to Mexicans going to Los Angeles. I noticed that their floor needed sweeping or mopping, so I asked if I could clean their office. The owner of the business, an American but not the blue-eyed or blond type we thought of as gringos, probably of Eastern European extraction, said, "Yeah! Go ahead." I began cleaning the place. I'd never done this kind of work in Peru, but here I was with a broom, strange mops, and unknown fluids. I did a good job. The man gave me a dollar, which for me was a lot of money. I opened my wallet and counted all my holdings—now I had one extra green Washington dollar. This was the country of opportunity, no question about it.

We boarded the beautiful, air-conditioned bus and set off for Los Angeles. The scenery was incredible, miles and miles of flat, green, fertile land with dark brown people working in the fields. From the bus we could see fancy houses with swimming pools, just like in the magazines.

From Los Angeles we went to La Puente, where Ernesto's sister-in-law lived with her parents. They were a Mexican family—their house was clean and well furnished. For the first time I saw a television set, and it was showing a beautiful Peruvian woman being crowned Miss Universe. I was glad for her, although I thought about the Indians, who make up the largest part of Peru's population. But then those were the times of glitter, and we were proud of her.

Ernesto had a car that his brother had left him, a 1948 Ford. We were planning to go to Utah in this car, but first we had to learn how to drive, especially on those Los Angeles freeways.

Like young people everywhere, we wanted to wear what American teenagers were wearing. In Peru, Levis jeans were for the rich and were a status symbol. Here everybody wore them. So we went to Sears and I bought myself a pair of jeans, some brownish shoes that were in fashion, and an Elvis-type shirt. It all cost just a few dollars. An incredibly cheap price! I knew I was down to less than fifty dollars, so no more buying. I just wanted to blend in. Then we went for a haircut. Man! did we get a crew cut, a professional one. Now I looked Japanese to some and American Indian to others; but whatever my face changed into, I felt American. I was doing what everyone else here was doing.

The days went by in Ernesto's relative's house, and I started cleaning the family's backyard, which needed some work; I did it for days, and they were thankful. I felt my stay was paid for with this work. They liked me and I liked them.

Finally, we were ready to leave for Provo, Utah, in that old 1948 clunker. The day before, this family had taken us to Disneyland, which was only two years old at the time. What a fantasy! To me it was the epitome of what the United States was. It was a treat I had never expected. No later visit would ever match the impact of that first one.

On our way to Utah we crossed the desert and stopped in Las Vegas. We spent some money, but not much. In those days the town had more of a cowboy atmosphere and was less opulent than it is now. In the clear night sky of the desert we saw *Sputnik*; now I was really getting into the twentieth century.

We arrived in Provo, a small, clean university town. Its people were extremely nice to us. Mrs. Muirhead took us into her home in rooms that she rented to foreign students. This college town came to be part of my life for five years. It was where the start of what I am now began; even my family's roots are there. The people of this area and of this state were Mormons and very religious: Brigham Young University was also a Mormon university.

This was a new environment, almost alien. As I recall (thank God!) it was a place where a young person could go to school and feel like it was a family. The campus was beautiful and the university was most helpful to foreign students from all over the world. Before enrolling, one had to sign a contract not to drink or smoke, which was just fine with me as I did neither.

My main problem was how to support myself. My parents used to send me money, but dollars were scarce then. I started to work at menial jobs while going to school. I used to work in the fields from 5 A.M. until sunset when school was out of session.

The fields were where I became aware of prejudicial attitudes towards Mexicans; and now this was going to be my problem as well. During the summer there was plenty of work harvesting apples and strawberries. Many people would go to the fields and wait for their turn to be called while sitting outside the orchards.

Among us all were American kids waiting for their turn to work. The blond, blue-eyed youngsters would enter the field first and pick up many apples from the ground just by shaking the trees. Next came another bunch of privileged kids who picked the fruit from the branches that were easy to grab. Then by midday, when the sun was hottest, we, the Mexicans and others, would be called and given a ladder to pick the remaining fruit. Well, by then there were very few apples left on the trees, and those only in the high branches at the top. So in one day's work I think I picked two bushels and made eighty-five cents. Yes, I remember it very well! Still, it was good money, and we were not upset by favoritism we could do nothing about. I thought that was a part of life in this country. At least one was not forced to work, and the white kids were doing the same work we were doing, albeit with some advantage.

I also worked in a cannery, starting at 4 A.M. and working all day. The pay was seventy-five cents an hour, a good wage if one could get it. I remember being given the worst assignment, which was to be at the receiving end of the belt carrying all the canned peas and other vegetables to be packed into containers. I had to put the hot cans, as fast as they came, into a cardboard box, which when full was heavy to lift. There was no rest; if I stopped, the whole assembly line would get behind, and I would be in trouble. Talk about monotony and tedious work; how could a person do this for a living? All the workers had only one two-to-three-minute break an hour and we were so tired we could have just fallen where we stood. It was hot, steamy, and noisy, but all the workers were students having fun and making good money. I was thankful and I was learning the American ethic, which in those days was to work and work hard.

Then I got a job on an iris plantation working for Mr. Mülenstein, a kind Mormon who gave me all the work I could handle. I labored in the fields on non-school days, mostly Saturdays and Sundays, from sunrise to sunset, the most beautiful parts of the day. The work was hard but pleasant, and the beauty of the Uinta Mountains reminded me of the Andes. My moment of rest, while holding my shovel against the ground, was spent counting the cars of passing freight trains, which were miles long and seemed endless. I admired those monsters as their metallic noises echoed against the snowy mountains, and I realized the strength of this country.

As my English improved, I started to take more serious courses, and by the end of the first year I had a steady job on campus, as a custodian cleaning classrooms. The work was from 4 A.M. to 7 A.M. at seventy-five cents an hour. I did this job for the next five years.

One early morning when the light of the rising sun first appeared, I saw a new worker while we were waiting for the door of the big building to be opened. The girl was wearing a heavy, long, dark, European-style coat. She was a new foreign student from Norway. She was good-looking and appeared very young, so I engaged her in conversation without shyness. Her name was Anja Hovland. By then I was somewhat sure of myself, or at least I felt I could put on a good front. We entered the science building, which had large paintings hanging on the walls. I pointed out to her the works of art and explained to her a few of my opinions. I was unaware that she was an accomplished artist in her own right in her country, spoke five or six languages, and was a devout Mormon with two years of missionary work in Finland. Well, I guess she was getting to know Latins and I was getting to know Europeans. We became friends, and in time I fell in love with her.

My life became more secure; I felt I had someone I could consider a part of me in this great country where I had no one close. During the summers while school was out, we looked for work in other states, which offered higher pay. Usually that meant California. By now I had a car, a red-and-black '56 Mercury, the only model that had those colors. It was my second car.

My first car had been a grey 1949 Oldsmobile, automatic with a tapered back, right out of the '40s movies. It cost a hundred dollars. One Thanksgiving, some of the foreign students were invited to a Mormon family's large house on a farm, and we went in this old car. That was to be my first memorable Thanksgiving dinner, and it was right out of a Norman Rockwell painting. The food was so plentiful and so different from our usual canned food diet that we ate turkey with all the trimmings "for ten days ahead and ten days back." At the end of the dinner I invited the daughter of our host for a ride in my newly purchased old automobile. She was blond and beautiful. Of course, there were no romantic ideas, as Provo was a city of complete innocence, whether chosen or imposed. As I was driving her around on the narrow dirt roads, my car broke down and started to open like a frog. The front axle split right in the middle and the car was flat on its front end. The embarrassment was hilarious; one could call it my first date. Her father came and helped me out of this mechanical fix.

Those early days in college were spent learning English and the customs of this country and adjusting to Mormon life. By then I was reading all kinds of books, especially philosophy. Books were plentiful and available as I had never known. I started to daydream about Peru as if I were helping my country. I kept giving speeches in my mind about how I thought the Indians and the criollos could get together and work for a great nation. Somewhere in my readings I found a phrase that to this day has been in my mind: "Study and prepare yourself and when your time comes then you will be ready to help your country."

Back then, the immigration service used to be very tough, especially on foreigners with student visas. We had to get special permission to work full-time during the summer, and we got such permission only if we maintained good grades or remained in school. If any problems were found, many foreign students were sent back home without questions asked.

I was one of the few foreign students with a car. One summer we decided to go to Los Angeles, the place where good money and work could be found.

Anja went to work as a tutor for a rich family's children in Santa Ana, California, and I went to look for a job. Leaving Provo and going to other big cities was like going from heaven to hell or to Sodom and Gomorrah. I dropped some of my friends and Anja at their destinations in the Los Angeles area, and then I was alone in a big city full of freeways with people who were not like the friendly Mormons.

I started to look for work. For days I drove all over Los Angeles and Long Beach, usually sleeping in my car. I had no skills and I was only looking for a summer job, but there was no work to be found. I also noticed for the first time raw discrimination. In those days there were not too many Mexicans in this country, and if there were, they stayed in the background. I was naive; I wanted to be and thought I was in the mainstream of American society. In my country, I saw discrimination, but rarely felt it myself, rather in the skin of others.

Very soon, I had stopped at all the hamburger and hot dog joints, and there were no jobs. The usual practice was for all the young, blue-eyed American kids to get the jobs.

One time I stopped at a hamburger place and inquired about work . The manager was an Anglo and he gave me the application. I was surprised, because most of the time I was told flatly or sarcastically, "*No hay trabajo,*" "no work." This time, I filled out the application along with some American youngsters. As I started to drive off, I realized that I had forgotten to write my social security number on the form. So I went back inside and asked the manager to give me back my form so I could finish it and write in the number. He mumbled something without any hesitation and pointed to my application crumpled up in the wastebasket. That was the way of life in those days.

As I was driving, still looking for work, on a clean street with beautiful houses, I saw some underground construction. I went to inquire about work, noticing that all the ditch-diggers were Mexican. An old Mexican man called loudly from below that there was no work. He climbed out of the open trench and looked at me with compassion, repeating that there was no need of another worker at the site, and gave me a dollar bill. In my mind I did not see myself as a beggar, but the act of this good person made me stop to think, and I started to realize I was in the same condition as they were. Finally I realized that my situation was not getting better.

One day, someone recommended me to a Peruvian man who was well-to-do in his country, and who was now working on a farm as a caretaker, with free housing. He let me sleep at his home, and through his connections he got me a job at the West Covina Country Club. I was hired as a dishwasher. Finally, I had a place to sleep and a place to work.

Here I saw both opulence and waste. There were big parties at the country club. One time they had a "luau" and on each plate was an entire chicken with Hawaiian trimmings. As I cleaned the plates, I had to throw untouched and unfinished food into the garbage. I could not believe it. These good people smoked and drank a lot; they were different from the Mormons. At work I was beginning to be identified as a Mormon, although I had never stopped being a Catholic, but that was fine with me. The help, including the chef who was the boss, used to make fun of the duality of my religion. I also started to notice among the kitchen and other serving crew some dislike for me, or worse yet, some sarcasm because I was a college student. I guess they could not accept a "Mexican"-Peruvian-Catholic-Mormon college student as a dishwasher. They called me "Pancho," as most Mexicans were called in those days.

In any event, summer ended, and I went back to BYU with money and new experiences. I was not bitter; I began to realize that this nation was big and diverse, and people were so different from where I came from that discrimination did not have such a great impact on me as it did in my own country. I expected it to happen in North America.

Deep in my heart I was not interested in engineering, although I was registered in that college at the wish of my father. I even used to carry a slide rule in my belt like a pistol, as all other engineering students did. I also kept taking general education classes.

Another summer came and I went back to Los Angeles, this time a pro at washing dishes. I looked for that kind of work and usually found it, so long as I did not ask for waiter or even busboy work. If I stayed in the kitchen, there was no problem.

By now I was reading a lot and I was living at the house of Dr. Evans, a Mormon doctor in Tustin, Orange County. My room was in the basement. It was full of books, and there I found a novel by American writer Morton Thompson, *Not as a Stranger*, the story of a young physician with all the idealism that any young doctor could have in those days. The book impressed me and made me realize that I had always wanted to be a doctor, that I wanted to go and help the poor, especially in Peru. The dream of becoming a doctor in this country became an awesome task to undertake, as unlikely if not more so than coming to the United States had seemed.

The 1950s were the golden age of American medicine. To be a doctor was the highest status symbol, and usually only the most privileged, smart, rich, and daring could become one. This country was (and still is) the cradle and the mecca of medicine in the world. For anyone to say, "I want to become a doctor," implied some visual and pragmatic credibility. People had a notion of what a doctor looked like— definitely not like a dishwasher. Certainly not a "Mexican-Peruvian." Well, the more I read Thompson's novel (which was made into a movie starring Robert Mitchum), the more enthusiastic and optimistic I became.

Finally I told Anja that I wanted to be a doctor. She surely believed me, no question about it. We discussed it, and I told her my dream of going to Peru to help the poor. Wealth was never the issue; my idealism was like a religion.

By now I was an experienced dishwasher. I got a job at the Branding Iron Steak House in Tustin. Many of my co-workers, the cook, and the waitresses got to know me. They learned that I was going to college, and they wanted to know what I was studying. The first time I started to tell them that I wanted to be a doctor, the response was laughter. The comment was, "Look at Pancho, he is going to be a doctor!" More laughter followed. Well, thanks to those people, my drive and desire to be a doctor became even stronger.

More and more I was seeing some resentment from the other workers, and my macho defense mechanisms were also more obvious, and I was fired many times. I became expert at operating automatic dishwashers and I figured out that I could study at the same time. I would put a wire hanger by the steamy dishwasher belt and place the book as a conductor places his score before a symphony orchestra. I could clear the leftover food and rinse the plates with a special hose and put the dishes on the belt automatically and efficiently without looking at them, all the while focusing my eyes on the book. It worked, especially when I did this for ten to twelve hours and sometimes twenty hours a day when I held two jobs. Once I was thrown out of a place along with my book because the manager thought I was doing this to show off and put others down. In those days relatively few people went to college, and Mexicans or Latins like myself were a rarity.

Another summer went by, and I went back to BYU more experienced. By now I was making more money than my father, but my mother was selling clothes without his knowledge, in the offices in Peru, so she could send me more funds. She really thought I was having a hard time, although I wrote her in my letters that this country was great, which it was.

At last I declared my major, premedicine. That was not actually unusual, because one-third of the students were premed and predentistry, and another third were prelaw. To get there, however, was another story.

My counselors, teachers, and friends became a little concerned with what they considered my ostentatious and unattainable desire to be a doctor. I started to take more advanced courses; the competition in the premed club was keen. The only acceptable grade was A-plus. Some students would take only one or two required subjects in order to get good grades. I used to take as many credits as possible a semester. My thirst for knowledge was voracious and I figured that I could take more classes without increasing tuition costs. That was a mistake, but eventually it became a blessing in disguise.

I started to inquire about admission into medical schools. All the responses were astounding rejections, and some stated flatly that no foreign students were admitted and advised me to look into something else. I even went to the University of Utah to talk with the medical admissions office. The secretary of the school of medicine asked me what I wanted. I told her I would like to enter their medical school. She looked at me and said that it sounded impossible, unless I was an exceptional student or had done some special research or discovered something. She mentioned a Japanese student who had been admitted, but he was a genius. Well, I was none of the above, so that was the end of it.

At BYU I found a teacher who believed in me, Dr. Clark G. Gubbler, chairman of the biochemistry department. Dr. Gubbler introduced me to an aspiring premedical student, Sheldon Sofer, a typical go-getter researcher. He wanted to enter medical school the unconventional way, by discovering a cure for seizures or mental illness. Sheldon was amazing. He was forceful and could convince anyone. He used to get grants for research in brain chemistry, studying the pathways of serotonin and its possible effects on seizures. He became a good friend, and put me to work on his investigative project. Now I was a respectable biochemistry researcher, with a white coat and my overgrown pet rodent. I must have severed the heads of thousands of poor innocent white rats. We would inject them with various drugs, remove their adrenal glands and brain, grind them up, and study their serotonin contents.

Sheldon had never taken classes in biochemistry, but he could discuss the intricacies of his research project with the best of chemists. I admired him. He made me feel so humble that I continued studying hard while he was going after that glorious day of discovery and admission to medical school and possibly the Nobel Prize in medicine.

I was now a psychology and biochemistry major, but still I was working as a custodian from 4 A.M. to 7 A.M. every day.

I used to fall asleep in classes. At times all I could think about was sleep—I became a walking zombie.

Again in my monotonous work I invented a way to kill the boredom of polishing and sweeping large classrooms and halls. I concocted a hook on the buffer or aspirator machine, just as I had on the dishwasher conveyor, where I could put my book and study while working. This helped me a lot, because time was of the essence, and those were my more-awake and alert hours.

Another summer came; this time marriage was on the horizon. Right after finals, on June 3, 1960, Anja and I were married. Because Anja would not marry a non-Mormon, I had converted the previous summer in Orange County while staying with Dr. Evans. There I read the Book of Mormon and the Bible, which were also required reading in religion courses at BYU. I became mystical and prayed as the Mormons do, asking God for help, the same God I had prayed to since I was a child. One day, on a beautiful, Sunday morning, I was baptized by Dr. Evans and became a Mormon. This conversion came more out of personal conviction and a desire to become part of these good Mormon people, who were like my family. They mostly practiced what they preached. Ours was not a fancy wedding, nor was it in the Mormon Temple; I never became a "good enough" Mormon to enter the temple.

Unlike most other young married students, I bought a thirty-eight-foot trailer house and moved my new wife to a nice place by the river. Summers and winters were intolerable in this mobile home, and so we used to stay in the library all day. It was clean and warm in winter and cool in the summer, and besides we did not have much money for heating or air conditioning.

By now I had taken the MCAT (Medical College Admissions Test) two times, the second time an improvement, with better scores. The point was that I persevered no matter what.

I started to apply to medical schools more seriously, and the rejections were more stern. In those days of the early

1960s, there were no minority or affirmative action programs. The fact is that even for an above-average American student it was hard to get into medical school—the competition was fierce. This reminded me of Peru, and this time it was worse, because over here there was open discrimination in this field. Even the large sum of money needed was a big obstacle.

Another summer came, and Ernesto and another Peruvian friend, Armando, and I went to San Francisco to find work. This time I went without my wife. We became entrepreneurs and decided to paint houses. It went well until we were picketed by union painters who gave us a hard time wherever we were working. It was just like in the old movies, union bosses harassing nonunion workers. They took us to their union headquarters, an old rundown building where some rough guys were playing billiards and smoking like chimneys. The smoke was so thick we could not even see the face of the person we were talking to. The boss wanted us to stop taking their jobs; furthermore, he did not want us to join the union, perhaps because we were foreigners or did not have enough money for dues, perhaps for racial reasons. We continued painting houses, mainly those that the union members did not want or could not paint. The houses we worked on in Marin County were in an Italian area on those famous, steep, hilly streets where there was no place to put the ladder at a horizontal level. We just took our chances and adjusted the ladder so that one leg of the ladder sat on "terra firma" and the other leg in God's hand. The houses were tall and of ornate design, with ornamentation that was difficult to get to. Those areas were easy to miss, and those Italian owners would look at every crevice we missed, and they would shout from below in Italian and tell us to sand and paint the bypassed spots. One house in particular took us a long time, but the two old retired Italian brothers liked us and used to invite us every night to eat a hearty Italian dinner, so we just did a good job and lost money, but they made us feel like real people. Italians and Latins have similarities, so we could understand each other. They also protected us from the union members. They were tough, and there were no pickets around their houses.

My wife was alone and we missed each other. So she joined me and we took a room in the Mission district of downtown San Francisco where she and I started to get a glimpse of the Mexican-American way of life. It was certainly different from life in the suburbs and 180 degrees different from Provo, Utah.

Somehow, we saved money for school and went back to Provo. I was already in my fourth year at BYU. Most of the European foreign students had finished school, and those who stayed were given nonmanual jobs as librarians, office clerks, and even teaching assistants. Many of the Latin or Third World country students were lagging behind or had left school. The few who were left were still doing menial work. I was still a custodian, and my wife, who was getting her master's, was working in the art department.

My foreign student English course classmates were from all over the world. My best friend was Jim Magueru from Kenya. He was black and had the most distinctive accent. Although people were nice to him, I could sense it was not always sincere. I was merciless to him and I teased him a lot. He became like my brother. I remember he was short of funds, so I told him to write to Tarzan and maybe he would send him some money since he made his movies in Africa and got rich off people like Jim. He just laughed and thought that was funny. Now that would not be politically correct to say, but among foreign students we used to tease each other about our countries of origin. He also wanted to be a doctor, but I never heard from him after I left BYU.

One early morning I was cleaning the floors all alone in the science building. Anja came and told me that she was expecting. We were both happy. I became philosophical. Life's events touch us as we go through time and here I was going to become a man with a family. I kept cleaning the green marble floor looking at the intricacies of each mosaic pattern and thinking how far I had come and that I was only just beginning.

By now my applications to medical schools were more persistent, some of them for the second or third time, and the rejections kept coming. The repeat applications had better MCAT scores, grades, and more credits, but still no deal.

Dr. Gubbler, my biochemistry professor/mentor, and Dr. Allen, a professor of embryology, both wrote letters of recommendation. I had done very well in their difficult and competitive courses. Also, the dean of students listened to my desire to become a doctor and to help people. He believed in my sincerity, and he wrote some letters for me.

Finally, in my fifth year in this country and in premed, I got a letter from St. Louis University School of Medicine in Missouri. They wanted to interview me, which was a sure way of saying, "Yes, we want you," but first they wanted to see me. So they asked me to come to St. Louis for the interview.

Airplanes were not the cheapest way to travel then, so I took the famous passenger trains portrayed in countless movies. I borrowed some money, bought a good suit at Sears, and left by rail for St. Louis. Again I traveled in the cheapest class, and once more said an unforgettable good-bye, this time to my wife. Some pain and uncertainty came over me, as I felt this trip was going to be the trip of my life; it meant everything to me.

So far I had not ventured to the East. The train departed and, as in old films, a black person manned the departure. He was dressed in a dark uniform and sturdy blue cap and he was shouting loudly, "Saaiinnnt Loouuiiii, allll abooaaarrrd" in a peculiar accent typical of train conductors of the times. The steam, the bells, and the whistle were sounds that brought me sadness and remembrances of Peru. I was sensitive to departures, especially this one.

As the train traveled for hour after hour, I could see the beautiful mountains and wide open nature passing by quickly, and my thoughts went back to when I used to travel in the high Andes. I could only think of the vastness of life, of the uncertainties of our future, and the unpredictability of it all.

Money was short. I had my thoughts and my books as my pillars of strength. I wanted to get a soda, so I went to the lounge car. My mistake, because there were several big guys like in the western movies drinking scotch and smoking cigars with their feet on the tables, and there were no Mexicans around. I bashfully passed their comfortable tables and couches and went to the bartender and asked for a soft drink. He was big, his voice was coarse, and he had been looking at me from the time I entered. In any event, he responded loudly and arrogantly, saying, "We don't serve Indians here." I guess I looked like an American Indian; I had a crew cut, thick black straight hair, and strong features, so I could not blame him. I just went back to my cheap seat and had my sandwich with water. I still was confident that had the bartender known I was a premed student and on the verge of being accepted into medical school, things would have been different. Besides, I felt, as Mormons feel, that I was in a better situation than they were. I was a good kid, I did not smoke or drink, and my future was bright. So I thought and I felt not discriminated against, but misunderstood.

The train kept going. The only thing that would console my thoughts of fear and possibilities of failure were the open spaces, the solitude of the mountains, and the continuous, mesmerizing sound of the locomotive. We passed many towns where passengers got off and on, and the difference in speech and manners was evident in comparison to the Mormons. The towns and people looked older, and seemed somewhat harsher.

Finally I arrived in St. Louis, the Gateway to the West. To imagine that this was the point of departure in the early days of the conquest of the American West! This was the place where new immigrants from Europe would begin their journey to find success in the West. Now I was going the opposite way. I arrived in the afternoon at the downtown St. Louis train station, which looked as if it were right out of the 1930s. The place was packed with people. The smell of smoke was persistent, and I felt more lonesome and lost than when I arrived in the United States in Calexico.

I picked up my small suitcase and walked to the street. This town looked more like the America I had imagined in Peru, but by now I was used to the clean, friendly, small university town of Provo. I felt that if I did not get accepted to medical school here I would not mind, because this town was too different, too old, and the people seemed unfriendly.

I did not know where the school of medicine was. I just took a trolley and asked the conductor to drop me off at St. Louis University. There it was, smack in the center of the old city with worn-out red-black brick buildings, some almost completely sealed with small windows. I was left on Grand Avenue. Then I found out that the school of medicine was a couple of miles farther north. I had no place to stay and I had to find accommodations, preferably a cheap hotel. My funds were low. I saw an old, rundown hotel down the street. I thought a hotel was a hotel, but this was, as I later found out, a place for pickups, drunks, and elderly people. I walked to this antique structure that was almost hidden by two large buildings. I think its name was Hotel Florida. The entrance hall was full of smoke and greasy chairs. The manager, who was black, stood behind a barred window and asked how he could help me. There were a lot of black people in this town. In Provo there was only one, and he was my buddy. I asked for a room, hoping it would be cheap. To my surprise, it cost only two dollars. I took the keys and went to the second floor. I opened the door, and it was a disaster. The bed frame was probably what the pioneers brought when they came to St. Louis. There was no water or bathroom, just one room, and the pillows and linen were so dirty that the wooden floor seemed cleaner.

This is the United States! I thought. I sit in filth and yet I am at the door of the biggest windfall of all professions. Yes, this is what this country was about and I had no regrets. I opened a big, old wooden window that had not been used for years. I had to force it and pull it slowly. I could hear the squeaking sounds as the windows resisted parting from each other. There they were, pigeons nesting with their baby chicks. I was so happy and careful. I was glad to see animals in this desolate part of the city. I made an effort not to disturb them, and I do not think they were concerned. I guess they were used to people.

The view was blocked by big buildings. I could only see the sky, but across the street were the relentless red brick buildings. I pulled my newly purchased suit out of the suitcase and put it neatly on a chair. My appointment was the next day at 8:30 A.M. I was exhausted and afraid. My future had never looked so grim as in this hotel. Somehow I managed to fix the bed, pick a clean spot, and lie down to sleep. At about midnight, someone knocked on the door. I jumped off my bed and asked who it was. A female voice answered, asking me if I wanted her to come in. I did not realize she was a prostitute, but I said no.

Cautiously I fell back to sleep. Looking through the half-open window I could see the dark blue sky and listen to the movement of the pigeons. It was winter but the room was hot and musty.

I woke up the next morning to the pigeons making a lot of love noises. The morning was crisp and cold as I went down the hall to the only bathroom on the floor. No shower, just an antique bathtub with dark rings at all levels on the peeling white porcelain. The knobs were missing and replaced with broken pliers. Time was running out, and I still did not know how to get to the medical school. I cleaned the tub and filled it with lukewarm water falling slowly out of the rusty, worn-out faucet. I scarcely took a bath, trying not to touch anything. My thoughts went to Puno, the Peruvian altiplano town, where there was not even this kind of tub. We had to boil the water in a tin bucket, take it to the back of the house, and bathe only one-half of the body—and that was once a week, mainly because of the freezing weather. Yet, already I was disappointed with this luxury! The morning was cold; the bathroom had no heater and no door, only an old mildewed plastic curtain.

I walked on my toes back to my room, and as I dressed my thoughts were on the interview, and my appearance was the most important thing now.

I walked out onto the cold street, Grand Avenue, lined with nearly bare maple trees with half of their brown leaves on the snowy ground. The view of elderly, lonesome people walking the streets was depressing. The church was on the corner, a very fine Gothic building. I entered to pray and ask for help. Well, yes, I was a Mormon, but I was still a Catholic at heart. This was my childhood faith, and the saints, especially Padre Urraca, were helpful to me.

I took the bus, as if it were the last ride in my short life. There it was, the school of medicine, a dignified red brick building with chapel-like architecture. The shieldlike emblem in the main entrance read "Santi Ludovici Medicini–1818." I had seen this picture in the brochures. Now it was in front of me. The medical students in pure white were crossing to the Fermin Desloge Hospital, an impressive stone building that seemed to match the old medical school. Oh, would I ever wear that pure white uniform with my stethoscope in my side pocket? Those young doctors looked smart—tall, no blacks, no Mexicans. It seemed an impossible illusion that I could ever be there.

I entered the medical school building for the first time. I felt a reverence just as if I were going to the Sistine Chapel in Rome. The smells of the hospital and chemistry labs permeated the entire building, giving me a queasy feeling. I climbed the ample, worn-out marble stairs and went to the admissions office. The middle-aged secretary welcomed me and told me to go back to Grand Avenue and then to Cardinal Glennon, Children's Hospital, which was not too far from the medical school, where my interview was going to take place. I walked down the grey marble stairs, went to the street, and now my legs were shaking, either due to the cold or anxiety. The final walk was agony. I saw the hospital, and it looked like a church. I entered it and asked for directions to the interview room.

I was directed to the X-ray department. I waited in the receiving room. Those moments were infinite, and my thoughts were on the meaninglessness of our doings. Dr. Armand Brodeur appeared and called me to come in. Drs. C. Rollins Hanlon and Vallee L. Willman were seated, impeccably dressed in starched, stiff white coats. Their faces commanded my profound respect and fear. They were both renowned surgeons, but I did not know it then. Dr. Armand Brodeur, a pediatric radiologist, was more down-to-earth, and his coat was white and crumpled. He wore a bow tie and was always smiling, as if he were trying to soften the two surgeons' moods. He was my hope. He ignited that last spark of optimism in my heart. "Sit down, Mr. Sánchez," he said, and all six eyes looked at me as if they were going to cut me open and really get to my soul.

"How did you get here?" they asked.

"I came by train, Doctor."

"When did you get here?"

"Last night, Doctor."

"Where did you stay?"

I paused and could not tell them where I spent the night. They probably knew of this hotel and its seedy character.

I said, "At the Claridge Hotel," which was a big hotel by the train station that I had seen and which I thought was a more reputable establishment. Later on I found out that it was no better. They just shook their heads.

They looked at my application, recommendations, my letter of why I wanted to be a doctor, and they looked at my grades.

"Oh! you have a D in square dance?"

"Yes, Doctor. I took it while I was learning the language and I thought it would be easy, but it was hard, because none of the girls wanted to pick me as a partner. I was an awful dancer and the female students didn't want to flunk by dancing with me. The D was an act of mercy by the teacher."

"I see you have a C but took the course again and got a B?"

"Yes, American history was hard and involved a lot of reading. I had to use a dictionary to translate many words I didn't know."

"I see you have taken biochemistry, but we teach this course here. You didn't need to take that subject."

"Yes, Doctor, but I was in research."

"What? Research? Tell us about it."

So I went on, discussing the pathways of phenylalanine and serotonin. I talked about the defect in the metabolism of phenylketonuria and how we often tried different drugs and sacrificed so many rats trying to find a cure for seizures and mental illness. I guess for a brown-skinned premed this was big talk. (Thank you, Sheldon Sofer; your ways of impressing people helped me and I felt good.) I knew the stuff, and they too were impressed.

"How are you going to pay for school? You are a foreigner and you cannot get any government loans. Worse yet, you won't have time to work."

"Well, my father will pay for it."

"Are you married?"

"Yes, and I have a son."

They all looked at each other. I felt things were getting worse.

"Are you a Mormon?"

"Yes."

They were Catholic, but perhaps they knew that somehow I was also Catholic, and they could see that I was a clean-cut, straight-arrow student. BYU was known for that, and that was a plus for me.

Finally, Dr. Hanlon asked me how I would fix a broken toaster. I said I had never owned one. They laughed and looked at their watches. Dr. Willman and Dr. Hanlon still looked somber, regal, and professorial. Even if I got in, those doctors could do me in quickly. It was hopeless; I was on the first step of a ladder full of loose steps.

Dr. Brodeur, still with a smiling face, talked to me like a regular person and led me to the door. I think he felt sympathy for my predicament, especially my economic situation. He was a genuinely good man, but so were Drs. Willman and Hanlon—they just had to be what they were supposed to be, surgeons and professors.

After the interview I was free, my soul and my spirit were weightless. I had no more worries. I walked the cold, windy, frozen streets of St. Louis, went to a café, and finally enjoyed a salami sandwich, the best food I had eaten in days. I did not care if I ever got accepted to medical school in this cold smoky city. I was ready to go to Provito, Little Provo, to my wife and son. I took the train back and this time I enjoyed the scenery. I did not go to the bar and just stayed in my seat reading my biology book. It was all a dream. I had tried my best. I knew I would be a doctor here or in China; it did not matter where.

CHAPTER EIGHT

"See One, Do One, and Teach . . ."

Two weeks later an envelope arrived with "St. Louis University School of Medicine, Admissions Department" in the left-hand corner. This was it! I quickly opened it and glanced at its contents. "We are glad to accept you to the school year of 1962. Please send a $100.00 deposit to secure your spot." Oh, tears streamed down my face. I ran home down the empty forestlike pathway at BYU, the letter clutched to my chest. I stopped to open it again. Yes, I was accepted. I showed it to Anja and we danced in the trailer. I could not stand still. I carried that letter with me and shared it with some of my friends.

Later on, some people changed their attitudes toward me. My premed classmates were not too happy. My name was listed with about seven or eight others on the wall of the biology building where all the students looked to see who had been accepted. Some would say, "Sánchez? How?" and the same for the other accepted premeds. It was hard then for anyone to get into medical school, and minority or racial quotas were unheard of.

We sold the trailer and moved to a one-bedroom basement apartment and put Roy, our baby son, in a cabinet drawer for a bed. We collected all the money we could get by selling my books, our bicycles, anything we could spare.

In July 1962 we traveled to St. Louis in my red-and-black Mercury. Good-bye, Provo, you had been a part of my life, you lighted the spark of optimism in my soul, and made it possible to go on with my ideals. This is home and I always will go back in thought to this oasis of spiritual tranquility in a worried future. I suppose that with the passing of time, all difficult moments become a spice in one's life, becoming little triumphs in a world full of vicissitudes. So, BYU will always be as pure as the fresh white snow that I saw for the first time in Utah. BYU is my beloved alma mater.

Oh, St. Louis, here I come! Land of the unknown, city of hope with its decaying panorama, hot and humid summers. I knew no one in this city. Anja had lived before in the old cities of the Nordic lands. She was accustomed to the old buildings, the old people, and the bitter winter cold.

Money was always a problem. We were told of cheap apartments near City Hospital and we knew a dental student, Larry Moss, a Mormon and a good friend of mine, who lived there, so we went to see him. The weather was so sweltering it was almost unbearable, like in the jungle, but without trees. We finally found an apartment on the seventh floor of a new complex known as "the projects." It was built mainly for inner-city poor blacks. The place was new, and it smelled fresh. The apartment had no furnishings or carpeting. The view was of flat St. Louis, with not a single mountain, only factory smokestacks, tall dark houses with chimneys, and red brick buildings.

The first thing was to get to the clean, new bathtub. I filled it with cold water and got in and felt refreshed from the heat and my spirit lightened up. We were home. This was it and we made the best of it.

We met other struggling dental and medical students. They were the only whites in this project, which, I guess, included me. We helped each other exchanging tips on how to get by and how to get jobs for the wives.

We shopped at the Goodwill thrift shop to buy essential furnishings—an old table, wooden chairs, a heavy office desk missing a leg, and a large blue couch with no legs in the back. Pretty soon the house looked livable. We were used to old things, so it was no problem.

School started and I had to buy books and a microscope. Money was short, but I bought books ahead of food. In the first days of school we were about 160 or so students, with different, strange names. There were three women, one of them African-American, one African-American male, one Hawaiian, one Korean, and one Latino—me. The rest were Italian, Jewish, and Irish.

We all shared a common bond—fear of the school's rigorous curriculum—and we became brothers instantly. We picked our friends almost immediately. We were all innocent looking, some of us carrying the weight of family and money problems; some were single and wealthy; others were smart and sure of themselves.

In our first classes—anatomy, pathology, and histology—the professors were prepared for carnage during the first two weeks. They knew one-third of us would be gone by then. Just as in the Normandy landing, it was a war zone. The school was there to flunk you, to test you, to make sure you could make it under all adversities. It was not there to help you, it was there for you to become strong and wise and eventually to help people. But first you had to prove yourself.

Anatomy was the first course, the most feared. Here was the first trench in the war; either you made it or you were out. Two or three days would pass and we would be asking what happened to the guy with the mustache, the freckles, the accent, anything we could identify him by, because we did not know names yet. Well, by then a few had left school. Something had been too much for them, maybe the dead bodies, maybe the professors.

We shared a cadaver between two students, and the dental students also dissected in the same amphitheater. My dissecting partner was Larry Schainker, and working together on this thin, old woman, our cadaver, we became almost brothers. We started anatomy by studying the leg and were supposed to get used to dissecting the dead by beginning in the lower extremities, which were the easiest parts. Anyone could learn these few long muscles, bones, and nerves. Sure enough, the first test came. I thought I had studied and dissected hard and did well. The grades were posted. I looked for my name on the medical students' list. It was not present, at least not in the first or middle columns with the higher grades, but it was in the last column. Oh, what an embarrassment, there it was, my name, in black and white. I went to Dr. Christensen, professor of anatomy and histology, an old-timer and admirer of Pablo Cajal, a well-known Spanish histologist who advanced the study of this subject. Not revealing himself, he just said, "I doubted you would make it. Many are already packing up. There are three more tests and this was the easiest part. When the head and neck comes up, you won't even know where you are."

Then and there I realized that in medical school if one is not doing well, one studies the books until the letters disappear and tears the cadaver to pieces until one knows the subject by heart.

Finally, my name was moved higher on the list, and kept going up, not to the top, but I was there with respectable grades. By now we had lost quite a few students and we had picked our friends. The Italians stuck together and they took me in as their peer. I guess their parents were more recent immigrants from the Old Country and they took a liking to me. My friends were Bob Rich, Anthony Puopolo, Ted Pepper, Sam Romeo, Bill Sears, and others. I was a new specimen to them. They had never had much to do with a Peruvian before. They used to tease me, calling me "Indian," "Spick," "Pancho," but it was all in fun. We were friends, and I never took offense.

I actually liked their joking, and I also learned their place of origin nicknames and teased them back, as was and still is customary in the United States, although somewhat subdued.

One of my best friends was my dissecting partner, Larry Schainker, a well-to-do St. Louisian, shy and always worried like me, in spite of being studious and smart. I actually had to calm him down, especially during exams. He was like a cane to me; he gave me confidence, moral support, and made me feel a part of his hometown. Once I invited him to my house. He could not believe where I lived. But he was humble and understood. He lived in the Ladu area, a fancy part of St. Louis.

Money remained a problem, and many times I did not have a dime for lunch. I would go to the cafeteria and eat the free crackers and ketchup. Larry would lend me ten or twenty-five cents and I would have barley soup. Oh, that was a luxury. I saw Larry years later and he had not changed. He even took notes of the speech that was given in our honor during our five-year reunions. Good old Larry! I wonder if he will ever relax. Now he is a well-known and prosperous physician with a great family on the East Coast.

The attrition in school was ferocious. Everybody was paranoid: "Will I be next?" Students were called to the medical school dean's office and told by the dean through a speaker in his secretary's adjacent office that they were "finished in school and to leave." That was it! Years of premed, years of hope gone in one lousy sentence through a speaker— not even in person or with an explanation.

I walked to the physiology lab. Forty dogs were by the table's legs wagging their tails. There were going to be several experiments until all the dogs were dead. I thought of Etico and the animals I had owned. I felt helpless. I would have liked to save their lives, but I was powerless. This was my first lesson in inhumanity and my first lesson in how to withstand it for the cause of medicine, although I have my doubts now.

Time came and went fast. The rigors of medical school, especially the first two years, were hard. Money was the perennial problem. My father and mother sent some money. Anja also worked at the university teaching Spanish, although she had a master's degree in art. Still there was only enough money to buy books and pay tuition. Because of my foreign status, I was ineligible for government or school loans. Also, I could not work, because my studies took up almost twenty hours around the clock.

By now Braulio had come to the United States. He had been a policeman in Peru, and I helped him to come here. He had had a hard time, discrimination was harder on him, jobs were difficult to get, but he eventually made it and brought his young family. *Now his son is a promising doctor, trained in Columbia, Missouri, and his daughter is a registered nurse working in one of the busiest Level 1 emergency rooms in St. Louis.* Yes, Braulio, my uncle Jilgero, the little Indian child whom I first met in Andahuaylillas, Cuzco, was now also speaking English. He worked hard and also helped me through medical school, even with the little money he made.

Once when we did not have a single penny and my wife was pregnant with our second child, we had nothing to eat. I went to the local rundown market and asked for credit to buy some food. I told the owner I was a doctor. He answered, "If you are a doctor, you can afford it." Desperate, I went to the back of the market and scavenged through all the edible items disposed of. To my disbelief, there were vegetables, fruits, and other canned items that were discarded simply because they did not look fresh or the cans had dents in them. I arrived home with a load of them. My wife was incredulous at what I had found.

Another time I needed tuition money desperately. Anja was teaching an evening class; one of the students, a wealthy banker's wife, Mrs. Fox, liked her, and we were invited to dinner at their elegant home. Somehow during our conversation they realized our financial situation. Mr. Fox, who himself had risen to the top through hard work, said, "Anja, come and see me tomorrow at the bank." The next day she went downtown to the large, prestigious St. Louis bank, timidly entered, and asked for the president of the bank. The tellers would not allow her in, but suddenly his office door flung wide open and he approached her with outstretched arms, saying, "Mrs. Sánchez, please come in." He was a typical banker, and a self-made American who understood our problem and knew about our need of money for school purposes. He loaned us a large sum, five hundred dollars, on our word only, not even a signed paper. Here is where discrimination is balanced out: In one place a person is treated like dirt, in other places one is treated better than gold. The point is to balance this dichotomy in one's life. I did and I still do.

As the second year came, life was either a little easier or I was more used to the rigors of school. The subjects were more bearable, and by then I had joined a group of young dental and medical students who used to cater parties for wealthy families in St. Louis. We were marketed as medical student busboys, and the rich people used that as part of their extravagance for sumptuous parties. We used to bring leftovers home by the bagful and save them in the freezer for lean days to come. This was the best food and it was untouched. Those rich people helped us and they did not look down on us. In Latin American countries this type of work for a future doctor would be unheard-of, whereas in this country the work ethic has no boundaries and honestly earned money is good from any source.

My wife went back to Provo to have our second child while I went to the University of Michigan School of Medicine to make up a course in microbiology that I and other medical students were unable to finish due to President Kennedy's assassination. This tragedy affected us deeply, and we could not study or concentrate for days. We all liked him, and I think it did harm the spirit of the country. Once more there was a family separation, and in hard times like this it was difficult. I do not know where we got the money to live on. We must have lived frugally, but we survived.

It was a hot summer in July 1964, and I was in my first rotation at the well-known St. Louis City Hospital. This hospital, built in the 1800s, was located right in the heart of the old downtown area where most of the poor lived, a short walking distance from my home in the projects. It was a classic—the type described in Thompson's novel *Not as a Stranger*, and in old movies. The hospital was huge, built with blackish red bricks and a domed entrance. It even had porches for the horse-drawn carriage ambulances of the past. The last paint job had probably been done at the end of the last century! The dim light bulbs were hung from high ceilings on what looked like threads. The large, accordion-like, steel-door elevator was manned by a black man as if it were a train. The wards were big with high ceilings and huge barred windows. In each ward there were forty to sixty rusty iron beds with peeling white paint that were filled with patients from the most destitute social and financial conditions imaginable, usually alcoholics, derelicts, and poor—black and white. I rarely saw Mexicans among them. Somehow this pathetic picture added a touch of romance to my new world of medicine.

As a third-year medical student I now wore a full suit of white, pants, shirt, and coat, and carried a stethoscope in my right-hand pocket. My dream had come true, I was living Thompson's novel. Now I was going to help people. This was it, the actual touch of the living, ill person.

My first patients were assigned to me. This ward was full of sick people. The hospital and the city could not afford nurses, orderlies, or doctors—we were it. We worked as a team. The chief resident was supreme commander, the residents and interns were the professors and consultants, fourth-year students were like interns, well seasoned and worthy of respect because they had made it this far. The third-year medical students, at the bottom of the hierarchy, were the working doctors, nurses, laboratory technologists, X-ray technicians, orderlies, anything that a patient needed. Each student was assigned ten to fifteen patients who were his responsibility. The adage "See one, do one, and teach the next one" was a fact of life in this place. Here we learned medicine right out of the inhumanity of hard labor and compassion for the patients.

My first patient was an old, heavyset white gentleman who had had a heart attack. There were no intensive care units or continuous monitoring as in today's sophisticated units. I was it, a new rookie, given the privilege to save the life of this half-corpse who was unconscious, drowning in his yellow fetid secretions, barely maintaining his blood pressure.

Oh, this was it! How was I to save the life or at least maintain the life of this big human being? This was the test; here either I made it or I would be in trouble.

I spent every hour, every minute, suctioning the thick mucous from his throat. I was monitoring his intravenous solutions with lifesaving vasopressors and keeping his oxygen mask properly in place. The oxygen came out of a large, green, rusty iron bottle that looked like an old cannon. As I worked hard through the night, my thoughts went to passages in Morton's novel. This was the real world of disease, a place for altruistic medicine, and I loved every minute of it.

After being awake all night, by 7 A.M. I was exhausted, my eyes were red, I had not eaten or even gone to the bathroom. I secured my patient, once again suctioning his gurgling secretions, fixed his oxygen mask, and checked his falling blood pressure, adjusting my IV vasopressor. The feared professors were coming for rounds, and I needed to be presentable.

I went to the fourth floor rapidly, climbing the large, worn-out stairs with bloodstains of years gone by, brushed my teeth, used the toilet, and put cold water on my bloodshot eyes. I then rushed down to the ward where my patient was. Oh no, I thought I was lost in this big hospital. My patient was not in the bed where I thought I had left him still breathing and stable. He was gone, and the empty room still had his fetid smell of death. My first patient, and I had let him die—this was a big blow to me. I could see myself packing my things and being thrown out of medical school, and I knew it could happen.

Yes, it was Room 312. The stern professors, the residents, and the other doctors on their rounds approached my patient's room. They all looked serious, and their coats were pure white and hard as the collar of a priest. Their faces were well-shaven; they had slept all night, and probably had had a good, hearty breakfast. Now they came for the kill, they were the Inquisition. They wanted to know what we did wrong, they wanted to know if we were good. If not, they did not want us there. They needed only good doctors; yes, we were doctors, not medical students then.

To my disbelief, as I was ready to present my case and explain myself, the professors looked at the half-lit, foul-smelling room and somberly walked away, saying that Mr. So-and-So had died and the room was greatly needed. They did not even look at me. They just moved on to the next ward. My soul shattered like a broken IV bottle. I was also learning the humanity of inhumanity. I had lost a patient, I had confronted death, and I had done everything possible. Those professors knew that. Just standing in the room of this dying man for a whole night was a lesson in itself: life and disease had its terms, there was no need to prolong it. We did what was best and available at that time.

The patients who came to St. Louis City Hospital were in the worst states imaginable. Their bodies were so diseased and full of pathology that it was an open medical book. Diagnosing and treating them was such a challenge that we took pride in it. We worked hard out of compassion and we learned fast out of necessity. If a patient needed blood, we drew it; we walked the empty, dark, ghostly cold, long halls in the early morning with the silent snow falling outside—those were our moments of rest. We talked to the lab technicians. We begged for blood as if it was for our own family; once in hand we rushed it to the ward and gave it to our dying patient. Then we knew we had done our job when we saw our patient come alive and refer to us as "my doctor." We held their hands, and nothing in the books could have ever taught us better how to become a good and caring doctor. Yes! St. Louis University School of Medicine was known for being a school where one learned clinical medicine in the real world. The school was not interested in our doing research or applying for grants; they wanted us to be doctors first, seasoned in the hardest of battle zones, the wards of St. Louis City Hospital.

Time went on, nights were like days. We stayed awake for thirty-six hours and whatever time was left was for studying what we saw. Our nice white uniforms became stained with blood, urine, and dirt, but we kept our dignity. Admissions came in and we took care of them until they left the hospital or died. Many of them became regulars, and we knew their lives as well as our own. I identified with them because they were as destitute as I was, but some had lost faith in themselves, society, and their families. We were their last link to the humanity of man and we never failed them. We were the final spark of hope in their most desperate moments and, if they died alone, our hands were the last they held. We suffered, because we could not improve their lot or even save their lives.

Once we wore those white outfits with our stethoscopes on our side pockets, we were well respected and could walk anywhere in St. Louis in this attire. Dressed in my uniform, I went down to the huge, old St. Louis train station to welcome my wife and our new child. He was not a pretty baby; I just did not like his looks. Poor Robert, I do not even have his baby picture. Now he is a handsome young man, but I guess my soul was hardened by all the ugliness of the city hospital, and nothing was beautiful anymore.

By now we could work in any hospital or emergency room in the city. We were doctors, no question about it—people trusted young, budding physicians.

I got a job at St. Mary's Hospital Emergency Room. I started to see patients who were in better shape than those at St. Louis City Hospital, and as a matter of fact, their ailments were minor. I realized that it was easier to know what to do for a very sick or dying patient than for a patient with a simple rash, sore throat, or depression.

One night an old man was rushed in by ambulance with two private nurses. I did not know who he was, but he was dying. His mouth was full of secretions, he had no teeth, he looked blue, and he was barely breathing. I jumped to his gurney and put my mouth to his and pushed in air as hard as I could till help came, and we revived the man. Later on, his private nurse gave me a hundred dollars. She said, "You saved his life." Of course, it took more than that to save his life, but he happened to be a wealthy St. Louis resident whom no one except his private physician was even supposed to touch. He had the best doctors in town, and here I was, a third-year medical student now also working with those doctors and the rich.

Unfortunately, discrimination was again beginning to appear in the picture. Some students and doctors were from California, New Mexico, Texas, and parts of the South. They had preconceived ideas of what a Mexican was and they would not hesitate to tell me right to my face; it did not matter to them where I was from. Some of them had the power of rank in medicine, which was just the same, if not worse, than in the military.

One particular doctor, an orthopedic surgeon, was well known in the hospital for not having patience with anybody he did not like. I think he disliked my accent, and when I examined his patients in the emergency room and talked to him over the phone about the problem, he would shout at me sarcastically and ask me to "speak English." He was arrogant and always in a hurry. I believe just a call from anybody was enough to bother him. He was powerful and gave many people a hard time in the emergency room. However, I was finally making some money as a doctor and learning more medicine.

I went to Sears Roebuck and bought a nice leather coat with an imitation-fur collar for Anja. It cost me a hundred dollars and it represented the first hard-earned money I had made as a doctor. This was also the first time I could afford to buy something nice for my wife.

By then some of the medical students were working in fancy private hospitals administering anaesthesia, delivering babies, and getting paid well, but some of us had to go elsewhere. I found a hospital housed in a vintage wooden building that was, I think, older than City Hospital, right by the railyard. Its name was Mercy Hospital, and it was directed by white nuns. It was only for black patients and it was staffed by black doctors. They needed young interns, residents, or medical students to do histories and physicals and to stay at night as the doctor on duty.

I was, I suppose, the only "white" doctor in this hospital! Cases came in and I was the physician who first encountered them. Again, these patients were sick, poor, and in need of care. By now I was a seasoned doctor and I became more so in this place.

I remember my first delivery was here. The mother was a pleasant black woman who came in the middle of the night in full labor and, having had many previous babies, was not in the mood to wait for her doctor. I was nervously sweating because I was alone. I had never delivered a baby. But a blessed old black nurse calmly got the mother ready. She knew I was inexperienced and told me quietly, "Doctor, you can do it. I will show you." She was so experienced that she probably knew more than an obstetrician. She just put me at the front of the birth canal after she prepared the expectant mother. Then she went to the patient's head, and from there she comforted and relaxed her, and with signs and gestures of approval she gently helped me deliver the baby, cut the cord, and give the crying baby to her mother. She knew I was exhausted from fear. Kindly she told me, "Doctor, you are tired. Go to sleep, I will take care of the mother and the baby." That beautiful, white-haired black nurse! I went to my room and cried with joy. She was the best teacher I ever had, so gentle, so human.

My room at this hospital was large with yellow walls, which had in some places decaying, faded wallpaper with prints of old St. Louis. The window, the size of a door with jail-like bars, had a view of the innumerable train tracks and loaded freight trains screeching and making noise in the immense railyard. The busy panorama was so depressing that sleep came as a blessing. I was paid twenty dollars for a whole night of work. But the payment was even higher in the learning experience. I also assisted in surgery, and sometimes the doctor would let me perform it. They were good doctors, and they had also probably become physicians the hard way. They were not accepted in the mainstream of white medicine. They had been treated worse than me, a foreigner, but they seemed to be oblivious to this way of life. Perhaps medicine gave them the incentive to carry this burden with more dignity.

At this time I was suffering from severe tinnitus (ringing) and pressure in my right ear. I had had this affliction since childhood, dating back to my Amazon River swimming days. I was in my ENT (ear, nose, and throat) specialty rotation and asked the ENT resident to look at my right ear. He was amazed at what he saw. He talked to the professor and chairman of the department of otolaryngology, an experienced, knowledgeable old physician, Dr. William B. Harkins. Unlike most professors, he inspired confidence in the students and was approachable. He looked at my right ear through a newly adapted operating otic microscope and called the residents to look at the largest cholesteatoma, a benign ear tumor, that he had ever seen. It looked like an onion. Dr.

Harkins told me that I needed surgery as soon as possible. Well, I had no money, no insurance, no time, and, worse, the medical school would not put up with a sick medical student. We were supposed to be supermen and I knew that if they learned about my condition, I would be kicked out of school. Christmas was around the corner, the cold weather of St. Louis was getting into my heart, and the anguish of this moment cannot be described. I had a wife and two children, and I had an ear tumor, malignant by position, that needed delicate surgery to remove it.

I asked Dr. Harkins if he could keep it to himself and do the surgery during the Christmas recess. That kindhearted man; he was a true humanitarian and understood my worries. Christmastime came and I entered the large building, going to the tenth floor of Fermin Desloge Hospital. I went almost incognito. I did not tell my friends. I did not want my wife to visit me. I had the surgery; now I was a patient. I had been close to death before because of severe illnesses like typhoid and other tropical diseases in the jungles, but here I was more afraid of being alive.

When they put me to sleep, my thoughts went to the unending hardships of my life and to my never-ending fight for survival. I woke up in my hospital room hoping that no one who knew me—especially my professors, Dr. Hanlon, Dr. Willman, or Dr. Broadeur—would see me in this condition, because they were following my progress in school. I was not a regular medical student who could get lost in the crowd. I was as visible as a mole among all the others, and my background was even more noticeable.

The professors, residents, interns, and students would pass my room during the morning rounds. I would cover my bandaged head with a sheet, and I could hear them say, "Oh, that is an ENT case, nothing to learn from this," and they would go to the next patient.

After three or four days, with a bandaged head, and barely able to walk because of dizziness, I left the imposing hospital.

Carefully and tentatively, I crossed the street and walked slowly to the bus stop. The day was cold, and snow was falling. The buildings looked old and dark, and my life did not look much better. The bus drove down Chateau Avenue past the old houses of the long-gone era of the rich, white St. Louisians, in which now only poor black people lived. I was going home. At least there would be no school for a while. I could not work, and we had no money for Christmas (not that we had before), but at least I was well and that was all that was needed.

I took the elevator in this by-now dirty and run-down project building. The elevator was dark and had fresh puddles of urine. I crossed the long deserted passageways, with the rats running out of my way quickly. The black kids looked at my bandaged head and perhaps felt sorry for me or were afraid of me; I must have looked like Frankenstein to them.

I entered apartment 704 at 1251 Hickory Street. I found my two children playing after a bath, laughing and giggling. I held their naked little bodies and felt their warmth. I was alive and I was holding them and I was so happy. Now I could enjoy my family: no school, no hospital, no professors, just my family until I got well. I could watch TV with them, see what they ate, and see what they did. It was Christmas, and we were almost destitute, but we had each other. I would make it, yes, I would!

The dark, cold winter was alive with the green lights of Christmas in the old city. Everybody was happy, my bandages were off, and New Year's came. I went to visit Bill Sears, Bob Rich, Anthony Puopolo, and Ted Pepper at the Phi Rho Sigma fraternity house near the medical school. They did not know what had happened to me. I was at their same level, whole, strong, and unharmed. They started to make jokes about me and my country, as usual. They asked me if we had Christmas in Peru. Bob said, "Damn Peruvian Indians don't know what that is." I laughed at their jokes. They were my buddies and did not offend me in any way, but I also knew Italian and Irish jokes, which I fired back at them.

The fraternity house was full of empty beer cans, uneaten leftover food, end-of-the-year party trinkets, balloons, and a large Christmas tree. They needed to get rid of the food and the decorated tree. I told them I would take it home. We cut the green giant in half and they helped me to put it on top of my car along with the food and other Christmas items, and I drove home with presents. Finally I had a nice, big dry tree, and it was not too late. Yes, we would have Christmas after all! Thanks, Bill, Rich, Puopolo, and Pepper—we were great friends and always would be.

We started the fourth year of medical school minus a few classmates. We heard about two students a year ahead of us and two weeks away from graduation who had been thrown out of school because of poor bedside manners and, I think, drugs. Incredible! Eight to ten years of school, so close to graduation, and now they were out. We all panicked; we did not know how to protect ourselves. Everybody thought they were next, and this fear was ever-present in our minds.

I was scrubbing to assist Dr. Hanlon in heart surgery. It was a procedure that carries his name, the Blalock-Hanlon operation, which is used to repair a form of congenital heart disease. There were about ten people in the operating room, and the other medical students and I were holding retractors to keep the chest cavity open for the surgeons to work on. We were literally under the armpit of a surgical resident who treated us as part of the instrument when they needed more retraction or visibility.

The loudspeaker called out loud and clear, "Dr. Sánchez to the dean's office right now." Well, that was it, the call I was dreading. Finally it had come; my soul came to a standstill, almost thankful for this moment; there would be no more struggling, no more anxiety. Now my family would be free of this sacrifice.

Slowly, somberly, almost embarrassed to be there, I went upstairs to our seldom used sleeping quarters. I changed into my white uniform, cleaned myself the best I could, and shined my shoes. Tears fell from my eyes. My heart ached as if a member of my family had died. My throat was strangled by the tension of my desperation. I took the elevator down to the first level and walked on the lightly snow-covered streets. I was oblivious to the traffic, and the soft, cold, winter air gave me a gentle slap in my face as I crossed the street half-alive.

I came to the dean's office, and the secretary made me wait in her office. For some time the school of medicine had been trying to recruit a dean. Meanwhile, we had substitutes, physicians of renowned academic backgrounds who were, however, not too interested in the job. Finally they found a professor of psychiatry, well known and with managerial skills as founder and first director of the National Institute of Mental Health, Dr. Robert H. Felix. He improved the medical school and morale of its students. I saw the old brown desk speaker through which many a medical student had been told to pack up and go home. I was waiting for that call. This moment was like a thousand days with no ending. Dr. Felix called, "Come in, Dr. Sánchez." The secretary took me in by the arm, and I saw for the first time this kind-looking, short, and pleasant man, our new dean. I started to hold back tears in my red, sleepless eyes and my voice went hoarse. Dr. Felix put his hands on my shoulder and tapped me gently. "Dr. Sánchez, we know you have it hard. You cannot get loans and you have a family. We are aware of your economic problems. Cheer up and do not worry, here is a check for four hundred dollars. Some anonymous person gave it to us for a medical student in need." My tears came finally to my cheeks and my throat closed almost to the point of asphyxiation. I could barely say thank you and I left feeling the humblest I had ever felt before in my life. I was awestruck at the kindness and humanity in this world. I think I was never the same after this incident. (To this day, I still donate money to my medical school for the same purpose.) But I had more professors and rotations to go through, and the inevitable possibility of being thrown out of school for any reason was always looming over the horizon. We were just that close to such an eventuality.

Now we could rotate to other institutions besides City Hospital. I was sent to the Veterans Administration (V.A.) Hospital, which was like a jungle. The chief resident was a tyrant known for his ability to get rid of medical students with a snap of his fingers. This was to be another hurdle. If I survived this rotation, then I would probably make it.

The first part of the rotation was the medical floor. There were many old and sick veterans from World Wars I and II, and even a couple of old-timers from Theodore Roosevelt's era. I was assigned an older all-American gentleman who seemed a little out of touch with reality, a World War II veteran. He was half asleep. I was supposed to do a physical and history on him. Cautiously I woke him up, saying, "Good morning, sir." He looked at me, became agitated, and covered himself with his sheets shouting, "I don't want a Jap doctor. Get away from me. Don't touch me!" One could imagine my embarrassment as I tried to calm him down. I did not want the other medical students to hear him. That would be the joke of the day. Also, what would it do to my reputation for bedside manners? Worse yet, how would the revered and feared chief resident take it? Somehow, I switched patients with Larry Schainker, and my first day ended pretty well.

I took up more moonlighting in other hospitals. I moved my family to a new complex that was a better place to live. For a change I could walk to my house at late hours, because this new place was in a newly renovated part of the old town. We were happy just to be safe, but my money problems were far from over. Even Harry Owens, son of the famous bandleader Harry Owens of the 1940s in Hawaii, helped me with a loan that I paid back twenty years later, after I met him in the Brazilian Amazon.

We were fourth-year medical students, making names for ourselves and planning internships and specialties. Most people knew what they wanted to do. I was still recovering from my years of struggle.

I was assigned to the tuberculosis ward at the large V.A. Hospital. It was like sending me to Siberia. It was a place in which forty or fifty patients were locked away because of their active, contagious infection. They could not come out. I was told just to look at them through a window, follow their progress, and make sure they were taking their medications and receiving their injections. Well, here we go again! Because of my nature or my experience after reading Thompson's novel, I wanted to change this. I was not afraid to get TB. I wanted to go inside and touch these patients. I put on my white linen gown, cap, and cloth mask worn in the old days and opened the glass door. The smell of the crowded men came through my mask to my nose as if the TB germs were trying to enter my nostrils. All those patients surrounded me and started to pull and shout at me. They wanted to get out. They told me their last sputum culture was negative, and I was holding them back. I barely made it out. They were mad because they had been enclosed for months in that ward with no contact from the outside.

I started to review their records and was told by an intern that the patients used to exchange their sputum among themselves so that a patient who was negative, or noninfectious, would cough up in the sample box for the infectious or positive patients. Eventually I gained their confidence and I straightened out their records and at least got the cured ones out. It was not that the patients were not taken care of; it was just that manpower was short. We were the medical students, but we also were already doctors taking care of social problems as part of our duty. I guess I could have read about tuberculosis in an outdated textbook in a fancy library and called that learning. But not in this school. Here we learned medicine right out of real life and we knew we made a difference to our patients. I would never trade the way I learned medicine; besides, it fit my temperament and upbringing.

By now we had lost a few classmates and gained a few repeaters from the previous class. So far it looked as if I was going to make it through school in four years, without repeating a single year (which was not uncommon), and I did! Dean Felix made a difference in uplifting the morale of the students. As a professor of psychiatry he knew about the stress we were under. Actually, we were paranoid, even the top students. We felt and knew that the professors were looking for any reason to get rid of students who they thought were not suited to be good physicians. Even the psychiatry rotation, I found out later, was in part a way to see if we were mentally fit and had no psychological problems. We lost two medical students via this rotation, and one ended up in a mental hospital.

Things were getting better. Some well-to-do students were already playing golf on Wednesdays, imitating the habits of some wealthy doctors. We had a party for our class. A socialite medical student rented a place in a country club, or elite golf club, and many of us went. It would be the first fancy place I had ever stepped into as a guest.

Once in the elegant dining room, I went looking for my buddies, Bob, Bill, and Ted. I could not find them, and they never showed up, nor did some other medical students. I found out the next day they had refused to go out of solidarity because blacks were not allowed in this club. That meant our two black classmates could not have gone, and I felt uneasy. What about me—I was brown-skinned, a foreigner, not even an American citizen, and I was allowed in this segregated club. I guess I should have been grateful, but I was very distressed. But now one could see that as the medical students were gaining confidence, some of them were showing their discriminatory patterns. The social climbing became more noticeable, and cliques developed among us—the Irish, Jewish, and Italians. I stayed with the Italians.

St. Louis seemed so much better now. Even the famous arch, a symbol of the Gateway to the West, was about to be completed. Roy (named after Roy Rogers, the cowboy actor), my first son, was walking and growing steadily. I even went to the movies with him to see *Mary Poppins*, which I loved. I bought a used record player from Goodwill and I listened to a borrowed library recording of Beethoven.

We went through another specialty rotation—this time at City Hospital in obstetrics and gynecology. Eight of us were chosen to go for three months, and that group included my buddies and a few others. We were together day and night delivering every baby, and there were many. Again there was the same motto, "See one, do one, and teach the next one." Ted Pepper did not get to see one. He was called on to do one, nevertheless: In the midst of the delivery, with his hands in the womb of a mother, the resident asked him, "How are you doing, Ted?" "Fine, Doctor. I can feel the midline sutures of the baby's head." However, that turned out to be the buttocks of the baby. The presentation was breech and was delivered by the obstetric resident. Well, no harm done; we just laughed and teased Pepper for days. He didn't like clinical medicine that much anyway. Now he is a successful radiologist in St. Louis. Lucky for new mothers and babies! As usual, I was the mascot of the group. These guys would get bored and pick me up and put me in a huge, linen dumpster, buttocks down and face and legs up, so that I could not get out. They would send me down an old seldom used service elevator to the first floor, where I stayed until somebody would punch the button. We were like kids. One time Livingston, a wealthy St. Louisian and a member of our obstetric-gynecology rotation, came in raving mad in the middle of the night. "What is it?" we asked. He started to tell us how he had asked an expectant mother if she was in labor, and she had answered that "she never worked." He was really mad, but we just laughed ourselves almost to death.

Oh, those days of medical school! They will live forever in my heart, and the memories cherished forever, because it was an eternity that only in retrospect feels as if it went so fast. Those medical students were my family, and every five years at reunions my wounds are opened when I go to St. Louis, and every five years my wounds are healed when I see them. So as always, we must say good-bye to all good and bad dreams. Graduation time came and we all tried on our beautiful black and green gowns. Everybody purchased a graduation ring, but I could not afford it because it cost about forty dollars. I was already in debt to the school. Again Bill, Ted, and Bob collected money and bought me the class ring, which had a beautiful green stone in the center with St. Louis on his horse on one side and the medical school symbol on the other. I still look at the depth of this precious rock and those four years crystallize in the beautiful green emerald of hope of this stone. I pray I will never misplace this most cherished ring.

Graduation day arrived, and my father came to St. Louis. He had retired earlier as a commander just to attend my medical school graduation. Four years earlier, at my bachelor's graduation at BYU, I had been alone. No family member was present at that event—my wife was having our first child.

The commencement began. Dean Felix spoke of his accomplishments and how he found the state of mind of the medical students, and he mentioned his encounter with a medical student—me—to the entire large audience in this impressive St. Louis cathedral. My thoughts went to that little boy in the jungles of Peru with no shoes and no school. Now I was part of the dean's speech. All because of my perseverance and the humanity of the people who understood my desire to do good for mankind.

CHAPTER NINE

Burned at the Door of the Oven

It was the 1960s, and the country was in an uproar. There was racial tension, social upheaval, and a war that would affect even me.

I got an internship at San Jòaquin General Hospital. In those days we prided ourselves on getting the hardest, worst-paid internship possible if the training was good. We still believed in learning the hard way. Many of us stayed away from private hospitals, because there we would not be given direct responsibility for the patients; we were not considered real doctors. So I elected a county hospital in the farming area of Stockton, California, which was well known for its training, where one was in charge of one's patients and no one else. This suited me: "California, here I come."

By now the rotating internship was repetitive, almost a copy of my fourth year in medical school. During internships St. Louis graduates worked with recent graduates from other medical schools. We were able to compare our abilities to theirs and we fared well. Another reason I went to Stockton was to be close to my friend Harry Owens, who was an altruistic physician and also a hard worker with the same ideals I had.

In Stockton I began to see the problems of the farm-workers, who composed almost 90 percent of our patients. This was so different from St. Louis. My Spanish, which I had not been using, had become rusty, but here I had a chance to use it full-time. The social problems were different. Unlike the St. Louis poor, these people worked hard, but their income was miserable and their social conditions worse. Many were braceros (Mexican field-workers), illegals, and transients. I almost felt as if I were back in Peru. The emergency room was full of people with multiple kinds of farm injury. One time a Mexican worker was brought in unconscious because he had mistakenly taken a gulp of a fatal pesticide thinking it was water. By the time we got him it was too late. We worked on him for hours, but he did not make it. His wife and numerous children were asking for him. When I told them that he died, I knew they were left alone in this foreign country with no one else to care for them. I could see the anguish on the face of the mother. She almost reminded me of my mother when my father left us in Iquitos.

In those days Mexicans or Mexican-Americans had very little knowledge of their rights. They were very humble people and appreciative of whatever was done for them.

We had some hotshot specialty residents from San Francisco who used to come to see interesting cases for surgery. These doctors would pick up most of the English-speaking patients and give me all the Spanish-speaking ones, almost in a disrespectful manner. This was aggravating, and I would deliberately speak only English to the Spanish-speaking patients, even using translators. I thought these people deserved the care of a more knowledgeable specialist and not that of an intern. Eventually those residents got the message, and this practice stopped.

San Joaquin General Hospital was a tough and busy rotating internship with adequate pay, but I still had to moonlight. At least we had food and a house, my kids were happy, and my wife was pregnant with our third child and only daughter.

For years the Selective Service had been after me. In Provo, as soon as I had changed my student visa to resident status, they took me to Salt Lake City for an army induction and classification physical. I even slept in the army barracks. They needed people for the Korean conflict, and I was game. Nevertheless, I was classified 4F due to my partial right ear deafness. So I was exempted from service in the late 1950s.

Now, however, the Vietnam conflict was getting worse. I was a prized physician in the late 1960s, because the army was drafting all the new doctors, especially young ones out of internships and especially residents in training. Since I was a foreigner, with a 4F status, and had served in my country in a military school, I thought I was foolproof for the draft. The hospitals needed residents in any field who were not going to be drafted in the middle of their programs, and I had my pick.

I even secured a surgical residence because of the fact that I would not be drafted. Lo and behold, at the end of my internship, I got a letter from the Selective Service System asking me if I was practicing medicine. I said, of course. Well, they said, your 4F status is changed to 1A, and you are draftable since we need you as a doctor and not as a soldier. The Vietnam conflict was not World War II, in which I or anyone would have joined *ipso facto* to serve without hesitation, as I had dreamed of in all those John Wayne and Van Johnson war movies. Many people were avoiding the Vietnam-era draft, however, and some doctors were going to Canada. Many of those who stayed were using their connections with well-known hospital programs to save them from the draft. They would go into specialties that made it necessary to keep them in the country and the hospitals would write on their behalf; others would enter the National Guard or Public Health Service. As it was, I had no connections and I was not in a hospital prominent enough to be exempted from the service.

I had one avenue: not to avoid the draft, but to use my rights as an immigrant. U.S. law states that if a person served in his country of origin, which I had, then he would not have to serve in another foreign army. I was a reserve officer in Peru, because I had gone to a military school and that was my rank upon graduation. The military in Peru mainly recruited men without schooling, usually Indians for the purpose of teaching them, and they rarely drafted high school or college graduates. The draft officer said, "Fine! We will call Mr. Berckmeyer, your ambassador from Peru in Washington, and see if this is true." Typical of some of my countrymen, who seldom took pride in its youth and talent, the ambassador's office staff simply answered that they did not know of such a law in Peru and that I could be drafted. They did not even bother to look at my military school records or their laws. Being drafted was more of a problem between my country of birth and me. It was not a battle that I wanted to fight. I did not know what lawyers could do and I could not have afforded legal help. I put up a lukewarm resistance and then accepted the decision without remorse. Doctors who were drafted then had a stigma of failure, as if one was not good enough to have one's school or someone fight for deferral. I could not join the National Guard or Public Health Service because I was a foreigner, or in any case I didn't even know it was a way to avoid actual combat duty. I did not look for any moves to avoid the draft; thus I accepted my destiny without further hesitation.

Instantly, I was without a job, without a future. I did not know what to do with my family, and now I had three young children. The draft board told me they would be fair to me. I could choose my branch: the army, navy, or air force. I remembered in Peru only the elite went into the navy, and it was the same here, so I asked for the navy. I imagined myself on those big ships in blue waters. I actually liked the idea of serving in the armed forces, especially the navy. I came from a military family, and it would be an honor for me to be in the mightiest navy in the world.

The draft officer said, "Good, we will try to get you into the navy, but it will take six to eight months just to clear your papers because you are a foreigner and we have to check your background." In those days communism was a threat and they needed to check everyone out.

There I was in the middle of the farm town of Stockton with no residence, no job, and with the possibility of going to Vietnam to become a casualty. The first medical officer who died in Vietnam was a St. Louis graduate.

Again separation and uncertainty came into my life. I had to send my family to Peru because I did not have anybody in this country who could take care of them and I did not know what was going to happen to me. We went to the desolate, small, dusty airport of Stockton and I said good-bye to my three children and my wife for perhaps the last time. Solitude and desperation came to me. I was left with our family cat. That night tears came to my spirit. I never had felt so lonely for my family, who had gone through so much with me. Now they were going so far away to a land that they did not even know.

I went to Bakersfield, California, and got a residency in internal medicine at Kern County General Hospital while the navy was making up its mind when to call me. It could be months, for all I knew, or I could be thrown out of the country if they found any problems. After all, we were just out of the McCarthy era and anyone was fair game to be denounced as a communist.

I entertained myself working hard and moonlighting, so at least money was not a problem, but uncertainty and the absence of my family was. Eight months later I received my orders. I was drafted as a navy lieutenant, equivalent to a captain in the army or air force, and I was told to be ready to go to Los Alamitos Naval Air Station in Long Beach for induction and training. At last I knew where I was going, and my new family was going to be the U.S. Navy. I was proud and happy. I just wished this war had more popular support, or better, that it was more like World War II. It seemed as if everything I baked so hard just burned at the door of the oven, as Cesar Vallejo, a Peruvian poet, had said in a poem. I never felt like going to Canada or back to Peru just to avoid the service. I took this call as part of life and accepted the challenge. This was a new experience, and I was sure there was a lot to learn.

CHAPTER TEN

As American as Apple Pie

I arrived at the Long Beach Naval Hospital, a beautiful hospital by the Pacific Ocean. The high brass were in this large, elegant hospital, all dressed in white uniforms with shiny gold stripes. The navy gave me five hundred dollars for my uniform allowance. I went to the PX (navy retail facility), gave them my rank, and they suited me up in a beautiful dark blue suit with two thick, gold stripes and the emblem of the medical corps on my sleeves, as well as a white hat with a big eagle on the front. The uniform looked just like those officers used to wear in the war movies I had seen in Peru years ago.

I took my newly purchased attire to the bachelor officer's quarters (BOQ) and tried it on. My roommates were young but seasoned navy pilots. These were new people to me. I had never had anything to do with this profession. Again, there were no Mexicans, no blacks, just me, a mole in this elite navy. They talked rough, smoked a lot, and boasted of their many female conquests. I was a Mormon, the perennial straight-arrow kid. I put on the uniform and felt proud and elegant. I had worn one as a high school cadet, so I knew the feeling, but somehow it did not look as good on me as on those hotshot pilots. The officers were polite to me, but I felt

I was proud to wear the uniform of the greatest and mightiest navy in the world.

alone and awkward among all those navy fliers. I followed what they did, so I put on my hat and followed them down-stairs. I arrived at the bar where everybody was smoking and having a good time, and nobody was standing alone except me. I took my hat off and sat at the bar, which was the only seat available. I do not think I had ever sat at a bar before, let alone drunk at one, which was not my intention.

The bartender, a typical old-timer, looked at my stripes and my medical corps insignia, and not necessarily my face, and asked me in a manner I had never heard before from an Anglo, "What can I serve you, sir?" Well, I did not know. I used to drink as a cadet, but it was more out of mischievous-ness than a fact of life. Not knowing what to ask for, I looked at the officer's drink next to me, a large tall glass with clean sparkling ice and water with a slice of lime, and so as not to be embarrassed I said, "One of those." That was it, my first introduction to real liquor. I think it was a Tom Collins. As I sipped slowly, a tough, middle-aged pilot, a commander, tapped on my shoulder and told me, "Doc, you have a price tag in the back of your uniform." I was a little embarrassed and told him and the other pilots that I was new in the navy and this was a new uniform, which I had just bought. Well, this was an excuse for all the officers to have fun and to drink to celebrate my new status, a young lieutenant in the navy medical corps. Again I became like a mascot. I had a few more drinks and we became friends, and I was accepted once more. They still made fun of me, but now they also respected me. As it turned out, doctors could easily ground them, stop them from flying, and any navy physician was a good ally for a pilot to have.

Still, I was alone, my family was far away, and the country was in disarray in the midst of a war with no end in sight. On television news, young protesters were always in the forefront, and one could not deny or forget that we had a big problem on our hands. Now I became part of this nation and its conflict—I was serving in the armed forces, the government's highest calling for any citizen.

I was very enthusiastic about being in the navy in spite of the political climate of the country. I was ready to be part of the team, and the military had always been in my blood. I presented myself to the executive officer of the hospital early in the morning according to my orders. At the door of the commander's office stood a highly decorated navy man full of stripes who I thought must be some sort of high-ranking officer. I saluted him, but this tall, blue-eyed, red-faced person stepped aside, somewhat embarrassed, and said to me, "Sir, I am the master chief petty officer of this hospital and you are a full lieutenant. I should salute you first." I learned to spot the brass in the hospital after his lecture. Little by little, I got acquainted with the ways of the navy.

I started to scrub and assist in all surgical cases at the hospital while I was waiting for my final assignment to sea, Vietnam, or God knew where. This was in 1967 and 1968, at the peak of the carnage of the war.

I could see some young doctors, who had been drafted like myself, using many ways to avoid bad duty stations. The well-known tactic of social climbing was one way. Another was to present oneself as a great doctor with a great future or career prospects. Some of them were going to be cardiac or plastic surgeons and had promised positions awaiting them. Eventually some of those doctors had the best of duty stations. They stayed at the naval hospitals already doing something like a residency while at the same time serving their two years of duty. On the other hand, doctors who had no social-climbing abilities and no prestigious residency programs to speak for them were meat for the cannon and no questions were asked.

Many young people were avoiding the draft by any means possible, and if they were already in the service, they were trying hard to avoid overseas duty. However, the vast majority of doctors took their orders as they came. Nonetheless, the general attitude toward this war was so different from that of World War II. There was no enthusiasm, there was no support from the country, and that made one's position in the armed service somewhat untenable, because the people were not behind it. I suppose seeing a Peruvian in the navy must have made this branch of the armed forces appear to be in real need of doctors, which it was.

My orders eventually came, and I was to go to the desert. I had been thinking that I would go to the blue waters of the ocean; instead, I was sent to the marine corps supply station in Barstow, California, a desolate, little desert town about halfway between San Diego and Las Vegas. Finally I had my permanent initial orders. I was able to bring my family back from Peru and reunite again in this isolated spot and live with the marines.

Professionally, the desert was not the best place for an aspiring young doctor in training, but the marines were good people, and they loved their doctors, corpsmen, and the other ancillary professionals provided by the navy. After this assignment many others came, and I eventually ended up in San Diego at the largest military hospital in the world. I worked there for a while, then I was sent for temporary duties to Camp Pendleton in Oceanside, California, and the Marine Corps Recruit Depot (MCRD) in San Diego. Time went by slowly, and I was awaiting orders to be shipped to Vietnam at any moment.

At that time there were not many minorities who were navy officers. I am sure I was the only Peruvian officer in the entire American navy, since there were very few Latino and African-American officers in the armed services.

Most of the top brass or older officers were veterans of World War II and they were disgusted with the antiwar sentiment in America. I sat at the table with the old-timers and listened to their unhappiness with the uprising of American youth in the streets. I could feel their discontent and see the distrust or antagonism toward the political climate. I would have enjoyed the navy more if the younger generation and the nation as a whole had been more enthusiastic about the war, but this was the 1960s and America was changing fast.

When I was transferred to the naval hospital in San Diego, I went to the officer's dining room and noticed that all the Filipinos and blacks were stewards. Few if any were of officer rank. As I walked into the place in my white uniform, I could feel the stares of all the officers, especially the high brass and admirals. I could see in their faces, "What is this guy doing here? Who is he?" With my Peruvian face, I surely was an enigma. I sat by myself in a corner and admired the elegant, busy dining room with all the paintings of the navy's past, old war ships, and distinguished admirals. My thoughts went again to the glorious war movies of World War II.

Thanks to my good training at St. Louis University, once I became acquainted with any nonbelievers, they became comfortable that I was their equal. Now I knew I had a solid crutch, and that was my all-American medical education. By now, I was more Americanized, but appearances are ever-present and difficult to change, although I was not discontent with mine. I seldom felt discriminated against. The navy never made me feel that way. These were all my solitary conjectures; I never put on a face or an attitude that I was either discriminated against or placed in a humbling situation. Actually I was always very confident and outgoing, perhaps to the astonishment of some people who met me. Wherever I went or on any occasion through the years, and especially nowadays, I feel as American as apple pie.

One group of enlisted people I will always remember were the corpsmen, the medics, or "docs" as they were called by the fighting men when they were in trouble. Those young people were the medical care teams who went to Vietnam to take care of the wounded in the battlefield. They were always so optimistic, so eager to learn and perform medical procedures, to the point that many were as good as any doctor, especially those returnees from Vietnam's battlefields. They would suture complex lacerations, remove tattoos, put on casts, and take care of many minor ailments. My nights on duty or days in the hospital or infirmary would have been routine except for the medics' continuous questions and thirst for knowledge. Those young corpsmen were doing everything and learning all the time in expectation of providing the best of care to their fallen fellow fighting men. On our nights on watch when we were not busy, we would discuss their problems. Many were days or weeks away from going to Vietnam and would express their fears or certainty that they would die there, however valiantly. They seemed more resigned than fearful, and it was just something that they wanted to talk about. Many of those young corpsmen, I would find out later, actually did die in combat. Each time, I would think about what good doctors they would have become. I used to urge them to go to medical school, telling them of my tenacity in getting into medical school and how they could do the same. I am sure many followed my advice and I know they probably are the most caring doctors. I never heard them complain about their situation—they were truly gallant.

My days at MCRD in San Diego were at times surrealistic. This was a place where young civilian recruits were transformed into fighting machines—marines. Their training was grueling, almost unbearable. Along with the carnage from Vietnam, one could feel the smell of battle in these training camps.

This is where I had to learn to put on some show of toughness. The drill instructors (DIs) were hard on the recruits as a part of their job, but in truth, they cared for their people despite their toughness. There was no other way. Some young men would crack under the intense stress and at times would malinger, feign illness, to avoid their situation. Then the medical officers had to come between the DI and the recruits. We were like arbitrators. At times we sided with the recruits if a bona fide medical reason was present; after all, we were doctors first, and our aim was to help the afflicted patient whatever the cause. This is where military medicine is learned, and eventually we would come to an understanding with the DIs, because they did care for their men. They knew when a young marine-to-be was not being truthful, and they were rarely wrong. We still had to deal with the budding marines and make them go back to training, and that was hard, but it usually was accomplished, especially if rank was used after determining the cause.

I will never forget this: I was sitting in my office reading a chart when a marine recruit came in and asked to be discharged because he had been a premature baby, about two pounds at birth (which probably was true). While I was listening to him, I kept reading my chart without looking at him, mimicking the usual disregard for enlisted men. I did not make eye contact. As he finished his story, I started to lift my head and I kept lifting it almost to the ceiling. There he was, a six-foot, two-hundred-pound marine in front of me, and I had to throw him out of my office. In cases like this, we could not have any sympathy for weakness and we learned to act like the DIs and cooperate with them for the good of the corps.

Once a group of recruits were brought to me because they could not run or keep up with the platoon. After I examined them and found them fit, I harassed them, implying that it was easy to finish the three miles required. Having said that, I decided to run with them. What a surprise! I found out I also could not keep up with them. It was then that I started to train and got attached to the practice of running up to three miles before lunch, so I could actually say from my own experience that it was possible.

Military medicine in these centers was often hazardous. We had epidemics and diseases such as flu and gastroenteritis, but occasionally there were serious cases such as meningitis. One recruit got sick with meningitis, and the word went out. The men found out that the signs and symptoms of meningitis were headaches and stiffness of the neck; by morning we had the whole regiment in for evaluation because they all had those symptoms. That was difficult, because many were trying to get out of duty. I really had to be on my diagnostic guard to weed out the malingerers.

One night when I was on call, a recruit known to be difficult came in complaining of headaches, as many others had, but he also was not following orders and was somewhat belligerent, so the corpsmen woke me up. I went to see him, resenting the sleep disturbance. As I was walking down the long hall I heard a big commotion. The medics were trying to restrain him. As I approached the infirmary, I was shouting and applying my rank to have him straightened out, but to no avail. Once I got close to him, I realized he was sick. I examined him quickly and did a spinal tap, which was not easy because he was fighting everybody, and he was big and strong. Sure enough, he was full of the disease, meningococcal meningitis. We immediately shipped him to the naval hospital with an intravenous penicillin drip. He made it, but that is how close things got. Needless to say, the next day on sick call we had to check the necks of hundreds of sick recruits to make sure they were not tender and had no other signs of this dreadful disease. This task was assigned to me and my colleagues, Lieutenants Warren, Sontag, Rasmussen, and others. For those who were not sick we gave them analgesic-balm for any of their ailments.

In the navy the sum total of my experience, however, is that the outfit was great and they were good to me. Although at first I thought I had lost two years, I now appreciate that experience. I paid my dues and answered the nation's call when I was needed, and I would do it again. I am sure medical school was more militaristic, tough, and stressful than the navy and could easily break one down. The professors and chief residents were more feared than the admirals. Then again, my viewpoint was that of a medical officer, and I could not speak for the regular soldier, marine, or professional officers.

Assignments came and went, and eventually my two-year tour of duty was up. I was discharged from the navy with all the honors conferred to officers. We even had the marine band play "Anchors Aweigh" for us, which brought tears to my eyes. I was getting used to the navy, but the war was winding down, and the navy did not need any more medical officers.

CHAPTER ELEVEN

The Children First

As every naval medical officer does, I fell in love with San Diego, and once discharged, stayed for residencies. I ended up in a large, local hospital to finish my remaining year of internal medicine, which had been disrupted by the war. Unfortunately, I had no desire for this type of training in a private hospital and I was uncomfortable. The resident was not in direct control of the patient's management, and that made this situation unsuitable for my way of learning medicine. I took the position just as a transitional move.

On May 31, 1970, a major earthquake struck in Peru. It affected a large region in the center of the country, including one of the cities that I grew up in, Huaraz. I read the papers and listened to the news and became very distressed. I was a doctor. I was trained to help people and here I was in this fancy hospital where I was not really needed. I asked for permission to go, since I was due vacation time. Somewhat reluctantly, they let me go, as if it was an act of irresponsibility on my part. It was my country of birth, and I wanted to help, but that was not understood. Eventually I was ready to leave and filled my backpack with medicines, needles, whatever I could find medically necessary, all for adults; up to this time my thinking was not focused on children.

I was going to Peru for the first time in twelve years, not as a tourist but with a mission and perhaps to face some hazards. A Peruvian airline I had been in contact with was planning to sponsor a group of doctors and gave me a free ticket, and I was placed in charge of a team of American doctors. The outpouring of help was tremendous, and the whole world was sending medical teams, medicines, and supplies.

I went to the Los Angeles airport and, with a few members of the team, we boarded the Peruvian plane. Already the peculiar smell of that region was in the air. I sat with my backpack full of medicines beside the window, my thoughts going to the country where I was born and that I had left over a decade ago. Now I was a doctor. I had changed, but my heart and soul were still concerned with the poor and the problems of that nation. We took off and through the window I saw the lights of the big city of Los Angeles. We traveled for hours. As we started to approach Lima, there was already a sensation of sadness and excitement. The fear of the past I had lived with came to me again; here I was coming to see more catastrophe than I had ever seen when I was young. Finally, I was going to do what I had promised.

The jet circled around Lima, with its unforgettable greyish, cloudy, misty, humid air that had been described by Pizarro himself. Crowds filled the airport. My parents were waiting for me; I had come full circle.

We were all given quick clearance and directed straightaway to the ministry of health headquarters downtown. All of us were eager to get to the mountains to help where the greatest damage occurred and where we were most needed.

Lima was in a state of panic. The earthquake had been so strong that even the capital of Peru was still shaking, and it was far away from the epicenter. We waited for transportation for hours. I had had no sleep or shower, but I was ready to go to Huaraz, or El Callejon de Huaylas, Valley of Huaylas, as were the other American doctors and international teams. We could see the streets full of people bringing bags of clothes, shoes, blankets, and other supplies to the ministry building. Eventually we were conducted by a military attaché to a room where a lady was welcoming foreigners who came to help. Unknowingly, I complained to this dignified-looking lady, thinking she was a secretary, urging that transportation should have been provided right away and that it was a waste of time to be around for this welcoming. She was polite and arranged rapid transportation somewhat apologetically. Later on I found out that she was the wife of the president of Peru, General Juan Velazco. I felt embarrassed, but then she understood our problem and probably knew that our intentions were to go and help as soon as possible; at least I hoped so.

I said good-bye to my parents from the bus and we left for Huaraz with the American team, which also included some Frenchmen. The trip was uneventful except for some altitude sickness, aggravated by bad roads and unfamiliar food.

We arrived at the port of Chimbote, the center of operations. We were stationed along with other foreign doctors and nurses in the stadium like prisoners. Marines from an American aircraft carrier were guarding the area: Here they were, my people with whom I had just spent time during my service in the navy.

We were kept for days awaiting orders and assignments. There was plenty of help, but no transportation. All the roads were closed and very few supplies and manpower could be moved. I presented myself to the commander of the carrier and, as an old navy hand, I was able to persuade him to mobilize my team. A big Huey helicopter came to pick us up and I managed to take two Peruvian medical students with me. Finally we left Chimbote. The noise of the helicopter was thunderous. We cruised over some big mountains and started to fly into the Callejon de Huaylas. We could see entire towns and villages buried by mud, and in places we could see the tops of churches and palm trees looking like sticks coming out of the mud. Many people were buried alive in those places; thousands of people lost their lives. As quoted in *LIFE*, May 1995:

> It dwarfs last year's Los Angeles quake, which killed 60; it dwarfs January's awful Kobe, Japan, quake, with its death toll of 5,000. Twenty-five years ago today, on May 31, 1970, in the Western Hemisphere's worst natural disaster on record, an earthquake in western Peru killed 67,000 people. The tremor, 7.75 on the Richter scale (the Kobe quake measured 7.2; Los Angeles, 6.8), shook loose a gigantic mass of ice, rock and mud from the two peaks of Peru's highest mountain, 22,000-foot Huascaran. The terrifying 200-mph avalanche swept over the northern town of Yungay, obliterating it and wreaking almost as much devastation in neighboring towns.

There was actually not much to do in areas covered by massive amounts of mud. The problems were in the smaller cities and towns on the hills that were disrupted by the quake and not by the avalanches. We arrived in Huaraz and found that medical teams were plentiful there. They wanted most of the foreigners to stay there where there were accommodations.

The town was in disarray. The stench of death, injury, dirt, and confusion was everywhere; it seemed as if no one was coordinating things. One could almost set up one's own tent and start to help. I heard of a place called Huata that was requesting help. There were no roads, but Huata had casualties and needed supplies. I convinced the U.S. Navy helicopter pilot to take us there. I decided to take along the two medical students and also a lot of supplies. We ascended to the top of the high mountains, where one could see the Cordillera Blanca y Negra, white and black Andes, so called because of the perpetual snow on one side and its absence on the other. The view was beautiful, but we could also see the extent of the devastation of all areas. The helicopter kept going over the black Andes, which were devoid of animal and plant life, full of rocks. It was so desolate that my heart felt empty. Eventually we could see a little speck of green in this vast land of nothingness. It was like an oasis in this imposing mountain of solitude. How could people live there? It almost gives one a sense of no purpose in life. People were born there, probably never left the area, and died in the same place. It was a town mainly of Indians who lived on a meager subsistence, and whatever little they had was lost with the earthquake.

The helicopter descended onto a patch of clear field that the children had used as a stadium to play football. As we descended, the people rushed to us as if they were going to assault us. We got out rapidly, while the rotors were still going, and put all our things on the ground. The navy pilot said, "Good-bye, we'll pick you up in two days." As soon as the aircraft left, the people started to try to take whatever we brought. I began to act like a DI and pulled off my belt and kept the people away. I climbed a stone fence and explained that we were doctors and we were trying to help. Eventually we erected our own tent. We had old Vietnam supplies, from C rations to American-made blankets, tents, and medicines.

I contacted the mayor of the town, who was a person of some means. He owned the only store in the area. He took us to see the village. It was devastated. No houses were left standing, and all the adobes were crumpled on top of one another. Bodies had been removed and buried already, but a lot of injured people waited in the town's central plaza. We immediately started to work, giving away blankets, C rations, and clothes. Our tent became the hospital, and we were busy all the time taking care of the wounded. People started to come from the higher mountains to be cared for. Almost every hour the ground shook, sometimes violently, as the aftershocks were still coming. At night while sleeping in our tents, the ground below us would be moving with a deafening unnatural sound. We could imagine the earth opening and us

He took us to see the village. It was devastated. No houses were left standing, and all the adobes were crumpled on top of one another.

falling into its depths, but at least we knew adobes would not fall on our heads, which was what caused most of the casualties.

We lost track of the days. Nobody was coming to or leaving this town. No planes or helicopters were flying by, and in fact we would later find out we had been forgotten.

One evening an exhausted young boy came, telling us that his father had broken his leg and was immobilized and in pain. I told him to see if he could bring him down since we were very busy with all the other sick. He said that the road was difficult and high in the mountains and could only be traveled by horse.

I discussed this with the mayor, and he volunteered his horse, called Napoleon. We left with the boy at 5 A.M. the next morning. The road went steeply uphill. Even the horse could not walk on this seldom traveled, rocky terrain, and at points we had to go by foot. Eventually we arrived at a fallen adobe hut where a man was lying down with a broken leg. He had been in agony and in bed, I think, for six days or so.

We immediately started to work, giving away blankets, C rations, and clothes. Our tent became the hospital and we were busy all the time taking care of the wounded..

Fortunately, there was no skin broken or compound fracture. Immediately I took out my plaster rolls. I had so little left that I used some branches to stabilize his leg and applied what little plaster I had. The cast looked good—at least it was solid. The man was in pain, but he did not complain. He had six children and they had a nice patch of land in this inhospitable place. As I came out of his hut to have something to eat in his makeshift outdoor kitchen, I could see the most enormous view of the white pure mountains, including the famous Huascaran, twenty-two-thousand feet high, the twenty-one-thousand-foot Huandoy, and the twenty-thousand-foot Nevado Huancarhuas. It was so breathtaking that I could not feel sorry for this man and his family. They had all of nature to themselves. The dichotomy of tremendous, desolate, clean poverty and beautiful, pristine nature came to haunt me on my trip back to Los Angeles. We stayed at this spot for a while just enjoying the spectacular view and letting

Immediately I took out my plaster rolls. I had so little left that I used some branches to stabilize his leg and applied what little plaster I had.

Napoleon rest. The climbing to this place was exhausting, but the trip downhill would be even more dangerous because of the stones and the steep slope. It took us almost the entire day to take care of this man.

Riding the horse in those mountains was one of my most memorable moments. I felt so rewarded for what I had done. It was as if all my ordeals to become a doctor had been worthwhile for this single experience.

My thoughts began to turn toward the future, and I started thinking about my purpose in life. Should I do this for life? But by now I had a family and a desire for more training. It was obvious that this country had no special programs to help the poor and the Indians. Nothing had changed in the twelve years since I had left. If anything, things had gotten worse, or at least my perception of the contrast was more striking. I started to feel the impotency of not being able to do anything. The problems of Peru are so deeply rooted that one feels helpless to solve them. One could come up with ideas of social reform and address them to the people and to the government, asking them to unite and help each other. It sounded so easy, yet it was so impossible. While daydreaming I often imagined myself giving speeches on how I could help this land get on its feet. When confronted with reality, however, I knew it was like climbing those high mountains, so daunting and treacherous. Frustrated, I would look at the infinity of the blue sky, at the purity of the mountains, and I knew I was home and unable to do much.

We arrived back at Huata, where our tent was near a small river. I was so tired that I took my C rations, ate some, and slept by the stream, breathing the clean air and having nightmares about the devastation that took place in this area and the futility of these people. By now we had been there more than six days, we had taken care of almost everybody, and we wanted to go somewhere else or be reassigned, but we had no contact with the outside world. We were unable to get transportation. Two planes flew by. We flashed our mirrors, but no answer. Eventually we had to send a team of rugged young people to get help, but we did not hear from them either. Finally we carried what we could and started to walk to the next village, where it was possible to call for transportation. This next town had more greenery, and there were also many sick people who needed help, so we set up our tent and started to work. Meanwhile, we sent someone to get us transportation. We spent a few days there, when at last an American helicopter came to pick us up. We were relieved. I was concerned I would be left in those areas for a long while, unable to return to the private hospital on time. Then I would be in trouble.

We quickly boarded the smaller, noisy helicopter, this time empty of supplies, filled only with memories of those people whom we had come to know so well. My heart felt heavy, my eyes became humid, it was like leaving my family. The pain was worse because they were left with no future in sight and I could do very little about it. It was like witnessing the futility of life. The helicopter rose and the dust looked like a little catastrophe. The people became small, their hands were waving at us, and their hearts were also sad. My soul was crying for them; I felt like a stone that has been thrown into the air and feels nothing but the vibrations of the rotors. The Peruvian medical students were also overtaken by the sadness of the place, but they were more stoic. They were more in touch with reality, and for them this was part of life.

It was so good to speak English with the pilot. He was a Vietnam veteran and was aware that I was a recent navy lieutenant. He could not visualize me in this duality of my life, especially in those places. Again we traveled the whole corridor of the valley and could see how the small towns were always in the path of the small river that came down from the high lakes. These lakes, like man-made dikes, could easily break during an earthquake and bury a town on their downward course.

Finally we got to Chimbote. Some of the other volunteers

We carried what we could and started to walk to the next village, where it was possible to get help. This next town had more greenery, and there were also many sick people who needed help.

were still there, eagerly awaiting to go out and help. They were almost envious of our trip. We waited a few days in this small concentration camp of doctors, nurses, and other helpers. Eventually we left for Lima in a Peruvian Air Force transport plane. Now I would have time to be with my parents. The capital had not changed much, although the Indian and mestizo population seemed to have increased. The criollos still had the same mentality toward people from the interior or provinces, although the earthquake made them realize that Indians existed in those inhospitable areas, and their spirit of help united the country. However, many catastrophes would be needed for this divided population to understand, love, and care for one another in times of peace and absence of natural disasters.

For a long time, almost as far back as I can remember, my constant thinking has been about how I could help my country to unite and fight for a common cause, to erase the past that haunts almost every Peruvian. Everyone has a way of coping with the problems of social injustice and social discrimination. Some completely detach themselves from their ancestral origin—even if they are the brothers of the oppressed. Others try to do away with the past by misconceived thoughts; some even joke that the problems of Peru can be solved by getting rid of the Indians. They mean, I suppose, that it would leave the criollos or lighter mestizos with a "better" country. Another solution, heard outside of Peru and in other Third World nations, as well, is that since the country is controlled by a few wealthy families or oligarchies, if they were done away with, the problems of Peru would be solved. These are all desperate ways of thinking. All sections of society—the Indians, criollos, mestizos, and the wealthy families—are Peruvians united by a common historical bond dating back to the arrival of the conquistadors. Now more than ever they need each other. With time they will become one and forge a great nation for their own good.

Unfortunately, most of the natural disasters occur in the Andean mountains where the majority of the Indians live, and it seems that Lima is oblivious of their plight—either because of its centralized government or because they have detached themselves from the Indian population.

Deep in my heart, I felt I was now getting a chance to help, although it was in a small way. Due to my circumstances, that was all I could do. I still was a young doctor in training with a growing family.

Nevertheless, thoughts of Peru have been in me for the last forty years of my intermittent absence. Most immigrants who come from Europe are able to shake their past, even their accent, almost as soon as they come to the United States. No ancestral upheaval haunts them. They may have recent memories of injustices, but by the time they have been in this country for as long as I have been here, they do not even remember their language. It is precisely this incongruence that has made and still makes my life philosophical. I have attained my professional goals, raised a great family, have no economic problems, and am well accepted by the American people. Yet there is this wound in my soul that will not heal and that continuously edges into every day and hour of my life, creating a continuous pain that obstructs the pursuit of happiness and my peace of mind.

So, here I am in Lima, as if the earthquake had never occurred. My parents and others think that what I have done was mostly of a waste of time. There is concern, but there is little they can do. They want the news of the catastrophe to cease so they can go on with their normal existence.

I visited some hospitals and clinics, but I was not overwhelmed by any lack of facilities, as compared to those in the United States, or for that matter, in the old St. Louis City Hospital. I saw the doctors providing care in the best way they could and often with the same concern of a good Samaritan. Those young Peruvian doctors were hardworking, altruistic, and enthusiastic, but their humanistic endeavors were somewhat petrified by the insurmountable problems and the inability to achieve much in their limited circumstances. Still, their valiant, individual approach was worthwhile, but it was not appreciated by the people or by the government. Perhaps it was because their endeavors were mainly to alleviate human suffering and had no bearing on the economy of the country.

I went to downtown Lima to confirm my return trip, and I saw again unkempt youngsters shining shoes. To me they were no longer innocent children—they were street-smart and able to handle the vicissitudes of life better than any college graduate. Their brown faces, dark shining eyes, and their hands and nails dirty with shoe polish were too much for me to bear. I wanted to help them, but all I could do was have them shine my already polished shoes once more and give them some extra money, while I was embarrassed for the tears in my eyes. I think that children who are either begging or working in demeaning jobs expose the very soul of a country. These children's existence is proof of the disdain of the very people who created them, of the government that tolerates their plight, and finally of the society that allows it to happen.

At the new airport I again encountered the familiar departures and the stress of separation. Who knows, it may have been for the last time, or perhaps I would return and see the same unimaginable solitude of this country. The poor and child vendors were running all over. Although modern, the airport had its peculiar smell, and the Inca relics and souvenirs for sale made me feel almost festive. I boarded the plane, took my seat, and sighed profoundly at the experience and hoped it would not be the last time I could be of service.

Now I was more determined to prepare myself so I could come back and help my mother country. I was going back to my rich, benevolent, continuously-trying-to-be-just uncle, the great United States. Even with its faults, it still is the cradle of dreams and possibilities, a place to wash away one's antiquated and anguished past. But this land is like a magnet. "Uncle Sam wants you," and you want him even more. One becomes so much a part of the United States that it requires the strength of a titan to break away for good to go to other places to create and spread the mentality of this great nation.

The plane had been in the air for a long time. I woke from my sleep as from a nightmare. I was sadder upon returning, yet I was comfortable that I had done this mission, in spite of the hospital's attitude.

The plane circled and approached Los Angeles, a huge city with house after house and trees that blend with the color of the smog. No clean mountains, no snowy peaks, no solitude of wild wilderness. Here one begins to feel the emptiness of crowded civilization in the absence of nature. I did not know whom to feel sorrier for—the Peruvian whose leg I fixed in his fallen adobe hut between two beautiful white and black mountains with a view more overpowering than the Swiss Alps, or those people who live like ants in the great Los Angeles metropolis. What a dichotomy, what an illusion, so hard to explain and yet easy to accept. The trip had ended. I was back to reality. I followed Uncle Sam's teachings, "Work hard and enlighten yourself and you will be part of this great nation."

I went back to my house. I embraced my wife and children, and I was happy, because I hoped my children would appreciate my deeds someday. I felt I was a human. I could still do things for others, and that is what I would always try to do. My depression or sadness lasted for days. My thoughts of Peru could not go away easily.

The hospital and its doctors were not interested in hearing about my humanitarian trip. They were concerned about their program, and I was ostracized. I felt if I had been someone else I would have been called a Good Samaritan, interviewed and on the glaring evening news. But as Latinos we had no capacity to do good, and if we did, it was irrelevant. Such is the duality of every society, and one must take things into context and keep on living and doing one's best.

By now I was concerned about my future in medicine. Although I was an accomplished generalist with a lot of experience gained in the navy, including surgery and obstetrics, I was still somewhat confused about a specialty. Originally I had been in a surgery program, but the Vietnam conflict had disrupted this endeavor and I lost three years of possible further training. My family was growing, and I felt like an eternal student. Thanks to the trip to Peru, I was able to clearly decide on a residency that suited my ideals. Through most of my years in medical school and internship, I noticed that most medical emphasis was on adult specialties. Pediatrics was a branch of medicine barely touched or sometimes avoided.

While I was in the earthquake area I had felt so inadequate with children, especially the sick ones. Even most of the supplies that I took were for adults; there was not a single needle sized for children. When I arrived in Huata, children were the most numerous and most serious patients we had. Even the adults who were injured would tell me or the

It was in the beautiful mountainous desert of Huata that I decided to go into pediatrics, a specialty I had never before considered.

other doctors, "Please take care of the children first." We had seen dehydration, malnutrition, meningitis, and other severe cases. Most of the sick were children, and their deaths were the ones that were most devastating to us as well as their parents. It was in the beautiful mountainous desert of Huata that I decided to go into pediatrics, a specialty I had never before considered. As did most other young doctors and even the main character of *Not as a Stranger*, I wanted to be a surgeon. There was no question that for my future endeavors to help people in those Third World countries, pediatrics would be the most needed and welcome specialty. Thus I put my efforts into looking for a good pediatric residency and ending my affair with the older population that I was already comfortably accustomed to. I would be entering an almost completely new field, much like starting over again, with very little of my past training to take with me.

CHAPTER TWELVE

To Make a Difference

Fortunately, the pediatrics residency program at the University of California at San Diego (UCSD) School of Medicine had an opening under the chairmanship of a great pediatrician and mentor, Dr. William A. Nyhan, a superb clinician and well-known academic physician and researcher. (A genetic disease, the Lesh-Nyhan syndrome, was named after Nyhan and his coworker.) Dr. Nyhan interviewed me and understood my desire and motivation for becoming a children's physician. I was accepted to his program, which was the most sought-after and difficult-to-get-into program because of the intense competition among young doctors just out of full pediatric internships at prestigious East Coast teaching hospitals.

One of the perennial challenges of medicine is that it may take more than a decade to advance from premed to formal training in a specialty. It never ceases being a new experience and a new station, and as one gets to the top, one has to step down and start again. First one is a premed, then after getting an undergraduate degree, one becomes a first-year medical student. Then as one gets through the fourth year, one is suddenly the new intern, just a beginner. Then after years of residency and going into practice, or entering the armed forces, one is considered a young doctor in town or a young general medical officer (GMO), and somehow the freshman-year feeling never seems to end. Even now with so many changes in medicine, we are new to the challenges and have to start almost all over again.

So here I was, a new pediatric resident. I was older, and my training in internal medicine—even my having served in the navy during the Vietnam era—was a drawback in this ivory tower. Those years of residency were hard, and the competition was tough in this academic environment. UCSD was a much fancier institution than City Hospital in St. Louis. There seemed to be more physicians in training than patients, so each case was managed by many doctors and one had to assert oneself in handling a case, but the residents were still in control of the patient and not subservient to a private physician. Instead there were professors, and they were demanding for our own good, and that of the patient.

The hospital was close to the Mexican border. The worst cases came from Mexico or were Mexican-American, and my knowledge of the language came in handy. Most of the poor were either Hispanic or black, and they were the sickest. In St. Louis most of the patients had been African-American. In any event, I felt at home in this environment and I was glad to be in it.

To illustrate both the excellence and competitiveness of this training, I recount a case of Reye's syndrome, at that time a rare disease. A beautiful five-year-old Caucasian girl was brought in a comatose state. The professors' knowledge and all the literature were exhausted in an attempt to find a way to save this child's life. I and others were taking care of her constantly while some interns and residents were researching the illness. While we were monitoring the vital signs and maintaining the IV, word came in that the child was to have a complete blood exchange transfusion as a last resort. This was tedious work and there were few volunteers, because there were other interesting cases to see. So some of us spent most of the night exchanging the blood of this child. Suddenly by early morning this little angel started to move, and one of the interns aggressively came in to help. We let him take the case; we went to our quarters because we were exhausted and needed to sleep. Eventually the child came to. By the time we woke up, the press was at her bedside to report her miraculous recovery in the news. The next day we saw the picture of this "valiant and great young doctor" who saved the life of this child, with his name in bold letters in the newspaper headline. The press and the intern failed to mention the efforts of the many people involved in the care of the child. Nevertheless we worked as a team always for the best care of our patients with the best of professors.

We also used to go to Tijuana, across the Mexican border, to bring sick children back to the hospital. These were the most exotic cases, from which we learned much. I felt good about those trips. At that time it was not as expensive to take care of seriously ill patients, and I think we were more charitable than we are now, or perhaps state funds were more plentiful, but mainly we had generous grants for this purpose. *Now with skyrocketing costs of medical care, and their great economic and political ramifications, this has become impossible.*

I also joined the adult infectious disease leprosy team, which went to study and try out new drugs for people suffering from this disease in Tijuana. We visited old, run-down, dusty colonies of poor people, looking for new cases and following the progress of others to see whether their scarred faces and bodies were improving or deteriorating. We took samples of new drugs, followed the patients' course, and took statistics. My main function was translating and explaining their condition to the patients. The team doctors were very knowledgeable and caring while in the pursuit of research for a new cure.

It was hard to support three children on a resident's salary. Again I started to moonlight in my preferred capacity, the emergency rooms. During the day I was a young doctor in training, but at night or on weekends in the ER I was a full-fledged physician, able to take care of cardiac arrests, car accident victims, and other more mundane medical problems. This extracurricular activity had to be done in peripheral hospitals. The chairman of pediatrics discouraged his interns and residents from moonlighting, but I also did it because I enjoyed practicing this type of medicine, making my own decisions that by now were more seasoned. Thus I was able to provide a decent living for my family, and at the same time I was learning and keeping up with adult medicine.

After a superb training, including neonatology rotations under the excellent and demanding chairmanship of Dr. Gluck, a renowned neonatologist, I was through in two years. I did not want to prolong my student life in a fellowship and I opted to go into private practice. I still felt I wanted to do adult medicine, especially OB deliveries; I was ambivalent about a full pediatric practice. San Diego then had only one or two Hispanic physicians and I was in demand within the community, although few institutions or doctors asked me to join them. All the other residents had spots in La Jolla or other affluent places, but I had no red carpet. I was on the threshold of my professional life. I had finished my training and I was ready to enter the world that would be the culmination of my efforts. I had no more steps to climb, no more tasks to tackle, but in reality my soul was in deliberation.

It seemed that I had come this far so that I could go to places to help and be part of the process, especially in Peru. Being a mere pediatrician, although with the clearest of intentions, I began to realize I was in no position to do anything of the sort at this time. But my desires to help the poor, the destitute anywhere in the world, were becoming ever more present in my mind.

By now I had been in this nation long enough to have realized that there were also social ills to overcome in this country that indirectly affected me and for which I could lend support. Also, I owed much of what I had become to the United States. I began to empathize with this country's problems with the poor and the discriminated against, many of whom were Hispanics, who were becoming more numerous and visible. Just across the border, the Mexican poor were very similar to those in my country of birth, and it was right at my doorstep.

I decided to stay in San Diego while taking care of my family and establishing myself professionally. My plan was to become self-sufficient and to be able to go to those poor countries and help on my own, since I had no funding and no one was interested in supporting my endeavor. Initially, I chose to practice in the somewhat underserved area of southeast San Diego, with the help of a retiring pediatrician and general practitioner, Dr. Myron Homnick, who wanted to do anesthesiology. I took over the small practice, because I still wanted to see adult medicine and do some surgery, and this arrangement suited me fine.

I began to make connections with newly emerging community clinics. The country and the cities were beginning to be aware of social problems, and these clinics were formed by private citizens to take care of their poor.

I was delivering babies for the Chicano Clinic in distant hospitals so that my pediatric colleagues would not know about it. This was done in an effort to help, and I charged no fees.

My office began to fill up with Mexican-Americans who were poor and for the most part on welfare. The previous all-white, English-speaking, private paying patients of Dr. Homnick began to disappear. Soon I was short of office space and needed to expand.

I asked myself where the "worst" place in San Diego to start a practice would be—there I would go! I began to look for places and I found a run-down small building in south San Diego, in an area called Otay, five miles from the Mexican border. The building and the lot were vacant and nobody wanted to buy it. It was a meeting place for gangs, and two murders had occurred there.

I thought this was the perfect place to open an office and get to work. My colleagues were stunned and even questioned my soundness of mind. Twenty-five years ago there were not many doctors in town, and I could have put an office in any affluent area and I would have done well. However, I still identified with the poor and the socially disadvantaged, and I found them right here in the United States. I had found all the assistance that this country offers to anyone who wants to succeed, especially anyone who helps others by helping themselves. I went ahead with courage to start my own practice where very few would dare.

The old building and the land in Otay were almost a giveaway, as if the owner wanted to get rid of them. I got a loan from Bank of America, which was very helpful and did not question my chances of success in this area. The banker, Mrs. Linda Mulosky, was also very helpful. I think my enthusiasm touched her, and she assisted me in obtaining a loan of more than I needed. She thought the existing structure was too old and calculated the expense of repairs would cost more than building a new one.

I found Mr. Amato Teta, an architect, who drew the plans according to my specifications for a nine-hundred-square-foot small office. I put up a sign in this ugly place where nobody dared to walk at night that read: "Future Pediatric Office of Dr. Carlos J. Sánchez." The sign itself was an improvement in this dormant, small, inner-city community consisting mostly of Hispanics of poor means and backgrounds. No new buildings had gone up in years. All the houses were old and decaying. Across the street were some temporary huts where braceros used to stay.

My colleagues drove down to see what I was doing and they thought I was making a mistake. They were all renting space in posh places close to hospitals, in sterile environments. I wanted to create what I would have liked to do in a country with many poor people such as Peru, and I was doing it right here, because there was also a need here.

The building went up in ninety days due to my insistence and desire to move into my new quarters as soon as possible. The little office looked like a jewel, like a fresh scent of air in a moldy, run-down town. The street was wide with no sidewalks; still there are none even after I fought city hall. Across the street was an ugly hamburger joint that was a hangout for suspicious characters. On the other side of my office was an old house that served as the small grocery store in the neighborhood. The owner was an old, unkempt man who was not very friendly. His store smelled of old, rotten wood and peeling paint, and it had spoiled food items that people bought simply because of proximity. I talked to the gentleman, introducing myself as his new neighbor and possibly business partner. We had something in common—we had the guts to serve these people even if it was a dangerous neighborhood. He had been shot twice in the chest by one of his customers.

On the initial day of opening there was not much fanfare. My first patient, bless his little soul, was a Down's syndrome child whose mother was a well-to-do Mexican living in a suburb of San Diego, but she came to see me here, way down in Otay. God must have sent this child to bless my new office, because after him, people started to come; in four weeks patients were waiting outside and the small office space was inadequate.

Finally, I was my own man. I had no more people to judge me, I had no more individuals I had to perform for. I had no need to prove to anyone that I was capable on my own merits. At last I could forget about their judgmental and distorted ideas. Here the patients, who were from all different social strata, were my overseers. They held me in high esteem for what I was and were not disappointed for what I was not.

The joy of being my own boss, the feeling of mastering my own destiny according to my own abilities, background, experience, and soul was beyond my wildest dreams. Finally, I became a full-blown condor flying with wings as wide open as God could stretch them. With the mature and solemn face of a condor, I could now soar to the highest mountains of fulfillment or glide down to the precipice of failure. But as a great condor, I could also see in the distance, peaks and mountains of iniquities that were asking me to fly to them—to feel the flowing air of my optimism moving with the winds and the mist of those great valleys of desperation. Now the condor, bloated with his successes, circled high in space, content as if he had finished a great meal, looking all around for hours, days, and years, his soul always hammered by those faraway, cumbrous mountains that he needed to fly to.

I had created my own world in the United States, but this was not to be the culmination of all my efforts. I was sure there was more of a calling. I wanted to make a difference in a place like Peru.

Finally my children and my wife could rejoice in my humble accomplishments and the small but sufficient economic rewards. Although I was busy and seeing more welfare patients than most other physicians because of my location, my practice could never match the monetary reward of other doctors in affluent areas with high-paying private clientele.

At this point I finally had some money and could afford some longer stretches of free time. I started to appease my soul by going on many trips into the poor areas of Third World areas such as the Amazon of Brazil, Peru and the high Andean villages, and Mexico. The chronicles of those trips I will relate here, hoping that I may be able to raise social consciousness, so the aberrations of the past and present will not continue to occur. In the future, I hope young people can be allowed to pursue their lives with a clean conscience, not feeling guilty about their accomplishments because of past and present social injustices that surround us everywhere in the world.

Now I was a respectable biochemistry researcher, with a white coat and my overgrown pet rodent. (See page 118.)

There it was, the school of medicine, a dignified red brick building with chapel-like architecture. (See page 126.)

Riding the horse in those mountains was one of my most memorable moments. I felt so rewarded for what I had done. It was as if all my ordeals to become a doctor had been worthwhile for this single experience. (See page 176.)

As I came out of his hut to have something to eat in his makeshift outdoor kitchen, I could see the most enormous view of the white pure mountains. It was so breathtaking that I could not feel sorry for this man and his family. They had all of nature to themselves. The dichotomy of tremendous, desolate, clean poverty and beautiful, pristine nature came to haunt me on my trip back to Los Angeles. (See page 175.)

The Amazonic Hospital was situated on a hill overlooking Lake Yarinacocha, a former arm of the Ucayali River. (See page 210.)

The hospital was well accepted by the Peruvian government and the ministry of health. In this hospital I met Dr. Jim, a Canadian physician, devoted to his work and skillful at all kinds of surgeries. (See page 211.)

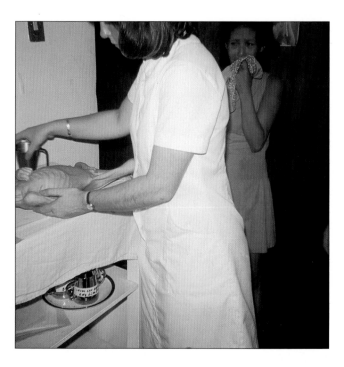

We were the final person who would tell them that they had carried enough sorrow and could now be at peace with their conscience, letting their children go to the cool, clean mists of heaven where they came from. (See page 218.)

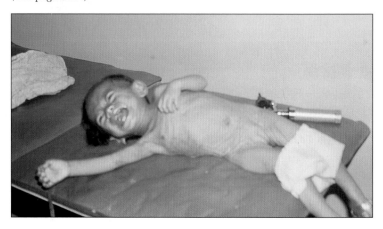

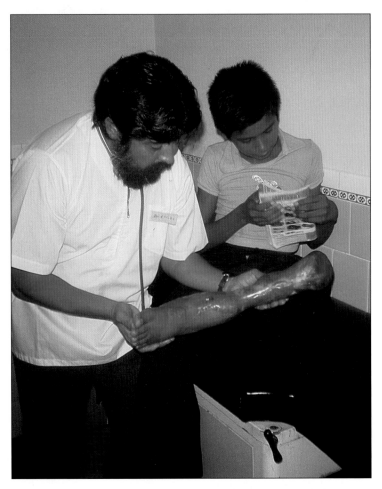

Now I was a doctor and I would dig my hands into any patient if for no other reason than to give that person some last hope. (See page 220.)

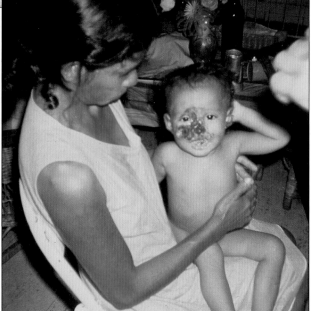

There was no use kidding ourselves—yes, we were helping, but it felt more like climbing mountains of the slipperiest soap, where with each step taken forward we slipped two steps back. We tried to use our hands—only to feel our fingers clutching the foam of hopelessness. (See page 217.)

Courtesy of Esperança Foundation.

Luke Tupper was so enterprising and full of ambition for this endeavor that he came to San Diego and bought and refurbished an old, discarded ferry-boat, the former Point Loma. I rode in that ferry when I was in the navy, and its captain was the father of one of my patients, whom I diagnosed and treated for TB meningitis when I started practicing in San Diego. *What a coincidence!* (See page 247.)

Their mother's milk would do the wonders of nature and give life to those children who would survive to perhaps suffer the same injustices of their parents. (See page 256.)

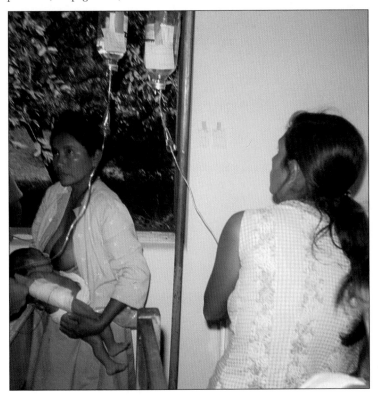

Their little innocent Indian faces are still in my mind, and I will always remember them. I am sure they are my guardian angels and grateful that I prolonged their lives to at least enjoy some of this great paradise, Earth, even if I could not save them from its inequities. (See page 258.)

By the time people went to bed from their New Year's parties, I was ready to take them home. (See page 256.)

Anja Hovland

This strong, aged man was stubborn and feisty as all Vikings are. He died riding his own craft on its maiden and last voyage, frozen by the Nordic waters. Through Anja, my lineage carries his blood and my Inca past has been appeased by this inheritance. My children will not suffer the pain of my ancestry anymore. The wounds have ended with me. (See page 238.)

CHAPTER THIRTEEN

Short of Money, Short of Time

As we grow older we tend to lose the humanitarianism and altruism of our youth. Citizens who do not take care of their young generation—as has been said of Third World countries—do a disservice to themselves. They seldom help their young people, especially the Indians, mestizos, and blacks. They do not appreciate them for what they are or make them feel like they belong. It is like parents who do not rejoice in the first small steps that their child takes. These countries actually truncate their children's early development, smothering their young people so that their souls become poor and meager.

Such a country's soul is so divided with class and social status that one segment of the people despises the other simply because of their skin color or degree of mix, with the advantage given to the lighter-skinned.

Discrimination in those developing nations is so pervasive, so ingrained, that it seems as if it were a new trait. One sees no progress towards its eradication. Only the forces of nature can mutate those genes and evolve those unfeeling people into new human beings who respect each other for the content of their souls, not for their color or social status.

While growing up, I saw so much disparity of social classes that it has harmed my inner spirit so that no matter where I am, no matter how rich I am, no matter how happy I am, there is always a sadness in my inner self. There is an existential solitude with a vastness of desperation added to the platitudes of our short existence and the inevitable end of our short lives that leaves us unable to do much to change it.

Each trip I have taken to help in needy countries has left me with a profound emptiness of heart, a deep frustration, especially because of my inability (and for that matter, everyone else's) to be able to do anything except pacify myself by frequent trips to help some people who are already dead in spirit but alive in sick bodies. However, I still receive immense moral reward from the people and countries I have helped.

How can one tackle such a disease of the conscience of a nation? How can one heal the scars of the past? How can one protect the young buds being shadowed by the great, giant trees of inequity? Oh! If one could have a gigantic pair of scissors and cut away the strong, stern branches of those old trees and make a passage of light, as dim as our hopes, but yet bright enough to give these young souls enough sun rays to grow above the big forests. These enlightened young souls could create vines that reach and absorb those large, monstrous, grotesque trunks scarred by the futile cries of the past and by the emptiness of time.

I could have lived like other doctors, fulfilled and accomplished, just continuing to work and reap the rewards, raising a happy family and living comfortably until retirement and death. That is the way of life in a great nation. That is the way of a fulfilled population and of a satisfied person who has not noticed the surroundings and seen the aberrations of society, even in a country as advanced as my adopted one. Yes, the United States has its injustices, but one has the freedom to choose whether or not to be involved without suffering the moral and spiritual devastation that one would in Third World countries.

The United States is a country whose beginnings were that of moral and spiritual enlightenment, although the country's history is also that of enslavement of blacks, annihilation of Indians, and discrimination against other societies. Somehow in the short 220 years of its existence as a new nation, the outcome is that of gradually cleansing the past with visible deeds of improvement for the people who were subjugated. However, this has not happened entirely by the charity or compassion of the people, or with the advantage of total political support; these changes were and are continually obtained by the oppressed themselves. Because the spirit of those people is alive; the will to fight is there. The chains of oppression can easily be broken. They are plastic, modern, and they have not been hardened by the passage of time, by the cruelty of hopelessness and sameness. The country is a sea of hope with sharks and beautiful fish all looking for a niche to protect themselves and enjoy the vastness of possibilities.

Now I have come to the plateau of the mountain and I could continue until it comes to the final cliff and the end of what my life would be. But no, I want small peaks and valleys on this mesa, hoping it could be as peaceful as the Grand Canyon, not as treacherous as the Pongo de Manseriche at the beginning of the Amazon.

It was at this stage of my life that I started to go abroad and to feel my way into the valley of the poor and destitute. As time went by, recollecting my trips, I felt that these were the most satisfying moments of my life. The beauty of nature enjoyed by those people and myself was beyond comparison to the riches acquired in a compact civilization where almost nothing is natural, where everything becomes ungodly, and where one becomes so materialistic in spirit, that the thirst of the soul can only be quenched by the acquisition of goods. So perhaps I will have the best of both worlds; but my confusion adds to the dilemma of having lived so long in two worlds so far apart.

I started to look for agencies that help people in need in distant countries, especially Brazil, Peru, and Mexico. I found few, and I realized that for the most part one had to act on one's own initiative and help with one's own means.

I took my second trip to Peru around 1974, this time to the Amazonic Hospital of Yarinacocha. This hospital was

built in 1960 by Europeans and Peruvians who were interested in helping the Indian tribes and the poor of this region
by giving free medical care. Many volunteers and donations
came from all over the world. It was a well-organized, non-
profit, nonreligious, nonpolitical institution. While one
stayed in this hospital, one could learn its history. Like many
other similar charitable institutions, it had a rather stormy
beginning due to lack of money, political problems, and internal difficulties. Besides free medical and surgical care, it
also attempted to promote preventive medicine, teaching hy-
giene and nutrition as well as mother and child care, and re-
ferring difficult cases to other hospitals if necessary.

The hospital's aim was also to help the Indians keep their
integrity and identity as unique Indian tribes, and to adapt to
ever-encroaching civilization without giving up their ways of
life, their customs, and their language.

The Amazonic Hospital was situated on a hill overlooking
Lake Yarinacocha , a former arm of the Ucayali River. Yarina
was the nearest village to the hospital. Pucallpa, the largest
nearby city, had thirty-five thousand inhabitants only ten years
earlier, but by 1974 its population had doubled. The hospital
was reached by paved and dirt roads that closed down when it
rained. Pucallpa and Yarina are closed in by jungle, a feature
that is especially striking when seen from the air. The distance
from Lima to Pucallpa is about 480 miles. Yarina is situated
444 feet above sea level and is close to the border of the Brazilian jungle. The climate is hot, with temperatures ranging from
about 68 degrees Fahrenheit to the mid-90s in the dry season.
There are only two seasons, one dry, lasting from May to November, and one rainy, from December to April.

The flight from Lima to Pucallpa took fifty minutes and
crossed the beautiful Andes. One could go by road during dry
weather, but that was an arduous thirty-to-forty-hour trip.

The hospital compound was mostly jungle and swamp,
with farms and houses for personnel. It had about forty beds,

divided into different specialties, and also a small morgue. Some buildings were made of brick and cement, others of wood; they all had tin roofs. The windows had mosquito wire netting and wooden shutters, and a few had glass panes. The facilities included a deep well for fresh, clean water; sewage treatment; and also generators for electricity.

Doctors were mostly guests from many countries who donated their services for weeks or months. There were also European medical students who came to study tropical medicine. A flying doctor service was available using the nearby missionaries' planes for villages deep in the jungle that could not be reached by boat.

The sanitarios, or "barefoot doctors," were young local people who were taught nursing skills and sent back to their villages to give first aid to their people. The hospital was well accepted by the Peruvian government and the ministry of health. In this hospital I met Dr. Jim, a Canadian physician, devoted to his work and skillful at all kinds of surgeries.

I made preparations for my trip, choosing Christmastime because of the prolonged holiday and the decrease in numbers of patient visits. I was filled with both a sense of duty and a sense of guilt for leaving my family at such a time. My finances were good, but usually only if I continuously worked and attended to my practice. I had no plans for retirement, and I carried neither life insurance nor health insurance; I was unaware of these necessities.

The nostalgia for Peru was already in my soul. My goal was to work hard, and I hoped the work would be challenging enough to satisfy my desire to help. I filled my red backpack full of medicines, syringes, and, this time, small needles for children. I bought army surplus gear and took no luxuries, no sought-after things like radios, televisions, or cameras. This time I went by jet. My appearance was unassuming, and by now I had a permanent beard that I had grown in the tumultuous 1960s and 1970s. The trip was rapid, the familiar misty Lima was on the horizon, and then the plane landed. The smell was as usual—a combination of humidity and food not produced in factories. I walked on the half-clean, greenish marble floor of the airport. The men in uniform with pistols in white holsters were ever-present with their suspicious looks but humble walk.

I went through customs. The officers were almost surprised that I traveled so light and brought nothing of worth, except for some medical instruments, needles, and medicines that they had no desire to impound or waste time with.

Outside was pandemonium: taxi cabs, small petty thieves, and people who came to greet the arrivals. My parents were waiting, their faces wrinkled and sadder than when I left last time. Their son was back, but he did not look prosperous! He was in fatigue clothes, army boots, and carrying a backpack. Was this the picture of a doctor who had graduated in the greatest country in the world and at such personal sacrifice? I could only see their faces of disappointment, yet they were happy to see me once more.

We got in my father's old car and left the noisy airport. As I looked through the dirty window, I could see people in dark clothes, their walk slow and their spirits looking sad, even when laughing. The streets were asphalt but full of potholes, with broken sidewalks. The houses of hard cement were attractive, but some had been under construction since I last left, and most were dusty with time and the lack of rain. My soul was sad, but my mind was happy to be where I was from; to see my parents who brought back my memories of the Amazon.

I arrived at the house where I had never lived but which we now owned. My parents were proud of their possession. The house had an air of still quietness; there was no hum of machines. The street was silent, with no nearby freeways, and all was peaceful.

We sat and reminisced about old times, and talked about my unscheduled, unplanned trip to the Amazonic Hospital. They thought I was out of my mind to go there because there was so much to see in Lima, so many modern things were happening. They wanted to take me to the best America-like places, especially in the beautiful areas of Lima—San Isidro and Miraflores. They did not understand that seeing nature and helping the poor were what I wanted, and that I hoped to work as hard as I could and to do as much as I could in a short time. Eventually they understood my feelings because they had previously seen how happy I was on my return from the 1970 earthquake in the Callejon of Huaylas. They knew I would only enjoy my last day in Peru after I did something that would cleanse my conscience like a confession.

I rearranged my backpack and we went to the airport the next day. By now I felt more like a Peruvian. The system got into me rapidly and I felt more comfortable. The smell of the city, the looks of the people, and the potholes in the streets were a delight. At the airport, lines of people with children and makeshift bags of goods were boarding small planes going to the interior of the country. There was no need for fancy clothes, neckties, or cameras. This was real life; the show was over. I took a small Faucett propeller plane to Pucallpa. As I sat in the cramped seat, memories came to me of my toucan with his large beak and colorful face who had shared oxygen with me years ago. I still could feel his claws in my hands that had not been weathered by hard manual work.

Oh, Lima, your scenery has not changed. You have just gotten bigger and more crowded. We crossed the frigid high Andes, terrified to think anything might happen here. But the view was beautiful, with perpetually snow-capped mountains that we now passed over quickly. Then the heat and humidity in the plane mounted as the green carpet of jungle below welcomed us. The long, snakelike Ucayali River and its tributaries started to play puzzles with me. A thought struck me: Wouldn't it be better to crash in this area; then, at least, our bodies would regenerate with abundant life in this jungle paradise, unlike in the desolate Andes.

We landed in an airport that was wide open to nature. I could feel the warm, humid breeze surround my body as if it were a giant welcoming friend.

I took a taxi to the Amazonic Hospital. Now they had automobiles and even pollution was present here. The car traveled the recently dried, bumpy dirt road. I rolled back and forth and my soul shook with enthusiasm. Trees and shrubbery were abundant at the side of the road, all green, all natural, and even the houses were made out of growing things.

The hospital was what a jungle hospital was supposed to look like. It smelled of antiseptics, the dying, and the sick. Everything rots there quickly. The dead have no time to

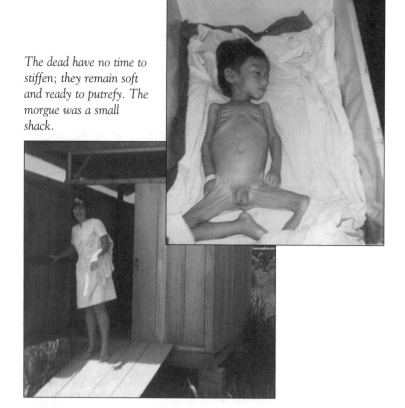

The dead have no time to stiffen; they remain soft and ready to putrefy. The morgue was a small shack.

stiffen; they remain soft and ready to putrefy. The morgue was a visible small shack.

I introduced myself to Dr. Jim, who was surrounded by working nurses in white aprons and several others. They all seemed to admire and revere him. Even I felt in awe of his air of humility and boundless energy. He had a crew cut, blue eyes, strong teeth, and was short in stature, but taller than me. He wore short pants and was always smiling, yet worried. His doctors were mostly Swedish and English, and there were several anthropologists from abroad studying the natives and also helping him with their social problems.

I could feel that he was suspicious of my intentions. I had no letter of introduction or recommendation, and he had no knowledge of me. I told him I was a pediatrician educated in the United States, and that I had experience in this type of work and was willing to do my best for one month. He eventually realized I was a foreigner like himself who wanted to help with no remuneration, but I think he still had some reservations on his mind about the reasons for my being there. He knew that physicians in the area did not volunteer, probably mostly for economic reasons.

Many doctors in Peru work under conditions of poor pay, lack of equipment, and most likely a severe division of class status, including enduring the perennial social climbing of some well-connected individuals. Nevertheless, most Peruvian doctors in the course of their daily work help a lot of people and get no credit. They are the likes of Good Samaritans, only they remain unknown. In any event, though one may speculate why people were not helping, I think physicians are sometimes unfairly judged, which is what makes our position untenable. The scrutiny creates more room for vulnerability.

I was a newcomer, but the workers in the Amazonic Hospital started to treat me like a regular. Soon after my arrival, I got a room in the foreign doctors and nurses quarters, quite modern and better equipped than the ones given to the Peruvian workers. I laid down my backpack, pulled off my stethoscope, and placed it on a wooden chair. It was as if it were my only companion. I felt a sense of belonging; this stethoscope was the only thing that would bring me credit and gain the friendship of people, especially the young children with their dirty little faces, rotten teeth, and warm smiles. It would also be the instrument that I would place on the chest of a dying person and hear no more the heart sounds that had once opened my pupils in delight when I first used it in medical school.

I took a warm "cold" shower that cleansed not the dirt, but the sweat and tiredness that in this climate was unbearable. I dressed in clean, light clothing and went to have dinner across the patio. The sounds and sights of the jungle were reminiscent of my youth—the noise of the thousands of insects, the crying of the big birds, the sight of the big frogs eating little frogs, and the big frogs being eaten by snakes. Life and death are continual; even one's own body is part of the mosquito's feast and could fall pray to the deadliest of diseases that are unknown in temperate climates.

After dinner, I went back to my empty room. I felt alone, and the darkness outside was alive with the sounds of animal life. My thoughts went to my family in the United States. A feeling of inertness came to me, almost a feeling of futility of life. I could hardly wait for the next day, to work until I was so tired that life had done its job and this emptiness was filled with the unknown of sleep. The morning came soon and the sun was strong. The insects were not as noisy and the heat was already burdensome. I dressed in my white surgical suit after a rapid warm shower. There is seldom cold water in the jungle.

I had a quick breakfast. Dr. Jim had already made rounds and was ready to go to surgery. I was assigned to the outpatient clinic and was taken there by a nurse. It looked like a market, people who looked old yet were young, babies suckling and hanging onto almost empty breasts, malnourished, pale children clinging to their parents. I looked like a giant compared to those people, and yet I was one of them. The smell was strong; their suffering was indefinable. I entered my examining room. It was furnished with a small, wooden desk, on top of which was an old Laennec wooden stethoscope, a replica of the first instrument invented by the French physician in the 1700s, which was still used in these areas.

Children started to arrive, their mothers eternally complaining about their lack of appetite, severe diarrhea, dehydration, and other symptoms. Again I felt as if I was in St. Louis at the City Hospital. I had to work hard out of compassion and learn fast out of necessity. The diseases I encountered were so uncommon in the United States that I was almost a neophyte in the field of tropical medicine, but the nurses and the other helpers had done this for years and they taught me the diagnoses and treatments immediately. The handling of the clinic had become so routine that their efficiency was welcome. Actually, the doctor was more a symbol of hope, a healer simply because he was a physician. These people were asking for miracles. The nurses knew that we could help a child, but the next day the child would be back, and the following week the same child might be dead.

The healing is not in the doctor or the medicines; the cure is in the hands of the government and society. The eradication of disease would be in the teaching of these masses, who reproduce at such an alarming rate, that the common denominator is death and the equalizer is the survival of the fittest.

There was no use kidding ourselves—yes, we were helping, but it felt more like climbing mountains of the slipperiest soap, where with each step taken forward we slipped two steps back. We tried to use our hands—only to feel our fingers clutching the foam of hopelessness. Yet we learned fast. There was no time to ponder; the people were waiting for us to see them. We had to give them something, and by the end of the day they were content because they themselves had done the best they could do, which was to see a doctor, and we fulfilled that desire. Those people had traveled for days and had sold all their possessions to bring their dying children to see us. When we told them about the impossibility of a cure, their faces and their souls became lighter, as if the weight of possibilities had been removed from their shoulders. They were sad but stoic, and also relieved, because they had done everything they could, and this was the last place to come. We were the final person who would tell them that they had carried enough sorrow and could now be at peace with their conscience, letting their children go to the cool, clean mists of heaven where they came from.

Dr. Jim's job was more rewarding, as it is for most surgeons. He cured diseases almost in front of the eyes of the people. He removed huge tumors, cataracts, and everything that can be eradicated, which produced an instant reward. Perhaps that is why he could bear it here for years. Every day each patient was a success. In a way I envied him because he had no time to dwell on esoteric things like life and death and why a healthy child had to succumb to simple diseases such as diarrhea, malnutrition, and dehydration. There was no magic instrument to cut this disease, and although we had diagnoses and medicines, the nature of the jungle itself was the origin of the disease. How can one cure that, unless there is a massive government effort to confront these problems? But it would not be in my or Dr. Jim's lifetime. Still the satisfaction was to save some lives, and Dr. Jim was doing a lot and so were the rest of us. What mattered in this scene of desperate people was that we could pull out of those Dantesque pictures some souls to live another day in this beautiful, treacherous jungle.

The days went by. I could have remained there for years and nothing would have changed. One learned about tropical diseases and, for that matter, its living pathology, almost in a day. Even one slide with a sample of stool had all the parasites one needed to see. A single patient could have all the tropical maladies, and in two or three days one could learn to diagnose most of the diseases, and probably treat none. One might alleviate the symptoms, but only for a limited time.

Dr. Jim was a kind man. He had a young family and they were very well adapted to the place and the people. In him I saw the absence of vanity and the rejection of social status. He felt that he was like everyone else, whereas many in his position would have their "head in the high clouds" and perhaps not even be worthy of helping this underprivileged class of citizens.

I remember a day long ago when I was in Huaraz and we had just finished our 28th of July independence parade. Another child and I had bought an ice cream cone from a street vendor. By evening I was sick with diarrhea that would not stop. My temperature was high, and by the next day I was dying of dehydration. The doctor came to the house but stayed outside on the patio. He did not enter my room to check me, but instead sent his assistant to examine me. He would loudly question the male nurse, "Is his belly tender? How is his tongue? Is his skin dry? What is his temperature?" and so on. Eventually his diagnosis was typhoid fever, and at the rate I was going there was not much that could be done. In those days penicillin was just arriving on the medical scene as a miracle drug, but not to this remote town far from the capital. He gave some well-intentioned but probably useless prescriptions and recommended that fluids be given at all times. My poor mother stayed day and night with me. She tried all kinds of herbs, and concocted potions that were folk remedies. Among them was the one of two lamb's testicles boiled in water until they burst. She fed me this soup daily as a last resort. Eventually my father went to Lima and got some penicillin that had to be injected intramuscularly every four hours around the clock by a sanitario sergeant who slept at our house while I was sick. Don't ask me how—I am sure my infectious disease colleagues are going to argue against penicillin as treatment for typhoid fever—but somehow, after a month and although I was scarcely more than a skeleton, I was alive.

Now I was a doctor and I would dig my hands into any patient if for no other reason than to give that person some last hope. I know that this is what was different about Dr. Jim and many other local doctors. They personally examined people with leprosy and other contagious diseases without hesitation.

As long as I have known doctors, I have seen arrogance in some. Maybe their reluctance to touch patients is because they know the futility of this gesture, or maybe it is because they have become hardened by the abundance of diseases. God knows, doctors are also human, and we are entitled to our idiosyncracies.

I cannot criticize this hospital, although there could be room for it; that would be an injustice. I was liked by everybody and I became part of the family. I brought laughter and joy because I am an outgoing and funny person, seldom talking about misery or acting somber. That is my way, to mask all my inner turmoil. I can make children laugh and I can talk to parents and know that I also lived like them in worse jungles and have not forgotten. I just wished I could do much more.

This is why now age and time are becoming a menace. Suddenly I realize I am not as young as I used to be, at least probably not as well adapted for the Andes where the air is so thin that even breathing is an effort. On the other hand, I have fought all odds and my added years are proof that I am a survivor; the body can accommodate a harsh climate given these circumstances if one takes the time to acclimatize to the areas.

Again time came to leave. I had made some good friends and I promised them I would return; they wanted me back soon. They took me to the airport. The familiar endurance of the pain of departure had already hardened my heart and I could only subdue it by the thought of coming back. Good-bye, Pucallpa. Good-bye, Dr. Jim. You were an unsung Albert Schweitzer. Hopefully this little paragraph does you justice.

I landed in Lima. Now I could enjoy this city, which has an interesting past full of beautiful colonial buildings and places to see, especially museums. I went to eat in typical places and visited my few friends. My heart was fulfilled. I was cleansed for another year or so. It was time to fly back to the United States, which I missed already. Each trip makes me realize what a good country the United States is and how much hope is there, but I also hope that I am an example of what makes this country great, which is its compassion.

Back in my practice in Otay, ugly Main Street looked deserted without sidewalks or people. Everything was in order, all the children were fat, nobody was really that sick, but I still managed to see seriously ill children because of the location and the type of population I worked with. My practice was booming despite the fact that my colleagues rarely sent people to this area. My patients were my source of referral, my allies. Now, even those colleagues were questioning my absence. They could not visualize what I was doing. Sometimes it was even embarrassing to tell them where I had been. But this country is so beautiful, because one can do as one pleases without the approval or disapproval of others, especially if one is one's own boss. What is more, one can make enough money to do those things that one wants to do. Instead of cruises or vacations, I was enjoying doing what I liked by working in the Amazon. I felt well rewarded after those trips, although my psyche was in a deplorable state and it took days just to get rid of the feeling and smell of the stench of diseases and misery of the jungle.

Meanwhile my already enlarged office was again beginning to feel small. I started to get ideas of building a large clinic for the Hispanic community, bringing Latin physicians in to take care of the welfare patients, the poor, and the needy. I started to contact Spanish-speaking doctors, usually foreign graduates. There were many who had come here because of the Vietnam-era lack of physicians. Many prestigious residency programs were filled with these doctors. Also, because of newly instituted affirmative action programs, many medical schools were graduating more minority physicians born in this country. Some were interested in coming to San Diego and starting a practice. So with this project in mind, I went to the Bank of America, and again sought the help of Mrs. Mulosky. They could not argue against success, and with a new loan I proceeded to build additional office space, plus an X-ray suite and a laboratory. I brought in an obstetrician and a pediatrician, both Mexican-American. Later, I brought in other doctors, and still others joined me, including one from Cuba, Dr. Ramon Moncada. We were all a happy family, and everyone got busy as soon as they hung their names outside the door. They were excellent doctors and their knowledge of Spanish helped their meteoric rise.

Once again, I was itching for a trip back to the Amazon. I knew Pucallpa, and I had good connections with Dr. Jim. As usual, I made no plans. I just got tired of the routine of my practice, and arranged for another pediatrician to take over in my absence. So I filled my backpack with needles and medicines and arranged my trip as before during the Christmas holidays. This time I took my older son, Roy, with me. We left the Los Angeles airport in army gear and backpacks—no presents, no TV, no nothing, just us. We stopped in Lima and the next day we went to Pucallpa, to the Amazonic Hospital. To my disbelief, the medical compound was closed. Some old workers I knew were still there, all looking sad. Their faces were empty of smiles, their optimism gone, and the place was deserted. It looked like a cemetery. The cries of children and the stench of disease were no longer there, and the foreign nurses, doctors, and anthropologists had left. For political reasons the hospital was closed. I began to realize that, as in many similar operations, the leadership of one individual made such institutions run well—one person like Dr. Jim—but when the leader left, that was the end of it. That person's enthusiasm, optimism, and hard work were contagious. This closure was destructive and detrimental for the community, because there was no continuity or plan to find another physician with Dr. Jim's philosophy.

An old employee told me to wait in the empty waiting room and the new director, a local doctor, would come to talk to me. I sat with my son, somewhat embarrassed. Roy thought I was going to be welcomed by a lot of people. I had told him that I would be working hard. I wanted to give him the joyful experience of helping others; unfortunately, the place was no longer what it had been.

The doctor came, a short, lighter-complexioned physician, smaller than me. He had perfectly groomed black hair, and was well dressed, as if for a party, with clean hands, no dirt under his fingernails. He seemed well rested with no apparent cares on his mind. He told the caretaker to have me wait until he had his breakfast and then to bring me to his office (Dr. Jim had no office). We patiently waited one or two hours, reading old magazines from the 1930s, and I tried to make excuses to my son. Finally I was taken to the director's office. I felt uncomfortable and humble, as if I were going into an important interview. For some reason I already felt uneasy with this man. I told him I was a doctor from the United States, a pediatrician, and ready to work, and that was the sole purpose of my trip. I mentioned that I had worked with Dr. Jim and that I was sorry to find he had left.

He said, "Whatever was done in the past in this hospital was not the best solution to the problem for the people in this Amazonic region." He and the government were looking for a better approach, studying the situation. When ready, it would be more efficient than the way the previous people had managed the place because it would cover larger areas and reach more people. It was a master plan, which probably was the thing to do, but everything was being studied in

Lima. In any event, my services were not needed and there were no patients. In my heart I knew what he was talking about, but Dr. Jim was only doing what one person could do. Wasn't it better to help a few while big grandiose schemes were being designed? In principle I agreed with the new plan, but in my mind to close such a hospital was deplorable. Of course, what I saw and heard was only the surface of the situation. I am sure there were just and unjust aspects that I cannot account for, and I could be wrong. I and other foreign doctors probably were naive, but then we were simple individuals trying to do something for a few sick human beings who crossed our path. We could not tackle the problems of a nation, although I would love to try it.

I asked the doctor if I could at least spend the night since I had planned to stay there. He was very helpful about that and gave me Dr. Jim's empty living quarters for the night. Roy and I went to this once-beautiful jungle house, which now had been closed for months. To our dismay, we found every corner of it was full of giant tarantulas and all kinds of insects. We spent the whole evening killing these arachnids just so we could find a place to sleep. Eventually we got tired of the carnage and decided to sleep on a table in the middle of the room, which we cleared of spiders. Sleep seemed impossible with the place loaded with tarantulas, but somehow we slept a little and in the morning we arranged our backpacks and left the once-busy hospital. We took a plane to Iquitos and from there we went by boat to Nauta, where the Marañon and Ucayali Rivers come together. The trip was a great experience. I felt as young as my son. We enjoyed the company of the people, and an American backpacker joined us for the trip. We arrived in Nauta, a small city with no doctors at that time. I went to the mayor of the town and told him I was a physician and I wanted to have his permission to set up my shop in the abandoned medical post. He was receptive and gave me a paper that read, "In the name of the revolutionary government, I authorize the

American doctor Carlos Sánchez to medically help the people of Nauta." He was the first to bring his children to be seen. Thereafter I worked without rest seeing lines of people with both minor and major ailments. Actually, this turn of events was more satisfying to me than working at the hospital, because I had to use my own entrepreneurship to handle the cases and to get medicines. I was also able to teach the sanitarios how to take care of the sick. I know my son was relieved for me because I was finally helping people. He entertained himself with his American tourist friend, Mr. Prell, and they were treated well on account of my celebrity.

We stayed there a few days, went on to another small village by the river, and did the same thing there. Our help was welcome. I was hatching ideas for doing the same type of work in the future, being my own agent and setting up a mobile makeshift clinic anywhere one was needed. However, my American mentality was still aware of possible medical-legal problems. I discussed my concerns with people in high places in the Amazon, and they laughed at the idea of malpractice suits. Now my thoughts were of building and staffing a hospital boat, traveling up and down the Amazon and its tributaries, and reaching more people in remote villages. I was full of plans, but short of money, and, more importantly, short of time. I set my projects aside for the future, hoping that someday I would have the time and resources to do this.

I also entertained the idea of becoming involved with the leaders of Peru, tackling all those problems in cooperation with the people and the government. Why not? My intentions were good and I was just as capable as any politician. I had a global overview and intimate knowledge of the needs of the country, obtained by my years of observing, living, and working in it.

Such practical experience is a better preparation for leadership than experience gained by one who is encircled by the political embroilment of the country. Stronger leadership will also come from one who understands the thinking of the leaders of other strong nations that dominate the economy of the world, especially those of the United States and the Western European countries.

This powerful country, the United States, has been forged around principles of moral rights and freedom. Here one uses the power of persuasion, the capacity to argue one's way into the hearts of people and institutions, even huge, monopolistic enterprises. The leaders will listen, and most of them are people who rise to the top through hard work, independence, honesty, resourcefulness, and persuasiveness, and many times they themselves came from humble beginnings. But they like to play hardball. They do not discount an individual because he or she is weak, black, brown, or poor, unless that person feels unworthy or unable to meet them as equals. One has to work hard to be heard, and eventually one comes to a consensus by the power of compromise, as stated so well in Profiles in Courage by John F. Kennedy. In developing countries, leaders are predetermined. In the Andean nations, it would be unthinkable to have an Indian or full mestizo as president. The attitude of the Indians or mestizos themselves is that they want to have a person in command who is a "man of presence," although this idea may now be changing.

Through the years, I have seen most of the leaders of my mother country seem to disappoint the people, or else they were good heads of state but the people were not united to support them. The accumulation of inherent problems and ancient social injustices can suffocate the most able and benevolent leader. The masses are hard to please, and with such a plurality of backgrounds—social and class distinction—good leadership is even more difficult to attain, but someday it must be done. Our world is getting smaller, and the countries in it are more aware of the needs of their citizens. People, through the information highway and mass media, are becoming more knowledgeable about what needs to be done. For that matter, the whole world needs to rearrange the affairs of this planet, which is decaying at a fast pace. Even powerful countries are unable to control the pilfering of nature and the disappearance of many species, in their own lands, and nobody wants to discuss overpopulation.

I am a believer, but I think that the paradise where good people go is a place like Earth. Before one goes to heaven that paradise is here. We have been to outer space, and so far all we have seen are planets that are melting hot or freezing cold, with unimaginable temperatures where only the atoms survive in tremendous, catastrophic turmoil. Where else but on Earth can one find crystal lakes, green forests, immense oceans, majestic mountains, and diverse varieties of life? If this is not paradise, I do not know what is. It is right in front of us, and we are looking to the galaxies in space for something that we already have here. What we need is peace of mind and peace of soul to enjoy this God-given blue dot in the universe that we call Earth, and we need to keep it intact and to preserve it as pristinely as possible. Man and nations are continuously thinking about improving their lot and that of others, but in the process they are destroying everything. This is what my inner self feels so strongly as I go through the passage of this short life, which perhaps in the end will make no significant contribution to change in my country of origin, my adopted country, or even myself.

I went back to Lima, and the routine was already all too common. I pondered on the psychology of the nation and the psychology of the people. I tried to understand what happened in the years I was gone, what I missed, and what I gained.

I went back again to the United States and my growing practice. Now the new Latino doctors were coming in great numbers. I remember in the early 1970s, when I went to a hospital staff meeting, there was no one to introduce me as the new member. They were all Americans and I was the only Latino. My aim was to merge with the crowd, to be counted as one of them, but initially I was visibly an outsider. I introduced myself with some jokes, and somehow laughter came from all of them, and I knew I was accepted and that their minds were a little moved by my remarks.

The new Hispanic physicians had formed a small group, and somehow I was the person who created a degree of comfort for some of them. I had no problems handling myself with any race or segment of people. I was glad that many were coming to give a boost to the Latino community. Some doctors came from privileged backgrounds and their agendas were different than mine.

But this country is so diverse and magnanimous. There is space for everybody, and sooner or later everyone will sense the true essence of what it is to be an American—not to be blond, blue-eyed, and white-skinned, but to work as part of a team and still be a rugged individual, a self-made person who can take pride in his humble background or beginnings and what he has made of himself on his own account, not because of family name, connections, money, or social status.

Seldom does one hear Americans boasting of their hereditary wealth or privileged status. They are, in fact, bashful about it, and appreciate people who have come up the hard way, whereas some newcomers bring with them deeply rooted ideas of class distinctions. That is why on most Hispanic television stations, one sees only one segment of people being represented. One would think that Latin American countries do not have Indians, blacks, mulattos, or mestizos, whereas on American television there are many races represented, although this did not come easy. The people fought for it; one must say racial equality is happening, probably not fast enough in the minds of the disadvantaged, but it is taking place in their lifetime, and I have witnessed and experienced the changes since I came here years ago.

What has my country of birth to do with this problem of racial inequality, which is psychosocial, cultural, and ancestral? Now the fragmentation of wealth and classes are more divisive and noticeable. The Indian and mestizo masses are reproducing at a high rate, whereas the criollos are leaving the country or reproducing less. Every race or class is part of a country and they should all work together. After all, they are made of the same earth with dif-

ferent shades of color, but they still love the country that gave them their first breath of air and rays of light. The privileged also have rights to the land that bore them. It is not their fault they were born in that social strata, but the problem is in the acceptance of each other for what they are—Peruvians who have lived and procreated there for five hundred years since the arrival of the conquistadors, and the Incas who have been there far longer. The United States is a great nation, and its greatness is still not rock solid, but it is getting there, not because of its wealth, but because of its acceptance of its diverse people and its respect for all, at times accomplished by applying just and strict laws. Uncle Sam is stubborn; the eagle is more rapacious than the condor, and its resourcefulness is seen in that beautiful eagle face.

CHAPTER FOURTEEN

The Old World and My Children

In the early 1970s I started to take extended backpacking trips in Europe, which became my second area of considerable travel. I began to acquaint myself with and understand the historical relationships of the Old World, especially those involving Peru and the Americas. Of course, this could be done by reading books, which I did, but one still has to see and know the people, their culture, their history, and their buildings to have an understanding of the place and to draw personal conclusions.

My first trip to Europe, in 1972, was with my family while on a three-month exchange program between UCSD medical school, where I was a resident, and the Karolinska Institute, division of pediatric medicine, in Stockholm, Sweden. This European city was just as I had imagined; history everywhere I walked. The people were sturdy and had no apparent problems visible to the eye or manifested on their faces. Their walk was firm, their language assured and almost devoid of any tales of misery that would balance their apparent complacency. They were very conscious of their rights and entitlements, such as strict labor codes of no more than forty hours of work per week and liberal social programs against the hardships of old age and childhood. Their taxes were heavy, but then the taxes were used to benefit those who paid them and the nation as a whole.

I arrived alone (my family was to join me later) at the Stockholm airport and went to my hotel by taxi, which was quite expensive. The ride was smooth, and the driver spoke better English than I did. I entered the old-fashioned hotel and took a room on the third floor, close to the old street. My thoughts went to the run-down hotel in St. Louis—somehow this place reminded me of it, although this older structure was indescribably clean. The windows were large and open to the outside, where there was silence; a few cars drove by gently so as not to cause any disturbance. I fell asleep at ease in a strange place, and yet it was not completely foreign. Somehow having a Norwegian/Finnish wife made me feel at home because I had dealt with Scandinavians in the United States, though not in their own country.

I was here to study under the great pediatrician Dr. John Lind, a tall, gentle professor who was very knowledgeable and who studied the diagnosis of some diseases of children by the way they cry.

At the Karolinska Institute I attended rounds to discuss or exchange medical ideas. Americans seem to be extroverts, perhaps even show-offs. These Swedes were very quiet. They almost had to be forced to express their feelings. I wanted to get to the core of what makes them who they are and perhaps to understand what makes me who I am.

The Karolinska Institute is a large central hospital. It is old and clean, and one sees hardly any turmoil, yet all the severe cases of almost the entire nation are treated there. One would think one was in a quiet church. I was excited to make rounds with all the doctors every day. The children had very exotic diseases, but they did not look sick. Their blond hair and beautiful faces showed no signs of misery like the ones I was accustomed to, even in the United States. These children were protected and respected. The doctors treated them like little adults; their problems were caused by their ailments, not by their lives. The mentally retarded, the youngsters with genetic abnormalities like Down's syndrome, looked very alert and responsive. They seemed to understand their problem, but conveyed an attitude that as part of this well-run society the security of being well cared for made their misfortune more tolerable to them and the rest of the citizens. It was amazing to me to see that the structure of the government could make some of life's vicissitudes more manageable, especially if the taxpayers' benevolence is not abused.

After a while I got restless in this hospital. There was no sign of human desperation—even mothers who were going to have sick newborns, like premature infants or other possible neonatal risks, were brought to this big center and handled in a subdued manner, never in a hurry, unlike in the United States.

In North America we still practice uncoordinated medicine at times. We relish the exhibitionism of medical feats. For example, when a mother with severe pregnancy risk factors gives birth anywhere, even in distant small hospitals lacking specialists, then the "cowboy" doctors are called to help the sick infant. This was part of the training I got in neonatal pediatrics. On one of those many occasions while at UCSD, we had a call from one of the hottest desert areas in the world, El Centro, to come and pick up a two-pound premature infant with respiratory distress syndrome. We called the Coast Guard to arrange for a helicopter, put our doctors and nurses together, ran to the airport, and flew to the desert. We arrived and stabilized the newborn with all our ready transport team knowledge and technology. We brought the child, after a bumpy and nerve-racking ride, to our neonatal intensive care unit (NICU), and by 6:00 P.M. we were in the news in blaring color and became instant heroes. The people were amazed at our endeavors, but little did they know that this was as backward as jungle medicine in most cases. In Sweden the public is spared those newsreel antics and they are the better for it. This is not a criticism; it is just a description of how things are done in different parts of the world.

On our routine rounds we went to the ward with children who had severe infectious diseases, which were not common at this large hospital. So far I felt I had not seen real disease, something that I could put my hands on and feel its fury and destruction. So I asked these polite Swedish doctors who seemed twice my size, "How do you treat your tuberculous meningitis patients?" because due to our proximity to the Mexican border, we had seen and treated a few cases in the United States and I was very up-to-date on that subject. The polite Swedish doctor responded almost laconically, if not sarcastically, "Dr. Sánchez, we haven't had a single case of TB in this country in the last twenty years."

I had mistakenly thought they were devoid of pathology; I was just told the reason: they had conquered most of the ills of their society, without fanfare and show, mainly through social awareness and legislation for the benefit of their nation.

Another time while all of us were making rounds in the neonatology unit, I saw an infant who had been severely ill, but there were no doctors or nurses in the room, only a priest and the parents holding the little baby's hand while the last rites were administered. Deep in myself I was itching to go and revive this dying newborn, to give mouth-to-mouth respiration, oxygen, intubate the child, start an IV, and prolong its agony. But those knowledgeable, stoic Swedish doctors attended to other matters because they knew they had done their best. They had worked all night and they knew when to stop. The relationship between medicine and society was of mutual respect and not adversarial as in the United States, where lawyers are an essential part of the medical team. Not with those Swedish physicians; they seemed so secure and sure of themselves, and their medical lives were not subject to legal dilemma or turmoil.

I noticed that though I was in the largest hospital in Stockholm they did not do bladder taps (inserting a needle into the bladder through the pubic area) on infants to diagnose genitourinary tract infections. At that time the procedure was more common in the United States than it is today. So they wanted to see the procedure done. They announced for all the young doctors to come to observe me insert a needle in the suprapubic area and aspirate urine (all this done against the will of the infant). They brought out a little blue-eyed, blond infant crying his lungs out. I told the beautiful young nurses to hold the child so I could do my tap. As I was about to explain the procedure, this tiny giant Swede let out the quickest and biggest stream of urine, without giving me time to stop it—it almost reached my face. Finally, I saw the Swedes laugh to their hearts' content. Luckily for the little patient, that was the end of it. He was not touched and the procedure was halted.

I made many friends at the institute and I was invited to their summer homes often. To them, I was a breath of fresh air from America, with a South American background to boot. Too soon, my three months were over. I had learned a lot and now my family joined me. My Swedish had improved and I teased my children with the few words I learned. I played in the streets with them, calling them "Sverige," which is the word for Sweden. I enjoyed the city walks. My wife spoke the language and knew the customs, which were basically easy to cope with. If one just behaved normally, not put on airs, one was a good Swede.

Somehow, I lost my sense of direction in Stockholm. I was accustomed to knowing the division of a town by its areas of poor and decay, as San Diego has Southeast San Diego, New York has the Bronx, and Lima has La Victoria. But in Sweden all the areas were the same, no richer, no poorer. A bus driver was as good as a doctor, at times better educated. Both spoke English and both received the same benefits.

This made me philosophical. I guess we need the poor to take our bearings in life. It is strange, but maybe the poor give more humanity to our existence; or better yet, poverty gives us something to fight for. In Sweden I only had to worry about myself. So I enjoyed my children; we played days on end, their laughter still in my heart, and I will always thank Sweden for that.

We departed for the lands of my wife, the lands of my children's other ancestors, Finland and Norway. We arrived in Turku, Finland, which was freezing cold, almost lifeless. The place was like a cold desert. My heart ached for its emptiness—people were scarce and difficult to establish a dialogue with, a world apart. My wife's relatives were nice but quiet in nature, and laughter was rare and well controlled. As I walked the desolate streets, my inner soul became somber and thoughtful. I saw an old building bearing a bronze plaque where Lenin had planned his anticapitalist uprising in Russia, and this place gave me a sense of those cold war days.

After a week's visit we took a ferryboat to Stockholm. My wife's two old aunts came to the port to bid us farewell. They were almost forgotten human beings who had never married and who had suffered the deprivations of World War II. Their lives had been so uneventful until my children filled their hearts with the renewal of life. My daughter, Helene, with her abundant, thick, chestnut hair, olive skin, and big dark eyes, gave these aged relatives the link that would connect the past of this Nordic people to the past of the Inca people. Their lives perhaps became fulfilled in seeing these beautiful children. When it came time to depart and as the huge boat was leaving, my little daughter cried as if she knew she would never see them again. She loved them for their gentleness. As the boat got farther away I could see those two little old ladies disappear in the snowy white, sad city until they became frozen dots. My heart began to cry for them and for my daughter, and we never saw them again. This probably was one of my saddest goodbyes. They were people I never knew, yet they were my family. Their blood was in my children. The world became smaller and the emptiness became greater.

In Stockholm we boarded a plane to Oslo. Oslo was cold but cheerful and it felt as if its people were at peace with their past. There was serenity in their buildings and political structure. There was no arousal of sentimentality or need to bring up instincts of protection. In those areas the inhabitants inspired self-confidence. There was no need to worry how to bend the laws of injustice. One's life, one's spirit enjoyed the dim light rays of sun that burst into one's heart in this midnight summer continent.

We boarded another plane in the reddish obscure night of the midday, and again I was in a familiar place where I could see nature from above. The scenery was that of mountains covered with pure white snow and sparse green vegetation. Although empty, it was not threatening. The land did not seem to create a melancholy of the heart, maybe because the people had conquered most of its difficult past and that gave them peace of mind. Perhaps we perceive the landscape for what its history had been, for what had been forgotten, and for what its future is. One cannot dissociate the natural scenery and the animals of a nation from the content of its people.

We arrived in Kirkenes, a small, frigid place, among the northernmost (70 degrees latitude) of all cities in Arctic Norway. The Condor had flown to the top of the world, where few if any of his ancestors had any connections—to the inhospitable places dominated by this sturdy people who could live months out of the year in semidarkness that could only be illuminated by the fire of inner content and freedom from social and emotional turmoil. Life without sunlight even for a day would be intolerable for people where misery and injustice are an everyday part of living.

In the book of my life, those days are a joyful memory. My family was connected to the past of this Viking people. The

absence of human misery set me and my mind free of the necessity to help the underprivileged. Here I could enjoy those
happy moments all for myself and my family. The only stories
I could tell are those of my encounter with the snow and the
low mountains where my skis made screechy noises on the
hard glassy ice and scattered the clean powder white snow. It
felt as if the world and I were as pure as God meant us to be.
I cross-country skied for hours and days, and my heart was
healed and refreshed with the coolness of this gentle yet merciless paradise of cold.

Just once I felt somber, when coming back at noontime
from skiing, with the sun as far away as if it were four in the
morning. As I was passing a cemetery I saw men slowly removing the hard, dark, solid frozen ground for a burial.
Somehow the sight was sad because the light was obscure. I
thought everybody should be buried when the sun was bright,
warming the last of the remains and also uplifting the hearts
of the mourners for another day of life. As I skied through
this macabre scene, cold vapor flowed out of my nose and my
body made the sounds of ice. I felt tired and thoughtful, but
my inner self had not been injured. How I wish the sun had
been shining for that dead person! But then his soul was gone
and the stars were more brilliant where he was going. After
this episode I continued enjoying this semidark country because there was light in the spirit of the people.

Through my father-in-law I could conjecture what the
Vikings had been like: sturdy, hard, almost defiant of the laws
of nature, cautious about the killing cold, and resilient as its
conqueror, yet at peace with their insignificance in nature. I
entered his workshop, where he built boats of solid wood.
The barnlike working building was cold and smelled of
freshly cut timber. It was like a place of worship. This old
man had created a sanctuary where he could peacefully sit,
smoke, and drink his coffee contemplating the fruit of his
work done with his bare hands. His long years had not di-

minished him; he could still create. He still wanted to put the wooden boats he built into the cold, Nordic waters and ride the waves as if defiant of the laws of life. This strong, aged man was stubborn and feisty as all Vikings are. He died years later doing exactly that, riding his own craft on its maiden and last voyage, frozen by the icy waters. Through Anja, my lineage carries his blood and my Inca past has been appeased by this proud and serene inheritance. My children are different for that and will not suffer the pain of my ancestry anymore. For that matter, I am the end of what happened to my ancestors. The wounds have ended with me. My progeny will be free of these psychological injuries.

I came back to the United States. The days were hot and bright as if to welcome the night. The delinquency of the people was increasing, and one felt as if one were in a torrential river where one either drowns or goes along with the current in order to survive. The competition was burdensome, the desire to surpass what was already achieved made my imagination build mountains to be climbed, creating my own obstacles, if only to prove that I was alive and felt like an ant, busy working as if the huge world would end. Now there were more doctors in my building, and I was adding more space for more Latino doctors—or anyone who wanted to practice where I was—and there were not many of them.

As time went on, the monotony of humble success made me fly to other worlds where I could be in touch with the perennially destitute in need of help and close to virgin nature.

Chapter Fifteen

No Time for Anger

One hot summer afternoon, in the ebb and flow of a busy practice, I felt the urge to go to where the great Amazon River continues. I had traveled and lived at the beginnings of its humble waters at its birth and cradle in the Andes of Peru, to where the young Amazon comes to adulthood in Iquitos. Then I went to where the river joins its bride, the Rio Negro, in Manaus. Santarem is at its middle age where the river eventually mingles with its blue-water mate. The Amazon rides to the edge of time and into the sunset of its life, ending in Belém at the Atlantic Ocean. There it dies like a big giant unwilling to disappear, where one can see its brown waters flowing deep into the womb of the great ocean, nurturing life for the world.

Such is my description of this majestic river that is so immense, so great. Yet the wormy imaginations of busy *Homo sapiens* would like to tame it, making it produce some inert pieces of comfort and contributing to the life of emptiness and the destruction of nature—a nature which God has given us to enjoy and revere.

The plane arrived in Manaus, Brazil. I felt the familiar embrace of the hot, humid air. I felt as if I were on an eternal vacation. I walked the crowded streets. Civilization had come in full force to this mid-Amazon jungle. Manaus had been growing since the day of the rubber barons, thanks to the natural product extracted from a tree, a white milklike sap called caucho, rubber, that now has been mostly replaced by man-made chemical products. The town had its magnificent beginnings in opulence and wealth that can still be seen in its old European-style buildings, including an opera house where the great Caruso sang. The city is still growing with the same vigor, but now it depends on not only a single source of wealth, but every possible resource exploited in this once-pristine, beautiful jungle. This land that produces so many natural products is underestimated in its beauty. The people are busy concocting ideas on how to extract its wealth and how to make the virgin rain forest into a giant parking lot and the wild Amazon River into a French Seine, where only swans swim peacefully in lifeless waters.

While in the city, I walked to the river's edge as if I were a turtle, guided by a biological compass to the shore. I saw and placed my hands in this brown water, the same that I had touched in my youth, which now brings the broken soil of my country and perhaps in it the dust of my ancestors. I felt at home. This was where I belonged. I saw the familiar double-decked boats with their hammocks hanging and their captains bargaining for passengers and cargo. I chose my boat by its resemblance to one of the past and haggled the price lower. Downward I went to Santarem, the place where the Esperança Clinic was and where I would work for the next few weeks and on future trips, a place where the spirit of help lightened the dark chambers of my heart so haunted by the predicament of some of the people of the Brazilian Amazon.

The Amazon River is joined by the Rio Negro, which is formed by tributaries that come from Colombia and Venezuela, becoming larger and larger as it gets to Manaus. In this city the two great rivers come together, but do not mix

This was where I belonged. I saw the familiar double-decked boats with their hammocks hanging and their captains bargaining for passengers and cargo.

their waters. As if they were bride and groom, the earthy brown Amazon and the blue-black Rio Negro "together but separately" run side-by-side on their wide course until they merge and become brown before disappearing into the vastness of the deep ocean. I embarked on my journey to Santarem in a small boat. The smells of the food and of the cargo were familiar and pleasing. Here the river was big, but it was not treacherous. The boat peacefully traveled its rapid, but calm, waters. There were no giant whirlpools that could swallow one at any time, as in Peru where the river begins. The people in the boat were friendly and exuberantly happy. They made music out of anything that made noise and sang all the time. I was navigating the same waters that once gave me my first feelings of sadness and joy. The happy times in the boat were like the moments of what one would like life to be, yet the trip was brief, only three days. We were getting closer to Santarem, still riding the brown macho side, not disturbing its bride, the beautiful blue half of the Amazon. As the boat approached the river's edge, the faintly forgotten sight of times gone by came into view. There was the coastline full of trees and small wooden houses, and the city with its bluish tile and European-style buildings weathered by time and storms.

The boat anchored in the busy harbor among hundreds of boats large and small. The people walked from one boat to the other as if they were in a parking lot. The smell of fish and fruits merged with the spirit of life, and I enjoyed the festive ambience.

I said good-bye to my friends on the boat. No one was judged for anything but accepted for what they were; there was no need to be competitive. Their lives were frosted like a cake with the sweetness of vibrant nature and the buoyant abundance of living.

I picked up my backpack and hammock and descended the wooden plank. I heard the gentle little waves of this great river. I climbed up the steep harbor, making my way between vendors and people looking for bargains. I made contact with their sweaty, sunbaked bodies, and their smiles were the welcoming of the people. This Amazon city was charming. The people knew each other well, and I was a stranger, but even in those places an Inca face was always visible. They wondered where I might be from. My pipe, my clothes, my beard were somewhat out of context; I was not a long-lived South American, but something else. I enjoyed the intrigue and their questioning looks. The children were as abundant as the fish in the Amazon. They all surrounded me. They liked the sight and smell of my pipe. Instantly I was liked by the youth, and they called me Cachimbo (pipe smoker), which was the name that I would have there. I always like to smoke a pipe while in the jungle. Although I am not a smoker, it is an occasional habit I learned from some of my clever medical school classmates. The aroma of the apple-scented tobacco refreshes the smell of the sometimes putrefying, humid air of the jungle; it also keeps the mosquitoes away and attracts attention, making me new friends.

Harry Owens, my good friend and classmate in medical school, was also a knight errant of the doctors for the poor. He made a life out of helping others and lived the existence of a loner, writing poems and immersing himself in the solitude of faraway places like the jungles of Brazil and Africa, and the coldest reaches of Alaska. I sent a child to tell Dr. Haroldo (as he was known by everybody) to come and meet me. In a short time and from a distance, I saw a gentle, bald-headed, grey-bearded man in white who approached me on a motor scooter. As he got closer, I recognized him and embraced Harry, my classmate of years ago. Our souls reminisced in silence about the hard days of

Harry Owens, son of the famous bandleader Harry Owens who conducted his Royal Hawaiians band in the 1940s. His father composed "Sweet Leilani," an Academy Award-winning classic.

Initially, the Esperança building was a typical Amazonic clinic for the poor, a one-story, cement structure, tin roof, painted blue, that looked cleaner than the rest of the buildings.

medical school, the very thing that made us brothers forever. This was the man who gave me moral support in my dark days of medical school. This was the friend who when I needed money loaned it to me without asking when I would pay him back. Even now I still owed him a thousand dollars and he had forgotten about it, but not me. I owed him much more than that. He always called me "Señor." Our faces were both lightly aged by the passage of time. Our joy was a delight to the children who surrounded us—two bearded men who looked as if they were mates like the Amazon, one light and one brown.

I jumped onto his motor scooter and we rode the bumpy, dusty streets. My heart was swollen with happiness as if I had found a long-lost brother. We arrived at the Esperança headquarters. It was a typical Amazonic clinic for the poor, a one-story, cement structure, tin roof, painted blue, that looked cleaner than the rest of the buildings. The heat was intolerable; there was no refuge from it. We entered the building, and all the people somehow already knew me. My face expressed all that I was. All they needed to know was my name, and from there on I was Dr. Carlos. The small, thin, dark-skinned ladies offered me cold lemonade. All the workers assisted me. The children touched me. I felt I was one of them. I was their family; this was what life was all about. This was a place where doctors, nurses, and others who wanted to help could go and, if in self-turmoil, they could find more happiness here than at luxurious hotels in France or the United States. There was no need to drink and no need to eat phony foods; the clinic's people were the substance that made one enjoy living.

As we told stories and made merry, next door we could see the familiar lines of the poor shoeless people, the sick-looking mothers with their babies at their empty breasts and youngsters of all ages clinging to their arms. The perspiration of hopelessness and the sadness of having a sick child were written on their faces. But this place was called Hope, in Portuguese *Esperança*, and that was what we represented and what made all those who worked here so happy. The goal was to give these people a little of our hearts, a small ray of hope, as the jungle trees give shadow from the oppressing sun.

Dr. Haroldo was busy with many patients, but he introduced me to all the American workers: Dr. Fred Hartman, the clinical director; his wife Mary, a nurse; and other volunteers such as Patty Payton, who were busy and full of stories. They were enthusiastic that I was a pediatrician. They knew that lack of pediatric care was their main problem, and their clinics were full of young patients who were very ill. I stayed in the clinic for the rest of the morning acquainting myself with the new environment.

By noon everybody was exhausted. All activity came to a standstill; we closed the clinic and went to have lunch and a nap.

Harry got a motor scooter for me, and I was happy as a kid with my new toy. I received my first lesson in driving it outside the clinic and all the children laughed at my poor dexterity.

We drove to a place for lunch where the lady cook was charming, and the food, although light and tasty, filled me as if I had eaten a huge banquet. The company and the conversation made the meal so much heartier. Afterward, we rode the scooter through the dusty streets and arrived at the house where I would stay with Harry. My room was empty. The bed was a hammock, the floor was cement, and the place was cool. I took the perennial warm shower that trickled in small droplets from a round, old, aluminum showerhead typical of the jungle. Here I was in the backyard of the greatest river in the world, with 20 percent of the freshwater supply on the planet, yet there was not enough water to take a shower! Such are the inconsistencies of these places, but one learns the ways of the people and one is liked for that, and not for one's criticism.

Dressed only in underwear, we took a midday nap that was obligatory in those jungle places, because the body becomes so weak that no one can continue the whole day working, or even stay awake for that matter.

Harry and I woke up one hour later and took another shower. We put on our thin, white clothes and headed back to the clinic on our motor scooters. The clinic was full of people; everybody was ready to work as if it were morning.

I was assigned to pediatrics, the busiest of all services. I saw again the familiar faces of mothers and children clinging to each other. The language was Portuguese, and my Spanish with its American accent of thirty years was good enough to sound Portuguese. I learned the singing intonation of the language, and my Brazilian Portuguese was just as good as if I had always lived there. The complaints could have been in Greek: I already knew what the problems were—diarrhea, vomiting, lack of appetite, some children's faces showing apathy and misery, their bodies copper in color, hair reddish, legs swollen, pot bellied—all typical signs of malnourishment and lack of protein.

The clinic was well organized, and had a good laboratory

with young Brazilian technicians who were trained on the spot and who could identify in these binocular microscopes a new universe of microorganisms such as amoebas, giardia, and malaria in all their stages. A new student could learn tropical medicine in a few days in this lab. The technicians were always so eager to show me the slides of my patients, but eventually I did not need to see them to diagnose the parasitic diseases. When clinically sure, and with their accurate reports, I just handed them packets of medicines and tried to remind the mothers to boil the water as they had been told a thousand times. Any of these children would be candidates for admission to hospitals in the United States, but in these places only the very sick were admitted and only if there was a possibility of saving their lives. Sometimes we had to send children away to die peacefully in the misery of their homes or we sent them back to the already-filled hospitals that they had just visited.

The clinic was not a hospital, and the children whom we kept were the malnourished ones like victims of kwashiorkor (lack of protein). It was possible to treat them. It was a matter of feeding them with a high-protein diet, slowly and gently. At the same time the nurses taught the parents and the people about the importance of protein. The custom of the parents was to boil the meat or fish and give the liquid to the children and the solid parts to the adults, because they thought the soup was the most nutritious part of the food.

Everybody worked hard. There was no time for political anger and there was no time for criticism. We did our best and tried to get along with the medical community of the town.

The Esperança Clinic was founded by a former navy doctor who had served in Vietnam and afterward had become a priest and gone to the Amazon as a Franciscan doctor. His name was Dr. Luke Tupper. He was so enterprising and full of ambition for this endeavor that he came to San Diego and bought and refurbished an old, discarded ferryboat, the former *Point Loma*. I rode in that ferry when I was in the navy, and its captain was the father of one of my patients, whom I diagnosed and treated for TB meningitis when I started practicing in San Diego. What a coincidence! Here I was full circle, and now this boat was in the Amazon serving as a hospital ship where all the surgical cases were done.

The days became routine. There was almost no time for anything else but medicine. When evening came, the clinic closed, the people went their way, and we were free in the warm, cool nights of the Amazon jungle city. We would go to the shore of the Amazon, to the Mascote Bar, and drink our cold beverages that refreshed our spirits. In those days, the early 1970s, there was no television in this area and the streets were full of people enjoying themselves with samba music, talking, and dancing. The tourist hotel was another popular spot because of its clean pool and cheap prices. The days were hard, but the nights were the best vacation I had ever had. The company was good and the stories worth hearing.

At that time, the clinic was struggling with the loss of Father Tupper, who had recently died. The situation was similar to that of the Amazonic Hospital in Peru after Dr. Jim left. The flaming spirit of one doctor or individual kept those missions flourishing, and when that person left or died, the whole enterprise's ideals and altruism died with them. What is sad, and in a way a great loss, is that no provisions were made for these clinics to become independent so that continuity of care could be counted on regardless of its founder or its most prolific worker. This clinic was just what Father Tupper started and probably what was in his mind for the future. Unfortunately, he died in a motorcycle accident (in the United States while training in ophthalmology) when he was full of ideas and plans for the benefit of the poor of Santarem.

However, a foundation was formed with the vision to perpetuate the desires and wishes of Father Tupper. Thanks to his family, especially his brother Jerry Tupper and other devoted people, the clinic kept operating, and it is still there. The organization grew big. Even I got lost when I went back again, because it had become so well run by the new leadership, director Chuck Post and Father Bill Dolan, M.D. Some of the romanticism of the initial clinic and hospital ship (which was replaced by a smaller boat) was lost, but it was all for the good of the people, and that is what matters most.

Dr. Fred Hartman and Dr. Harry Owens were the clinic's brightest stars in those difficult days, and they kept the clinic and the boat afloat. Volunteers like myself and other teams were the people who came and gave a moral boost to these overworked humanitarians. We were their link to the world of plenty.

The clinic took the initiative of bringing native Brazilians to work and learn the varied skills needed to keep people healthy. They were the so-called barefoot doctors, former patients whose lives had been saved and who had stayed at the organization to work. They were the best messengers and health education workers the clinic had.

It is here that I met my best friend, Dr. José Garcia, a Bolivian physician of slender body, eagle nose, and the resemblance of a mixture of less Indian and more Spanish. I called him "Almagro" because he looked like the skinny Spaniard who killed his partner, Francisco Pizarro, back in the old colonial days of the conquistadors in Peru. *Dr. José, as he is called, is a man with the heart of a dedicated doctor and he has been working at the clinic for many years.*

Dr. Garcia came from Sao Paulo. He was interviewed and hired; his qualifications were in order, but as was any new doctor he was monitored. I made immediate friends with him. He was alone, his family and children were away, his economic situation was bad, and apparently he was a former army doctor seeking political asylum from the revolutions of Bolivia. I could empathize with him. He was philosophical, altruistic, and well read.

After he was situated in our quarters with Harry and me, he was put to work the following day. Everybody was watching him. Even I wanted to know his medical skills and, more than anything else, his approach to patients, especially his compassion. This doctor was knowledgeable of all tropical diseases and a veteran of many clinics in the Amazon, but he also was shy and not a show-off. Sure enough, a young woman who was somewhat emaciated came in wheezing and short of breath, having what appeared to be acute asthma or advanced tuberculosis. Dr. Garcia made his diagnosis and gave medicines to the poor woman and sent her home. Dr. Fred was very concerned about the handling of the case and thought that the patient should have been hospitalized. Harry, Fred, and I sat together and went over the clinical records and brought José to give his clinical presentation of the patient. He presented the case in such an exquisite manner, even using Latin for some of the signs of her disease, that we were astounded and felt that his management of the patient was right for the area. What is more, he knew that there was nothing that could be done. He was aware that there was no hospital to take her to; in fact, she had just come from one. The lesson that we learned was that this doctor knew his medicine and took things as they are.

There was no need to hear the litany of how sad and inhumane the system was, which was supposed to be taken as a sign of being a conscientious physician or caretaker. This doctor spared us all that and went on to his next patient. All of us would have done the same thing after we had ruled out all other possibilities. Dr. José became well respected, and his knowledge and compassion were unquestionable. He has worked for years without fanfare or glory. He is truly a dedicated man. I am still in touch with him. I appreciated and miss his philosophical approach to life in the midst of the humid, hot city in the middle of the Amazon. The time went fast, the work was hard, and the friendships made were so lasting that when the time came to leave, I felt I was leaving my heart, and I knew I would come back to this place many times. My thoughts are always with this beautiful city of Santarem and its friendly and smiling people.

CHAPTER SIXTEEN

Where the Condor Flies Free

I returned to the United States, again back to my busy practice. The next day I was in the hospital as if nothing had
happened, my body still feeling the heat of the Amazon. I
had a big breakfast in the hospital doctor's dining room.
Everybody waved, "Hi, Carlos. Where were you?" I simply
answered, "In the Amazon." Well, they thought I had a hell
of a vacation, maybe went on a cruise, although they knew I
went on medical field trips often. My life quickly adjusted to
the rigors of competition and the hassles of running a practice. So the days became routine. My office was prosperous,
my work was hard, and the management of the practice
mounted to the point of stress, yet I had everything in this
country. I was already looking forward to going back to the
jungle or the Andes.

So it became a ritual and I started to travel every year,
sometimes twice a year, or as many times as I could steal away
from my practice and my finances could afford. This time I
decided to go to Cuzco to help at the place of my mother's
birth, Andahuaylillas, which is a few miles from the capital
of the Incas. It is the typical, little old Andean Indian town
that I described at the beginning of this book.

I arrived in Lima, then traveled to Cuzco, as usual with a backpack, simple clothes, my pipe, a harmonica, and of course my stethoscope and otoscope and some medicines. I went to the chief of health services of Cuzco to request permission to do medical work since I had no Peruvian license to practice medicine. I entered an old hospital where people made funeral arrangements as a part of the business of hospitalization. I asked to see the director, who was busy, and who obviously did not want to see me because of the strange request to work in a small town without pay. And I was supposed to be an American doctor! He simply thought I might be another funeral agent and avoided wasting his time on me. Still, I was persistent with his secretary and eventually got to his office. As usual, doctors of high position in these areas are very dictatorial and hard to convince. Eventually, to save time, he issued a letter stating that I had permission to do medical work in Andahuaylillas. I think he was flabbergasted that I was asking permission in the first place, because I could have done it on my own, no questions asked, but my legal mentality was cursed by the malpractice mania of the United States. I could not risk any illegalities, even in a remote place like this Andean town, which did not have a doctor. Happily, I clutched this piece of signed and sealed paper as I had my letter of acceptance to medical school.

Then I went to visit some relatives on my mother's side. I explained the reasons for my visit, and they seemed perplexed by the nature of my trip. They scratched their heads in disbelief: "To go and help people?" They thought I was not of sound mind and questioned my motives. If I was an American doctor, I should be squandering my dollars in the hotel suites of the "touristas" in Cuzco, if I was such a great physician, they thought. In any event, there was no encouragement from anyone, especially since it was New Year's Eve and the festivities were in full swing. Even the hospitals were slow to admit patients; if anything, they were mainly discharging patients. So I went alone to Andahuaylillas in a truck full of Indian people along with their chickens, pigs, sheep, and other animals. As usual, I made friends with them, and they liked the smell of the pipe tobacco that I smoked on purpose to sweeten the air.

As I jumped off the truck in Andahuaylillas, a place that was deep in my veins, a sense of the past came to my inner senses. I felt as if I had just been there; an eerie air of nostalgia hit me. My soul was not as happy there as in the jungle. The Andes made me conscious of my past, and it must not have been good. In these historical places, there is always that endless, indescribable melancholy that only departure from this life can make one forget. My heart cried like a sad huayno, melancholic dance music of the Andes played by Indians, and bled like a screeching yaraví, sadder than a huayno; one cannot even dance to this music. This is the land where the condor flies as free as the clouds and where the emptiness of the sky is filled with the wide wings of this bird that glides endlessly in the high mountains as if defiant of the tormented past of these people and this land. Only he has been spared the history of tyranny and despotism and only he knows that nothing has changed in the last five hundred years.

The place was as I had left it fifty years before—the old adobe church still there, the water faucet still in the center of the plaza, the two-story house of the Ballenas, with old Spanish murals fading on the walls, all still there. They had been the influential people of the town. Everything was as it was in the past, even the old trees; only I had changed and aged.

I visited some relatives whom I knew when we were children, and they took me to the sanitary post, doubtful of my endeavors but eager to help. This was the only place where the people could go for health care, dispensed by an old gentleman who, though technically the sanitario, was for all practical purposes the doctor.

I introduced myself as a Peruvian-American trained doctor who wanted to help and showed him the letter of recommendation from Cuzco and also a copy of my diplomas and
medical license from the United States. He was skeptical but
accepted my explanation and showed me to his clinic. The
place was a one-story house made of adobe with an outside
open waiting room. The floor was of dirt and there were some
sparse medicines and some old hospital instruments with no
particular purpose but to impress the patients. He seemed
caring, and people came to see him from distant places by
foot or any other means. He treated them accordingly and in-
structed them where to go if things were bad. He knew the
way medicine was practiced there.

It was New Year's Eve, and I suggested to the sanitario,
"Let's get to work. Have the people come and see us, or better yet, let's go and see anyone who may be sick at home." He
was astounded; he himself was preparing for a New Year's Eve
party. He told me there was nothing to do. However, he said
there were twins who had been discharged from the hospital
a few days earlier, but who got sick again with diarrhea and
were getting extremely dehydrated and possibly were going to
die. The hospital was miles away by car and the New Year's
festivities made transportation difficult to obtain.

We immediately went to see those children. We entered a
small hut built on the patio of a big house. The one dirt-floor
room was crowded with kitchen and bedroom furnishings. In
the semidarkness of this hut I saw two small infants moderately
dehydrated, lying in a pool of watery stool with their little arms
bearing the markings of previous IVs. The parents, a humble
young Indian couple, were ready to accept whatever fate
awaited the twins, prepared even for the worst. I immediately
asked the sanitario if we could take them to his medical post
and treat them. He said it was no use. He had no needles or IV
solutions for children. I said, "Whatever you have we will try
to use." We carried the children to the post in our arms.

Evening was approaching, and the cold was getting into our bones as we hurried to the empty sanitary station. We lit some candles and I began to look for needles and solutions. Luckily, we found some large adult needles and some normal saline and lactate ringers solution that were still sealed, but there were only two bottles. Of course, there was no laboratory for electrolytes or other tests. These children were 8 to 10 percent dehydrated, and any fluids would do them good.

It is an amazing thing: Often in pediatrics the life of an infant depends on as simple a procedure as starting an IV, sometimes placing a needle in a vein that is as thin as a hair. I was quite good at it: Using the light from the candles, I was able to place the needles in the thin larger veins of their heads, which I had previously shaved. They were crowned with the needles of life stuck into the feeble veins of their little skulls. Their cries of misery and the atmosphere of the place made my spirit sad, but my soul was happy, because I was doing something that I wanted to do and I was hoping it would work. New Year's Eve I spent the whole night checking my

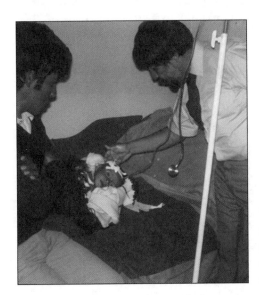

They were crowned with the needles of life stuck into the feeble veins of their little skulls.

IVs as if my own life depended on it. The faces of the children began to swell up, their little dry mouths began to have moisture, and their tearless, cloudy eyes began to brighten like the sheen of black amber stones. Their sunken skeleton-like orbital sockets began to fill in and they cried not like cats, but like little cougars.

The morning began to shed its cold, and golden light rays appeared in the dusty, dark room from the only god known to the Incas, the sun. My eyes were tired, my body was aching, but my fears began to disappear. I could see the success of such a simple thing as inserting a needle and two bottles of water. By the time people went to bed from their New Year's parties, I was ready to feed the children and take them home, where their mother's milk would do the wonders of nature and give life to those children who would survive to perhaps suffer the same injustices of their parents.

In the next few days, the story spread all over this small town, and I was invited to have a feast of guinea pigs cooked by the mother of the infants whom I had just saved. As the children got better, the parents asked me to be their padrino, spiritual father, at their baptism. The boys were christened in the ancient church where many of my ancestors had probably been baptized. I was the godfather, the church was full of people, and the children crowded around outside this church, which was to the townspeople as grand as the Sistine Chapel, waiting for the godfather's custom of throwing money all over the grounds of the church. The children picked up the coins as fast as I could throw them. This was the most glorious and rewarding moment of my trip. This was the "crowning moment of my profession." The saving of those lives was worth all my tenacity to become a doctor.

The mayor of the town made me an "honorary mayor" with all the regalia, and thanks by the townsfolk in attendance. In my euphoria, I promised more help, but little did they know that I was full of desire but short of means. Those enterprises required money and manpower and, as much as I tried, I could never get financial support. I could only use my own funds, which were not enough. The day came to say good-bye. I donated to the sanitary post my stethoscope, my otoscope, and many other things. I also was satisfied that I had taught the old gentleman some knowledge of medicine, especially pediatrics, which he graciously accepted while we worked the following days seeing regular patients in the post.

I left Andahuaylillas, as always with great hopes of coming back with more help. As I left Cuzco and took the plane to Lima and then to Los Angeles, my mind wandered to the many adventures of medicine and my insignificant contribution, which embarrassed me.

Back in my San Diego practice, I dealt with the advent of managed care and more bureaucracy. Patients were more demanding and the joy of medicine was being eroded by the lawyers and the litigious. Even if one was not involved in litigations, it was still an unpleasant environment to be in.

As I started to work in my office, I began to think: What if those twins had died while under my care? What would have been the outcome? Would the people have understood my failure or appreciated my efforts? Even now I shiver at the thought, because there were many people celebrating my deed. I am sure in the United States, I probably would have been questioned and possibly held responsible if anything had happened, and with good reason since I had no "real" business being there. The legal mentality of this advanced country was haunting me. So far, people in Third World places are usually thankful regardless of the outcome. They knew I did my best.

Five months later when I had all but forgotten those events, I received a letter from Andahuaylillas, from the same sanitario who worked with me helping people and saving the lives of those twins. His comments were incredible. I could not believe it: I almost destroyed the letter so as not to think it was real. The old gentleman accused me of being an imposter and not a real doctor. He charged me eight thousand soles for the needles, IV solutions, and the other things that I used in his infirmary to save those twins. He also accused me of having stolen the very instruments that I had left as a present, such as the otoscope and the ophthalmoscope, which are expensive there, and which I had hated to part with since they were from my medical school days.

Obviously, the accusations were untrue. The amount of money he was asking for was a trifle, forty to fifty dollars, but his ill-intentioned thoughts made an impression on me, because it represented the cruelty some people are capable of. It is this type of behavior that creates distrust. This was when I almost froze when I realized, "What if the twins had died?" The letter from this man would have been more threatening then, but even now my soul sometimes becomes dark with the deeds of some of my own countrymen. I guess this is what is so unsolvable, the harm people do to each other in many different ways.

I received news from my family in Lima that the parents and the twins had gone to their house and asked for help. My relatives helped them and I also sent money; after all, they were my godsons. The father did not find a job in Lima, and went back to Andahuaylillas. Months later I heard the twins died of some disease, probably the same illness I saved them from. I was very distressed. I felt I should have done more for them, but it was so impossible due to time and distance. Communications were so difficult. It just happened without my being able to help out. The deed of curing them was in vain; perhaps I did more harm in prolonging their misery. Their little innocent Indian faces are still in my mind, and I will always remember them. I am sure they are my guardian angels and grateful that I prolonged their lives to at least enjoy some of this great paradise, Earth, even if I could not save them from its inequities.

The routine of practice was at times bearable only because of its humanistic ends and also because I was doing

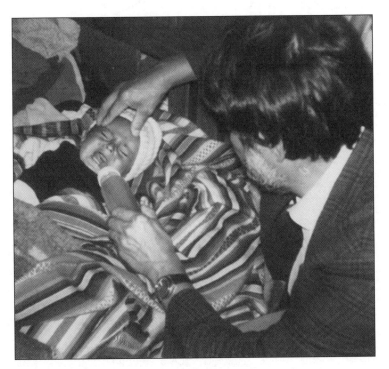

The deed of curing them was in vain; perhaps I did more harm in prolonging their misery.

what I was trained for and liked to do. Sometimes I feel sorry for the people who have to endure manual or boring jobs just so they can survive. Years of such an existence must be excruciating. Suppose for the last forty years I had been washing dishes or working in the fields with no sight of betterment? The thought itself is unnerving, yet probably most of the population live in this predicament. In Third World countries, this fate is part of life, and people are actually happy to get any job as long as they can feed their families. Yet here in the United States we try to get jobs that are rewarding to our psychological well-being, and if we find them we still look for more enhancement in our lives—but not everybody is that lucky.

CHAPTER SEVENTEEN

Immersed in a World of Poverty

In 1978, I made another trip to the Esperança Clinic in Santarem. On those trips, I was a courier for many expensive items for the clinic, including money that I had to carry tied to my waist at all times. Sometimes nights in a hammock on the boats of the Amazon were a sleepless and dangerous proposition with this cargo. The American doctors and the American help at the clinic were thankful for my trips, especially during the holidays.

Christmas holidays, despite the abundance that I had now acquired, did not have much meaning for me. My most memorable Christmas had been when I had very little and was in medical school. A discarded tree was my Christmas decoration, with little more beneath its dry branches than fallen needles as presents.

Somehow Christmas caused me anxiety. My guilt at having so much gave me the desire to help, especially in faraway places like the jungle. But now that my children are grown, I feel sad that I missed precious holidays with them.

The Amazon River was like a magnet. By now I had traveled almost all of its entirety. I went to Belém, Brazil, where this largest of all rivers ends. There the Amazon is majestic, so wide and endless as to be confused with the ocean. The beauty at sunset there is intoxicating. Belém is an old, beautiful, large metropolis with colonial buildings that give the city a flavor of its own. It is worth walking its streets even on hot, humid days, just to be mesmerized by the noise and the happiness of the people. I spent a New Year's Carnival there, dancing in the streets with thousands of Brazilians until my feet got swollen.

After the familiar touristic viewing of the town, I went to the shore of the river to get a boat to go up the Amazon to Santarem, which was a five-day trip. The streets by the port looked like those of days gone by. The stores had supplies that people buy to enter into the solitary life of the jungle. Here I saw the same things my father used to buy years ago in the jungles of Peru, usually for trade with tribes: Coleman lamps, curare paste, knives, old rifles, canned food, medieval-like instruments, medicines, and hammocks. The atmosphere was a feast for the eyes and the imagination. The merchandise was not fancy or expensive but a necessity for jungle people, certainly of no use to consumers in rich countries. I spent the whole day just browsing around and enjoying the smell of the festive street market. I bought a strong, ornate hammock. Finally, I went to look for my boat. As always, I chose boats by how much they reminded me of the ones in Peru and my childhood. I also was conscious of their prices, mainly from reminiscence and of the custom of haggling for lower fares.

I found a three-decked, white steamer that looked solid. Even the captain wore a white uniform. I purchased a ticket, not for first or second, but for third class, where the poor and the real jungle passengers traveled because of necessity rather than for tourism.

The cost of the ticket for a five-day trip was around five dollars. I could afford first class, but I just wanted to be with the Amazonian people and immerse myself in their world of poverty and gaiety. Many Brazilians may be poor or have very little, but their outlook on life is happy. There are no signs of sadness in their faces, and the samba is always there to enlighten their spirits. I always admired them for that—it was a feat that I had been trying to accomplish myself.

The lower deck was full of cargo and held the kitchen. The engine was below. The sounds and smells were ever-present, even in one's sleep. All the people entered the boat and ran for a good spot to hang their hammocks and make their own little world. I found a place in the narrow passage near the middle of the boat close to the rail, where I could see and hear the river all the time. That was the essence of my trip. I wanted to listen to the jungle sounds while the boat was breaking through the brown waters. I wanted to see the far-off shores and islands and hoped to hear the long-forgotten animals that I knew from my childhood in the deepest forest.

I had never been so comfortable as I was in this spot, with my backpack as a pillow and enough space to rock my hammock when I wanted a jungle breeze to stir the heat or to get away from the mosquitoes. People were everywhere; my neighbors were at half an arm's reach. We established conversation, and friendship was immediate. Even here I was handy for the mothers with their numerous children. Little did they know I was an American doctor! They welcomed my advice and help with some ill children.

To describe this trip one would have to be there, and it still would be unbelievable. The continuous sound of the propeller, the slow advancing of the boat against this great, giant river, silver-plated in the evenings by the clear, close moon, were what life on this boat and on the shores—for that matter life on Earth—were all about. Sometimes the monotony of the beauty would be interrupted by pouring rain that made the heat more tolerable, and it was always welcome. To see those big droplets of water fall onto this vast expanse of freshwater made me feel like a part of the revival of life. It felt like being in the biblical deluge where one was a creature in Noah's ark. The boat felt like it was the only craft on the entire, unstoppable, raining river.

This time I made the mistake of not buying my own survival supplies. I had neither utensils nor a dish, and in third class nothing is provided. When the time came to eat lunch, everybody went to the line just as prisoners in the old days went for their rations. They all had a deep plate and a spoon, but not me, and nobody had one to spare. I had half a small gourd, a souvenir from Peru, which I used for a plate. It was not big enough, but it held some food. For a spoon I cut a plastic medicine bottle in half. The food was a mixture of rice, beans, meat, and yucca. As I was eating, I noticed that some of the rice looked peculiar. Upon closer examination, I saw that what looked like rice were small maggots from the rotting meat. Eventually I got tired of separating them and I figured they were boiled and of no threat. I even went for a second serving. The Amazon rain can increase the appetite.

When the boat passed close by small villages, the children would get into their little canoes and come paddling fast to the moving boat for handouts. Passengers would throw anything on the water, and it was welcome in those isolated spots of the jungle. I felt so overwhelmed by this sight that I started to throw them all the things that I could part with. I even gave the shirt I was wearing. It was fun and sad to see the little brown children masterfully guide their small canoes to the floating items and retrieve them. If the present had a higher value, like my shirt, they raised their hands and gave me the thumbs up sign. My heart swelled with happiness and I cried for their happy poverty.

The days went fast. As we approached Santarem, we could see the big wide river with its two distinct colors, one side brown, and the other blue-black. We always traveled on the brown waters. The city's shore was more visible as we got closer. We stopped at the commercial port, where there were fewer boats and no market. I disembarked along with some other passengers, and I said good-bye to my friends. The boat continued to Manaus farther upriver. It had been a great trip. Here I was again, in the Esperança Clinic ready to work and renew my friendships. Many volunteers had left, but some new and old faces were present. The clinic was always in a continuous state of change. Surgical teams would stay for weeks, volunteers for months, but rarely was anyone there for two or three years, so the place was the same, but not the crews. This time Dr. Harry Owens was not there, and even the medical director, Dr. Fred Hartman, was packing up after a three-year stint. Only Dr. Garcia and I were old-timers, along with some of the Brazilian help.

On this trip, Dr. Pylon, an orthopedic surgeon from the United States who came to the Esperança Clinic frequently, was again helping with the children who had clubfoot deformities or other types of bone problems. He worked from morning until night. He never left the boat, on which he also performed all the surgery, not even to go to the tourist hotel to have a cold drink. He was truly a hard worker, with no time for philosophy or the romanticism of medicine in the jungle. He was a great surgeon, and his work on children was miraculous, especially in this Amazon city.

While all the nurses aided the surgeons in surgery, the nonsurgical staff handled the whole outpatient clinic, sometimes I alone and other times with Dr. Garcia. We did all the unrewarding work of treating diarrhea, malnutrition, and malaria, and sending people home to continue their suffering. In this clinic the plastic surgeons, ophthalmologists, orthopedists, or any other teams with surgical doctors and nurses, including anesthesiologists, were the most sought after, and they were the backbone of the foundation. In any event, we all worked as hard as we could and helped each other if there was need for consultation.

Usually, a surgical team stayed for no more than two weeks. In those fourteen days the work was excessive and grueling.

The teams had to accomplish all the complicated surgeries that should have been done in a year's time in that short span of time in order to finish all the cases scheduled. Once they left, the tranquility of the clinic returned and we could enjoy our work more peacefully regardless of the lack of commodities, which the teams were aware of, but which they never complained about. They were truly gallant missionaries of medicine.

The more often I went to Santarem, the more enthusiastic I was about the idea of a hospital ship in Peru, especially now that the Esperança boat in Santarem was coming close to its decommission. We even discussed the possibility of towing the old converted *Point Loma* ferry up the Amazon to Iquitos from Santarem. After a few weeks of continuous work in this clinic, I left Santarem, taking another smaller boat down the river to Belém, where I took a plane to Los Angeles. By now I was a veteran of many trips, and it had become a routine.

Through the years, I have noticed that the jungle has lost its virginity. Somehow it looks more civilized and that makes it more savage. Cars and televisions are anachronisms in this beautiful forest region. Even the people have lost their originality. I remember when I first went back to the Peruvian and Brazilian Amazon, there was no television. But when I went on subsequent trips, this already-old invention had arrived in full force, especially in Santarem. Before, when I visited poor families in their homes, the children, their parents, and I used to get together and have great times just talking, singing, eating, and even dancing. With the advent of television, however, I went to the same houses and all they could say was "hi." They all were glued to a miserable television set on the dirt floor, watching programs with no meaning. Their eyes were stuck to the tube, and I walked the deserted streets while everybody watched their favorite, empty telenovelas. The people have lost their innocence, they have lost their individual resourcefulness, and now they are packed in cities in great numbers. They are no longer masters of the jungle. They were once subservient only to the laws of this green disappearing giant. Now they look for someone to take care of them, and that attitude burdens the government with social ills, problems that would be difficult to alleviate for any type of infrastructure, unless the country destroys its jungle for questionable benefit and not necessarily for the people's. So this was how I started to perceive the places that I revisited year after year.

While in the United States, I went to the board meeting of the Esperança Foundation, in Phoenix, Arizona, to discuss the possibility of a similar clinic in the Peruvian Amazon or elsewhere. The people from the foundation treated me well, including Jerry, the brother of Father Tupper. I met old acquaintances whom I knew in the Amazon, like the outgoing director, Win Stewart, the new director, Chuck Post, and, of course, Harry Owens. I was given a few minutes at their board meeting to propose a plan for the Amazon boat in Iquitos, Peru. They were enthusiastic, but also skeptical about the project because of the political climate; also, they had been rejected years ago when they wanted to do that same thing in Peru.

I was able to get their consent and even an appropriation of a pledge of a few thousand dollars as seed money to explore the possibilities of putting a hospital boat in the Peruvian Amazon. The rest was up to me; I was to connect with the Peruvian authorities and get backing from the government, which was crucial for this type of enterprise.

With my optimism and persuasive attitude, I went to study the possibility of this project. I arrived in Lima with a feeling of a mission to accomplish. My parents had indirect connections, and I asked them for their help because I had none since I had lived so long in the United States. I had even lost touch with my friends from the military high school, some of whom were probably in high positions in the government. My relatives were not enthusiastic about the project. They knew that the people and the government would not be interested and, in fact, they felt sorry for me because of my certain disappointment.

I met with two Peruvian senators. The first was a woman who promised me the world, but in actuality, no real work was ever done to accomplish anything. The second senator received me in his congressional office and heard the proposal for a hospital boat on the Amazon. All we were asking for was permission—no money at all. A neighbor, a well-connected engineer, and the second senator were able to arrange for me to meet with the minister of health of Peru, the second-highest authority in health matters in the country after the president, just like our secretary of health.

The day of my appointment at the ministry of health building was the culmination of my efforts. Even getting the audience was a success in itself. I put on my best business suit and had my shoes polished by two shoe shine boys. The engineer and the senator could not go to the meeting, so I went alone. I entered the big, modern building that to me as a child had looked as if it were a place of impenetrable might. Now I was walking its halls to see its top official. The place was well secured with guards and many foreigners coming in and out. I got to the top floor and approached the receptionist, who matched my name against a list of visitors.

I was told to take a seat, but I preferred to walk around in this magnificent building. While my mind was working on how to get to the soul of this great person and convince this powerful politician, who was also a well-known physician in Lima, I strolled the hall mindful of the authoritarian posture of these doctors in high positions, and I felt somewhat uneasy and not too optimistic.

A well-dressed criollo and an almost Anglo-American-looking man, his attaché, came to receive me at the door. He interviewed me first and asked for the reasons for my visit in more detail. I gave him all the literature and a letter of intent from the Esperança Foundation, which he took, I suppose, for the purpose of advising the minister about who I was and what my request was. I was sure that his superior was a busy man with the monstrous task of fixing the health problems of Peru and that my visit was probably a nuisance to him.

After a while, I was led by the attaché to the office of the minister and I was asked to sit in a large waiting room, which had a green carpet on the floor just like in official buildings in the United States. In Peru, carpets were rarely used; usually there were mosaics and tiles on floors, especially in the older buildings. The view of the city was spectacular, and actually, from the top of this building the city looked beautiful. Eventually a dark, short man of heavy, if not obese, build came to meet me in the waiting room as he was saying goodbye to two Germans he had just met with in his adjoining private office (into which I was not invited). I presented myself politely and with a revived reverence and respect for the government representatives in high places. I introduced myself as an American graduate physician born in Peru who wanted to help his mother country. I could see in his face, which revealed more Indian blood than I expected for a high official, a "who cares" attitude. I went on to explain the idea of putting a hospital boat in the Amazon, just like the one in Santarem. I showed him pictures and described the work done by Esperança, the American organization. He listened very seriously, somewhat exasperated, but politely enough, getting ready to give me the final blow. His aide was beside him, and at times he gave me a faint smile of approval, but I think he was still aware of his boss. I finished my presentation, which was made in a humble if not begging manner, being careful not to offend this high official or at least not to sound like an arrogant American.

Finally his turn to talk came. He crossed his legs and pulled out some pictures of vintage World War II American warships acting as floating hospitals in the Amazon. They even had Red Cross signs on the sides of their hulls. He said that the Amazonic region did not need any more hospital ships. The country was taking care of these problems quite well. He also mentioned that the small amount of money proposed would not create an impact. In fact, he said that the two Germans who had just left brought financial help of millions of dollars for the same type of objective, though not necessarily boats.

I listened like a son to a father. He was older than I, and I was still a young doctor. I accepted his explanation, although I felt somewhat diminished by his refusal of the project. I was skeptical but also somewhat optimistic about his air of confidence. I thought that things in Peru might be getting better, and that finally, here was a man who was doing it, who did not need an American pediatrician from Peru to help in his efforts. My soul wanted to join my fellow Peruvians in a spirit of brotherhood and throw away all those acts of arrogance, which had always caused so much harm to Peru as a nation.

I left the huge office. The aide shook hands with me somewhat apologetically, and I walked down the long hall with my head lowered, without my project papers. As I savored the known path of rejection, I remembered the phrase that my father always repeated to me, "Nobody is a prophet in his own country." My thoughts went to the United States, and I missed its compassion and rather naive approach to these types of charitable enterprises.

Once again, I went to the Amazon and helped people in my own little way. After a few weeks, I flew back to the United States, almost defeated and sad for the people I had just been helping—where I had seen no big hospital ships.

On a February night in 1985, five days after my return from another medical trip to Peru, I suffered the severe accident with which I began my story at the beginning of this book. Ironically, a well-known Spanish cardiac surgeon, Count Juan Suros XII of Barcelona, took care of me, saving my life. Centuries ago, his ancestors decimated mine. Five hundred years later, I was saved by their aristocratic descendant. Thanks to Drs. Argoud, Rios, Aguirre, Gale, Cohen, and many others, my practice kept going. My family were instrumental in maintaining the office.

The first day I returned to work, I entered my office, and in its darkest corner I knelt and prayed to God for his help. I started to see my patients with the most respect and reverence for disease, because now I had suffered once more the smell of death. I became a more compassionate doctor, but I also became compassionate for myself. I wanted to get rid of the ghost of my past, and from then on I tried to live more in tune with the present.

A few months later, a devastating earthquake occurred in Mexico City. I decided that I had to go to help. I could not sit around hearing the news; besides, I had been in a more severe earthquake in Peru. Mexico was more advanced, and the news showed a more coordinated effort of help from around the world.

I left for Mexico City with a team of four doctors, including my old friend and intern from UCSD pediatric residence days, Dr. Phil Mattson, and nurses, all under the auspices of the Salvation Army. My practice was taken care of by two hired pediatricians and help from my colleagues.

We arrived in Mexico. The unforgettable turmoil that follows catastrophe and the camaraderie and bonds that are established are so familiar and universal in these circumstances. It was like a festivity, although it was sad. The work and the sense of duty dull one's anguished spirit, and friendships are formed that last forever. The common goal of helping others is a powerful chain that links everybody. Feelings of arrogance or distrust are discarded or at least held in check.

Compared to the Peruvian earthquake of 1970 and others, the Mexico City earthquake was less devastating. The people were under control after the initial destruction, which was very bad but which was rapidly taken care of. We came several days after, so I cannot say I was in the fury of it since the dead and seriously injured were already taken care of. As usual, I worked with children in the Salvation Army headquarters in Tepito, a poor area of Mexico City. I was amazed by their nutritional status. They were all robust and rarely did

I see any anemic or malnourished children. *Mexico has a temperate climate, although its polluted air will become more of a health hazard than parasites or tropical diseases, if it has not already. The spoiling of the environment can be a very difficult health problem to tackle, and I do not know who is going to address that situation. That takes technology, not humanity, but it must be done for the sake of our survival and preservation of our natural resources. That is what is more pressing in the world now.*

The ailments we saw were mainly what appeared to be "earthquake shock syndrome": headaches, lack of appetite, and an air of somberness. Our team was helpful, especially the nurses, who were skilled in uplifting the patient's moods. I was not too good at this. I was looking for more severely ill people so I could immerse myself in their medical problems. In any event, we did a good job, and the people were thankful for that. On my return, I flew over the incredibly smoky, dark brown landscape of Mexico City. When I got back to the United States, I felt more enthusiastic and eager to work and to get ready for other trips to other countries in need, maybe because everything had been so well organized by the Salvation Army for this earthquake.

Again, my practice started to boom. I formed a medical group with many physicians. The picture of medicine in the United States was changing and allowing me less time and money to undertake enterprises of the nature I was doing.

To release the stress of work I began to take trips for the sake of leisure and learning. I traveled quite frequently to Europe, still in regular class and with my backpack, just like a student. I visited Spain more than three times. I enjoyed its history and its connections to my past, even a sense of déjà vu came to me there. A sense of this phenomenon occurred in Cordova, where my surname is common. I believe that it was probably from Cordova that the Spanish part of my mixed ancestry came—probably a combination of Spaniard and Arab. But for sure I am more Indian than Spanish.

I took trips to Russia during the cold war and found the cities in good physical condition. I believe that any society is good if one does not see abject poverty, especially children begging in the streets. Russia had none of that, and, as a matter of fact, one was forbidden to even tip. I visited their hospitals, and although criticisms could be in order, they will not come from me. I know what constitutes complete decadence in a nation when I see it, and in this land the children were fat and happy. Children have no knowledge of the political system, they only know what will make them grow into healthy adults able to make their own judgments with a brain that has not suffered from hunger, despotism, and neglect by the country that gave them birth.

EPILOGUE

Reflections of the Soul

The original manuscript of this book was handwritten in a short time for compelling reasons. For years I have struggled to write about my life as a way of telling the history of my people and the experiences of being of Indian descent. However, many a time I picked up a pen and began scrawling down some notes only to find the flow of my thoughts was blanketed by the mist of uncertainty. It was like trying to make a hand made of rock move one line. The forces of my imagination were tangled like a ball of llama yarn that has entwined itself, futile to be used as string.

But now that this simple story has been written to show that the Indians are being bypassed by the consciousness of history and getting nowhere, I feel that a heavy burden has been lifted off my soul. With the solace and spiritual peacefulness of a long life, I will attempt to encounter serenely the vicissitudes of ongoing living and stretch out a hand, unhampered by my past, to the coming generations so that I will become part of a chain of good links. I hope my progeny will benefit from my swift stay on this good Earth. May the next generation's mission be to save nature and the remaining species that inhabit this beautiful Earth and to tell our own kind to reproduce less, because quantity creates a sense of cheapness of our own worth, if our lives are not lived to the best of our abilities free of the lessons of the ugly past.

As I come to the culmination of my most fertile years, I see in retrospect that most of my life has been spent trying to become someone—in spite of the contrary forces of destiny, discrimination, self-doubt, and absence from my own land. But nothing will overcome the inner turmoil created by the forces of history, the inequities which one's ancestry suffered through, especially when time, as infinite as it is, has not had light-years to erase it.

Perhaps these last five hundred years were crucial to our existence, because of the power to record all this information due to the inception of the printing of books and to the rapidly advancing embryonic computer age. Someday, perhaps even our emotions will be stored and recorded for remembrance and will no longer be imprinted in our chromosomes. Then we will become humanoids without a history to haunt us, and we will have only the future and no past, like light and time that have only one trajectory, forward forever, never going back. By then we will be superhuman beings, all holding hands and carrying our children forward. With our soft glowing, blowing gowns of the past, swiftly flowing into space, with no wounds on our hearts or souls, our chins and eyes will be fixed only on the infinity of the universe.

Each nation is molded according to its history, and its people will reflect that in their spirit. That spirit will create changes in the basic instincts of mankind for better or for worse. The nation's past will be either the ornamentation or the thorns in the soul of its people. As in a bouquet of roses, the arrangement will reflect only its creator's imagination, with stems full of the thorns of the ugly past to protect the delicate flower. Before nations were created, the lands were conquered and reconquered among a people of equals. But when the lands became continents, their people evolved into different types of human beings by the forces of time and evolution. The "inequality" was due to the laws of nature, and man with his flawed imagination mistook these people as an aberration of the works of God. The New World discoverer became a superhuman in the eyes of the natives by the simple fact of the reflection of light onto the skin pigment of these conquerors.

The aberrant history of their past was brought to this "new" continent, destroying those infant and growing civilizations forever, leaving centuries of human bondage that only time will reverse. Even at that, the product of its final evolution leads to speculation: Will they be superior or inferior beings?

As the world evolves and time passes, a new mankind will emerge. As they go to conquer other nations in space, they will not subdue the spirit of those aliens, having learned from the mistakes of the past for the good of the universe. Still, there are plenty of wounds to heal in our present planet, and we probably have time to save almost everything that God and nature gave us.

Thus this Condor, as he flies into the sunset of his life, can only ponder the future in the golden glow of the sun as it disappears below the horizon. Darkness will come and he will fly to the high mountains as if looking for the last rays of the departing sun to catch the final, fleeting, crepuscular, faraway reflections of this bright star. In his night of darkness, he will think of the ways that he can improve and uplift himself and how he can become a source of inspiration to those who have suffered, who now suffer, and who will continue to suffer.

As the early morning arrives, he will hope to get a glimpse of the first morning light that rises softly in the remote, inhospitable mountains from the Inca sun, to them, creator of all living things, that comes to warm our hearts and our desolate souls. This Condor will slowly open his huge wings. He will look north, south, east, and west, but decisions are hard to make, and he will soar toward the rising sun. At a distance he will see mountains upon mountains, and he will try to fly to them, because they will always be there. But with the weariness from his trip, he will glide into the oasis of spiritual reflection and see that mankind has a future: If each person does one act of good, the grains of good sand will bury the mountains of injustices of the past. The beautiful white sand of good deeds will be bathed by the waves of content, and this big Condor will have flown to the far oceans looking for that sunset and that rising of the sun.

Anja Hovland

Years will pass as time softens the edges of the mountains and the souls of men, my remaining soul will rejoice in the molecules of my dust, feeling the Indian children dancing and singing along with all the children of the world. As my dust dirties their little bodies, then I will know the burden of what has happened is gone to the end of the universe, where in the emptiness of space I will feel no more pain.

What Happened to the Incas?

The advent of Peruvian culture is known to be around 10,000 B.C. In distant times Peruvians were gatherers of plants and fruits as well as hunters until they acquired knowledge of agriculture. It is possible that they came from North America and traveled to South America through the Isthmus of Panama, eventually arriving in the Andean region. They slowly formed groups around strong leaders who directed the expeditions and mastered the hostile environment. Initially, these people traveled along streams and fields, nourished by such animals as llama and deer. If reserves of game diminished, they moved on. Once groups became established in one place, they began cultivating plants native to the continent, such as yucca, maize, potatoes, and many types of vegetables. With this new non-nomadic way of life, they could produce objects for personal use, as well as for trade, eventually mastering ceramics and metallurgy.

The extremes of Andean geography exceed those of any other South American country. Argentina, for example, is uniformly flat, and the topography of other nearby countries presents few extraordinary challenges. Peru's geography, however, includes great natural barriers for its inhabitants in all its regions. The Pacific Ocean to the west has two marine currents of opposing direction: the Humboldt current, named after the famous German explorer who studied this phenomenon, and the equatorial current, also known as "El Niño," the child, because its effect is most notable during December. The Humboldt current is cold because it comes from the South Pole. It traverses the entire Peruvian coast and turns west, encountering the southbound equatorial current, warming the Humboldt current, with a consequent abundance of fish. Both currents change the coastal climate. The cold Humboldt minimizes evaporation from the ocean and, in turn, rainfall on the coast, creating immense deserts with sand fine enough to ski on, as if on snow. El Niño, when it deviates off its course and approaches the northern coast of Peru, can create great tempests and catastrophes. Paradoxically, these natural problems also create a wealth of fish, and, since there is no rain, the guano, sea bird manure, collects in great amounts to be used as fertilizer.

Thus the coastal inhabitants fight to compensate for the lack of rain, but with their titanic resourcefulness, the little water that comes from the Andes is stored through large, ingenious irrigation systems.

The Andean region is the great theater where the early Peruvians mastered their environment and where the present-day inhabitants continue to struggle for the future of their land. The great Andes that cross the region longitudinally have cordilleras arranged in a stairlike manner. High and inhospitable, these peaks have an extreme configuration and are abysmal in nature. Thus the pueblos, cities, and aldeas in the Andes, or so-called serranias, see their progress truncated by the difficulty of the terrain, the excessive rains, and the frost, all of which harm the meager crops on the small plots of land. Added to this chaotic geography, the region is situated right in the "circle of fire of the Pacific," the most active seismic area of the world, where continual earthquakes destroy what took years of painful construction to build. Yet, like ants, and at tremendous costs, reconstruction is always the next step in the ladder of progress, which is sometimes not noticeable and appears to be static.

The selva, rain forest, is at the other side of the eastern trans-Andean cordillera. From its slopes, the vast, flat, forested region begins, crisscrossed by many great rivers, including the Amazon. This jungle area is now being exploited at such a ferocious pace that perhaps very soon nothing will be left of it because it is so sensitive and can be easily conquered and destroyed by man—unlike the Andes, which will not let anyone even flatten a peak. But these Andes have gently allowed the Incas to painstakingly cultivate their sloping hills enough to sustain a meager, hardworking few, eventually pushing them to unite and form a great empire out of necessity for the common good.

The primitive man of Peru can be recognized in the jungles where tribes still live, preserving organizations and customs similar to those of their ancestors. They are led by clans, or groups of families that are related by blood, vicinity, occupation, and customs. These people have a wide variety of myths and superstitions and revere the forces of nature.

There are about twelve tribes in the jungles of Peru, many of whom I had the privilege to know when I was a child. Among them are the Shipibos or Chamas, the Ahuarunas, the Huambisas, and the Jivaros. They are interspersed throughout the jungles. They make their own weapons for hunting and warfare, such as the pucuna, a carefully made, long hollow tube from which a needlelike wooden stick coated with curare is blown to kill game once so abundant. Others use the bow and arrow for hunting.

The development of the Andean civilization took place along the whole length of the Andes, from Panama to the south of Chile. Although Colombia, Ecuador, Bolivia, Chile, and Argentina had important manifestations of the Andean culture, it was in Peru where its splendor reached its highest degree of importance, equaling and even surpassing other cultures of the world. Thus the Peruvian people of antiquity were the creators of the pre-Inca and Inca civilizations. They were able to fight the forces of nature and create a culture of their own.

The pre-Inca civilization, in its primordial stage, had seven big cultural centers: Chavin, Paracas, Tiahuanaco, Mochica, Chimu, Nazca, and Cuzco.

The oldest pre-Inca culture was developed in Chavin, starting around 1000 B.C. and lasting until the start of the Christian era. The area has an altitude of approximately eleven thousand feet and is located near the beginning of the Marañon River, which feeds the Amazon. This culture left the great temple of Chavin, where one can see colossal stone sculptures of the Wiracocha god and obelisks with feline and human figures. There is also a condor chiseled onto a flat stone, representing this godlike animal (abundant in those regions) with its wide open wings and noticeable, stylized great garras, claws.

The Paracas culture, which developed around 900 B.C. and lasted until A.D. 200, was known for its underground funeral sanctuaries, medical skills, and knowledge of mummification. Skull operations, or "cranial trepanations," were performed to extract broken pieces of bone from the skull to repair injuries sustained in war. To prepare a patient for skull trepanation, the ancient Paracas used anesthetics such as coca derivatives. The knives, called tumis, served as both surgical and ceremonial instruments. Once the broken bones were removed, the opening was replaced with metallic pieces—usually gold plates of the same size—often with successful results.

Mummification consisted of removing all fat, as well as all visceral contents, then anointing the body with special herbs and oils. After this, the bodies were wrapped with exquisite mantles and placed in baskets and buried underground. They were well preserved because of the dry ground of the coast. The Paracans were so well known for their textiles that even now with modern technology we cannot equal their weaving and coloration. They used the finest fibers of cotton, alpaca, and vicuña, weaving up to two hundred to four hundred threads per square inch. The colors have lasted for centuries looking as if they were made yesterday.

The Tiahuanaco culture flourished between A.D. 900 and 1100 in the Kollao plains close to the highest lake in the world, Titicaca. The most distinctive relics of the Tiahuanaco culture were the chulpas, funeral tombs, made of skillfully crafted stone in the form of small round towers. In the palace of Kalasaya one can appreciate the entrance or portico to the sun, where the stone is sculpted in high and low relief depicting the Wiracocha god, who was believed to be the creator of the world and of man. They also worshiped the condor, the puma, and the serpent. They had a system of social organization called the Ayllu, a conglomeration of families, that was later adopted by the Inca empire.

It is amazing that those pre-Inca cultures were so old, some already in ruins, at the time of the Incas. The word *Tiahuanaco* is of Inca origin and was coined while one of the latter Incas was visiting these ruins. While in that area he received an important message brought rapidly by a chasqui, a fast runner. To glorify this man, the sovereign thought of the fastest animal of that time, the huanaco, and so he said to the exhausted marathon runner, "Tiahuanaco," which means "Sit down, huanaco" in Quechua, the Inca language.

The Mochica and Chimu pre-Inca cultures developed between A.D. 200 and 1500 in the northern coastal areas of Peru. Because of the shortage of water and the dry deserts, they became masters in the construction of channels for irrigation and water storage and in unifying small rivers to create more water volume. Vanquished prisoners were used to collect guano for fertilization purposes. Their architecture represented the sun and the goddess moon called Si. They thought the moon was more powerful than the sun because it could be seen both in the day and at night. They were masters in ceramics, creating the so-called huacos-retratos, picture ceramics, depicting pain, laughter, and joy. In metallurgy, they created fine work in twenty-karat gold.

The later Chimus may have communicated their thoughts through writing, using symbols inscribed in pallares, big legumes, which, unfortunately, have yet to be deciphered. They worshiped the god Kon, the ocean. They also built a huge wall like the Great Wall of China to defend themselves from the Incas coming from the south. The city of Chan-Chan, the capital of the great Chimu, is still partly intact. It is a large pre-Inca city, even bigger than early Trujillo, which was founded by Francisco Pizarro after he stopped and admired these great ruins where he noted temples, grain storage, water reservoirs, houses, and palaces decorated with artistic sculpted clay. The fall of the great Chimu civilization came in the fifteenth century when the Inca leader Pachacutec, with his powerful armies conquered the emperor of those ancient lands, "El Gran Chimu."

The Nazca culture existed between A.D. 300 and 1000, developing close to Lima. The Nazcans were skilled in agriculture, taking into account the lack of river and rainwater. They made subterranean channels to obtain water, forming aqueducts and reservoirs that are still used today. To the Nazca culture are attributed the topographical figures that on aerial view suggest to some people traces of airstrips or airports for long-gone extraterrestrial spaceships.

The Inca empire gradually became a multinational state when the above-described cultural centers unified with its center at Cuzco, retaining their own characteristics and regional customs when they were united. It is possible that each pre-Inca culture would have reached higher splendor and surpassed the Inca civilization, but once it was consolidated, the Inca empire was a powerful state, comparable to that of the Aztecs and to others around the world.

The newly unified empire was vast, as described by the conquistadors in 1532, spanning from Colombia in the north to Chile in the south, including present-day Ecuador, Bolivia, and Argentina. The population was between eleven and twelve million. Like the ancient Europeans the Inca people also had legends to explain their origin, similar to the myth of Romulus and Remus and the origin of Rome.

Foremost is the legend of Lake Titicaca. It tells that the sun, the father of all, noticed the corruptions of men, so he sent Manco Capac and his wife and sister Mama Ocllo, making them appear in the middle of Lake Titicaca. Manco Capac had a golden scepter and was told by the sun god to build a city where the golden bar could be easily buried in the ground as a sign of its fertility. This happened on a hill close to present-day Cuzco. Thus was founded the capital of the empire, which was called Kosco, later Castillianized by the Spaniards to Cuzco. Manco Capac taught the men work and civic duties, and Mama Ocllo taught the women their family duties.

The new empire was headed by a sovereign, called "Inca," who wore a special, symbolic attire for his high position. There were two dynasties, headed by thirteen Incas (Atahualpa, the fourteenth Inca, was never crowned a sovereign) who ruled for more than a hundred years (from 1400 to 1532). Each sovereign is described, because, like all leaders, each is remembered for great single or multiple feats.

Manco Capac, the founder of Cuzco and the Inca empire, built the first temple of the sun, called Inticancha, which still exists.

Sinchi Roca, also called "the warrior and the prudent," was the son of Manco Capac. He proclaimed himself the supreme descendant-leader of the Inca religion, thus creating a theocratic and political government.

Lloque Yupanqui started the confederation and fought the Collas of the Lake Titicaca area.

Mayta Capac finally vanquished the Collas, thus enlarging the empire. He also built a great bridge over the Apurimac River.

Capac Yupanqui added more provinces to the empire. His poisoning sparked great unrest among the Quechua people, almost to the point of anarchy.

Inca Roca reigned for about forty years. He established schools in Cuzco, Yachayhuasis, for teaching the nobility, and protected the amautas, wise men. He used the word *Inca* for the first time.

Yahuar Huaca, "the one who cries with tears of blood," was so named because he was abducted by the Ayamarcas when he was a child. It is said that his tears were blood, which discouraged his captors, and he was returned to his father, Inca Roca, who prepared him to lead the government. He fought and vanquished the aggressive Chancas in the battle of Yahuar-Pampa, the "plains of blood." It is said that the Wiracocha god helped the Incas because he transformed all the stones into warriors and they fought on the side of the Incas to win this great battle. Yahuar Huaca was assassinated, and a person of non-royal descent was elected as Inca.

Inca Wiracocha, near his end, named his son Urco as successor, in spite of the legitimate prince and noble successor Yupanqui. But when a surprise attack by the Chancas forced Wiracocha to leave Cuzco, Yupanqui took over the leadership and repelled the invaders, using this opportunity to make himself sovereign and changing his name to Pachacutec.

Pachacutec was the most brilliant Inca of the whole Incanato (Inca empire). His name in Quechua means "the one who changes the world." He was a great warrior and administrator. As a warrior, he conquered the Gran Chimu, expanding his territory extensively with the help of his son, Amaru Yupanqui. As an administrator, he established the royal overseer, the Tucuyricus, to assess the needs of the empire. He extended a vast network of roads throughout the empire and established the tambos that were used as places of rest for travelers. He created the chasquis, a postal system, using the empire's fastest runners. Moreover, Pachacutec divided the Inca empire into four regions, called the Tahuantinsuyo. He also reconstructed the sun temple, Coricancha, previously called Inticancha, and restored the famous Sacsayhuaman fortress. He established the mitimaes, loyal Inca communities who traveled together to distant places to keep his empire intact and under constant watch. Lastly, he unified the cult by proclaiming a supreme god, Ticci-Wiracocha-Pachacamac, translated from Quechua as "the creator of the world and the beginning of everything created."

Amaru Yupanqui cogoverned with his father; he was the last Inca to share this position.

Tupac Yupanqui conquered the Araucanos of Chile and beautified the temple of Coricancha, covering all the walls of this temple to the sun with pure gold. He navigated the oceans, possibly arriving in the Galapagos Islands, which were thought to be in Oceania.

Huayna Capac, son of Tupac Yupanqui, governed for twenty-five years; in his reign the decline of the empire began. He had to fight rebellion and border uprisings, thus limiting the extension of his empire. He established two longitudinal roads covering the whole length of the Tahuantinsuyo, one on the coastal side and the other in the Andes or Sierra. He lived mostly in Quito, Ecuador, and at the end of his life, he had trouble choosing a successor among his three sons. He named Huascar (who resided in Cuzco), but because his other two sons helped him in the northern battles, he changed his mind, first naming Ninan Cuyochi his successor (who died soon after without governing). Huayna Capac was poisoned in 1525 by a curaca, or lord, in Quito, and his mummified body was transported to Cuzco and interred with customary great pomp. His third son, Atahualpa, made himself governor of Ecuador and began to fight his brother Huascar in Cuzco.

The reign of these two last sovereigns, Huascar and Atahualpa, brought the downfall of the Inca empire and signaled the coming of the conquistadors. Huascar sent an army to Ecuador that was repelled by Atahualpa. In reprisal, Atahualpa sent troops to Cuzco under the command of two famous generals, Quisquis and Calcuchimac, who quickly marched to Cuzco and fought Huascar, defeating him and taking him prisoner. The triumphant General Quisquis ordered horrible slaughter in the capital of the empire, and even Huascar died in this first and final civil war of these great people. Atahualpa, before being named the sovereign, was executed by the newly arrived conquistadors.

Thus began the end of this great empire by the Spaniards, to the point that it has left the Inca descendants still in a somber state to this day—who knows for how much longer. That humiliating conquest is one of the reasons for writing this book and for subtitling it *A Forgotten Holocaust*. I am the product of this beginning and of the endless centuries of perpetual genocidal decimation in an insidious, hidden form of holocaust that needs to be expressed by one who has the pain of this pungent past and present and who tries to understand and do something about it. America has tempered my soul; I thank God and my adoptive country that my progeny will not feel the painful past.

For a better understanding, I would like to describe more fully the organization of the Inca empire and its greatness, explaining why the present-day descendants are in a state of disarray because a European type of culture was implanted that was not suited for the region—or at least was not suitable for the people.

The Inca social structure was hierarchical, with three different social classes: the Inca leader, the nobility, and the people, all having rights and duties. Nevertheless, in this empire there was no discord within classes. They collaborated among themselves for a better future for the society.

The base of the organization was a conglomeration of families of the same lineage, property, language, and religion, which was called Ayllu, a word meaning mutual help, common work, and collective bargaining. The Ayllus were led by a council of elders called curacas. A curaca was usually the eldest among his people and performed the duties of marriage, education, and uniting people for war. The Ayllu was a small world with a magical attraction; the mountains, rivers, caves, and other geographical obstacles were part of this community that created a special unity among the individuals, and were thought to conceal residences of the spirits. Although the Ayllus were pre-Inca, their magnificent social structure was adopted by the Incas as a social system.

The political organization of the empire was headed by the Inca, whose rule was absolute and theocratic, because he was the son of the sun; thus, his mandate was divine.

For the colossal task of governing, the Inca had an imperial advisory representing each region, who resided and worked in centrally located Cuzco. Due to the excellent governing system, the empire was always united because it had one supreme authority, one cult—the sun and the moon—one official language, one single administrative and economic system, and, finally, many well-built roads connecting the four suyos, or regions.

Although there was no system of writing, the Incas had a way of keeping statistics and historical accounts through the quipus, which was a bundle of wool cordons with knots at different points and of different sizes. This quipus could be read only by specialists called quipucamayocs, who were something like today's computer programmers.

To supervise all the officials, the Inca had the help of the tucuyricus, whose name means "the one who sees all." Tucuyricus existed throughout the empire and had the combined authority of a law enforcement agency and a court system, say, an FBI and Supreme Court in one. Thus they made sure that laws were obeyed. They heard petitions and complaints and also administered swift justice.

The greatness of the Inca empire was founded on three factors: political strength, economic organization, and military might. The empire was closely knit, which is why it was powerful, respected, and progressive. The land belonged to the state, and there was no private ownership. Once a person died, the land reverted back to the state and was given to another person who could not sell the lots he received to cultivate. Thus, it became perhaps the first socialist state in the world, along with few advanced civilizations in Europe and Egypt.

The distribution of work in the empire was a must for all, including the Inca himself. They even had a motto, "the one who doesn't work doesn't eat," thus maximizing production. The collective work was divided: for families, for the state, and for the Inca. Laziness was severely punished, and the people's industriousness is well known, as they were masters in textiles, ceramics, and metallurgy. They were famously skilled in work with lead, copper, bronze, silver, and gold, but they had not discovered iron.

The religion of the Inca empire was polytheist. They had many gods: great gods, private gods, and cults of the dead. The great gods were common to all the suyos: Kon was the ocean; Wiracocha was the god of the nobility; Inti was the sun; Quilla was the moon; Collur was the stars; Yllapa was thunder; Mamacocha was the goddess of the ocean; and Pachamama was the god of fertile soil.

The cult of the dead was similar to that in Egypt, and tremendous amounts of time and work were invested to procure all the necessities for the world beyond for the dead. The supreme priest of Coricancha (temple of the sun) in Cuzco was the Villac-Umu, something like today's pope. The Inca temples, those great works of architecture, were so solid that the Spaniards used them as bases on which they constructed their modern Christian sanctuaries. The foreign structures were usually destroyed by earthquakes, but the Inca structures remained impervious to the forces of nature.

Holy days were and still are great festivities that reveal the spiritual sentiment of the people. Among them is Inti-Raymi, which occurs in June and is dedicated to the sun, thanking it for the abundant harvest. In October is the Coya-Raymi, a feminine festivity that is dedicated to the goddess Quilla, the moon.

The art of the Incas, of which one sees vestiges in museums or in ruins, is aesthetically comparable to that of other great civilizations. Their music was pentaphonic, only five notes without intermediate notes, which is why it sounds and feels sad and monotonous. They had wind and percussion instruments, including the quena, flute. Allow me to expand on this for a moment. Readers who have listened to "El Condor Pasa" by the great Peruvian composer Daniel Alomias Robles will feel deep in their hearts the emptiness of the Andes, yet they will be uplifted by the winds of hope, to loft their soul into innermost introspection—because we are one people on this Earth, and all our feelings are the same. Robles is our Beethoven, and "El Condor Pasa" is our Fifth Symphony; the difference is that this Peruvian symphony is from beginning to end an unendurable musical experience of the depths of one's valleys where, alone, one has to uplift oneself to the heights of the spirit and reach the high peaks. For that, one must become a condor and soar into the emptiness of the frigid airless space rising above the mountains and clouds, floating and circling the unending dark valleys, leaving one to ponder what one has gone through to get there. Whereas Beethoven carries one through the deep valleys, he also takes one almost to the crown of the mountains, thus leaving one's soul cleansed and mesmerized with a certain inner peace.

Regarding education, the motto "ama sua, ama-llula, ama-quella" (do not steal, do not lie, do not be lazy) was the great moral principle adopted by the Inca culture. The social classes aspired to practice these teachings—from the sovereign Inca to the last yanacona, or helper. The schools, called Yachayhuasi, were places where members of the royal family and the nobility were educated by the amautas, wise men, who also had a rudimentary knowledge of astronomy, including references to the twelve months and the thirty days of each month. The children of the Ayllus studied such subjects as language, religion, laws, the significance of festivities, and agriculture. Some people were taught the use of herbal medicines: coca as an anesthetic and quinine bark for malaria.

The curacas administered justice in their Ayllus, punishing theft, murder, laziness, and adultery. The Inca and the imperial advisers were the only ones who could dictate the law. For unusual and special crimes, there was swift justice. The punishments were severe, sometimes disproportionate to the crime, and at times were extended to the relatives of the accused.

The infant was raised by the mother, who always took the baby on her back wrapped with a mantle secured to her body so she could have her hands free for work. The children helped their parents and usually learned and followed the occupation of their father. The state was in charge of the elderly, invalids, and widows, who were fed, clothed, and housed—unlike today where one can see so many elders in utter desperation, abandoned by their children, who want to live in overpopulated big cities.

The Quechua language was imposed over all others. It was called Runa-Simi, which means "general language," and there was also a highly stylized Quechua language for the nobility.

The military was well structured, and the Inca was the commander in chief of the army. Troops were divided into groups of men under the command of a close relative to the Inca. Each unit had a flag or banner that portrayed the seven colors of the rainbow and the image of the sun on one side.

The conquest of neighboring nations was peaceful rather than violent. When they tried to annex a nation or Ayllu peacefully, the Incas sent messengers to persuade the enemy to surrender, offering special conditions, at times resorting to bribery to incorporate them into the empire. Once annexed, the people were assimilated and given all considerations, keeping their status and noble titles. If violent action was necessary, the armies penetrated the borders, having previously ascertained the country's strength through spies. The object of their conquest was not to capriciously expand their territory, but to expand Inca culture following the mandates of the mighty Wiracocha god. This was no different than the Spaniards who brought the Catholic religion with them except that the Incas respected others' beliefs, gods, and customs.

Thus we come to the end of this young flourishing civilization that was just getting its foothold, only one hundred years old. One could only imagine what its future would have been if the circumstances had been different. After the great discoveries of the fifteenth and sixteenth centuries, the countries of Renaissance Europe started the conquest and colonization of newly found lands. Spain was the leader in this endeavor, a country that had just liberated itself from a seven-hundred-year Arab occupation.

The Spaniards led many expeditions and conquered many nations, beginning with Mexico by Hernando Cortés, and ending with Peru by Pizarro and Almagro, the prize of all conquests. What made the conquest of Peru possible? The reasons were both internal and external.

The primary internal cause of Peru's downfall was the discontent of the conquered nations in the Inca empire. Many chafed under the rigorous authority of some Curacas, especially when the Incas bribed those elders who were untouchable and abused their powers. The work regimen and the system of mitimaes, forced transfers of groups of people, were also causes of unrest. Although few in number, these opponents still facilitated the invasion and conquest by their desire for revenge against the Incas.

A second internal cause was the civil war between Atahualpa and Huascar and the death of their father, Huayna Capac, which diminished the defense forces of the empire. To this problem was the added surprise of the Indians at the presence of bearded men wearing armor, brandishing shining shields, carrying fine-pointed swords, and creating havoc with their arcabuzes and cannons, which were few but terrifying. The sight of horses especially intimidated the natives; at first they thought that man and beast were a single creature, like a centaur. But this initial fear did not last long, and eventually the desire to fight the intruders culminated in the uprising of Manco II.

The obvious external cause of Peru's downfall was the unstoppable desire of the conquistadors to acquire gold and wealth from the vanquished nations. The ambition of the Spanish royalty and other monarchs to obtain unknown and distant lands stimulated expeditions, giving the conquistadors advantageous treaties, titles of nobility, and privileges. Other Indian nations offered help to the conquistadors, showing them the roads and guiding them to the best economic resources, which explains the facility with which Pizarro took over Cajamarca and forfeited a treaty with Atahualpa after Pizarro got the gold, killing him, thus leaving the Inca empire without spiritual leadership.

After the conquest, there was no exchange of cultures; instead, one replaced the other. From an economic perspective, this "layering" of cultures had tremendous consequences in countries like Mexico and Peru, where their empires had had a manageable and just economy. Eventually, those countries were exploited for the benefit of the conquistadors and the Spanish crown. America became a rich source of raw materials destined to satisfy the needs of the already advanced manufacturing industries of Europe. What was the initial Indian reaction once the fear of horses and of the alien men dissipated? They began to learn to fight the intruders and to defend the Inca empire; however, a few Indians remained afraid and gave aid to the conquistadors, making the expulsion of the Spaniards impossible.

When Francisco Pizarro started his march to Cuzco in 1533, there had already been some Indian uprisings. Pizarro was valiant and intelligent and he sought the advice of the leaders and Orejones, the noblemen of the Inca empire. Upon their advice, he recognized as a successor Inca the younger brother of Atahualpa, Toparpa. This was a diplomatic move, but it did not work because Toparpa was recognized as a puppet Inca, and reaction to Pizarro's trip to Cuzco was hostile in many places. While traveling, the new puppet Inca died of mysterious causes. Guided by General Calcuchimac, Pizarro continued his trip to Cuzco. Eventually, Calcuchimac was accused of killing Toparpa to become emperor himself, for which crime he was burned alive. After a short fight, Pizarro entered Cuzco on November 15, 1533, and immediately took over the sanctuaries and palaces and stripped the city of all its gold and glory.

Since the legitimate Inca Huascar died, the imperial power went to Manco, descendant of Huayna Capac. To appease the Indian masses, Pizarro proclaimed him Manco II. The new ruler was a subject of Spain and he tried to govern the Inca empire in harmony with the Spaniards. However, the conquistadors ransacked the temples, converting them into horse stables and the palaces into forts without respect for the vanquished people's myths and customs.

Once Manco II realized he was an instrument of the Spaniards and only a puppet Inca of a nonexistent monarchy, the stage was set for a general uprising. When the Spaniards asked for more gold, Manco II promised them more bounty from nearby Cuzco. Hernando Pizarro let him go to get the precious metal, but Manco II used his trip as a pretense to reorganize an army, and on March 6, 1536, enormous masses of Indians marched to Cuzco under his leadership, taking over the fortress of Sacsayhuaman.

Just as when Atahualpa was taken hostage at the beginning of the conquest, the fight was again unequal, two hundred Spaniards against thousands of Indians following this new Inca warrior. One cannot dismiss the valor and heroism of the Spaniards, especially the brothers of Francisco Pizarro, Juan, Hernando, and Gonzalo. (Juan Pizarro died in this battle.) The Incas set fire to the city of Cuzco, causing such a sweltering heat that the Spaniards found refuge in the Plaza de Armas, main plaza, and from there defended themselves bravely, causing thousands of Indians to die. The Inca leaders were optimistic because there were other general uprisings in Peru, and the overthrow of the Spaniards seemed possible.

Francisco Pizarro, who founded and lived in Lima, was alarmed by the rebellion in Cuzco, and he requested help from Mexico and Panama, and at the same time sent troops to Cuzco. Meanwhile, the besieged Spaniards in Cuzco, with their arcabuzes and horses, broke out of their sequestration in the plaza and took over the fortress of Sacsayhuaman. The rebellion failed because of the help from Lima and the propitious return to Cuzco of Diego de Almagro (who had tried to conquer Chile but could not), whose returning armies attacked Manco II, completely subduing his troops. Manco II, knowing that he had lost the battle, escaped (possibly to Machu Picchu, a hidden and magnificent fortress). His successors were called Incas of Vilcabamba, and they mounted a continuous but disorganized resistance against the Spaniards.

So much cruelty and grief happened in the following 244 years. Suffice it to say that once Atahualpa was killed, the curacas aroused Indian nationalism to confront and eradicate the invader, beginning with Manco II and leading to Tupac Amaru II in 1780. The newly appointed caciques (a word coined in Central America), supplanting the curacas of the decaying Inca system, became leaders for the benefit of Spain. Some of these newly chosen and handpicked Indian rulers worked side-by-side with the Spanish exploiters, committing horrendous abuses against their own blood brothers to gain personal power.

The Spanish domination of Peru changed the economic and social Inca structure. The Indians quickly changed from the established regimen of subsistence without monetary gain to the new Spanish system that exploited all resources with the main goal of accumulating wealth for others. The transfer of land ownership was drastic. The Incas were accustomed to the collective agrarian system rather than the private property system. Production was no longer for the common good, but for the good of commerce and mercantilism brought from the Old World—itself coming out of the Middle Ages and crumbling feudalism. Obligatory work, accepted dutifully during the Inca empire, was imposed on the Indian, not for his benefit, but for the benefit of the conquistadors who practiced cruel and genocidal exploitation.

From an economic point of view, the Spanish domination specifically meant changing the Inca economic agricultural structure to a mining-based economy. Thus the Indians were displaced from their valleys of productivity to the high inhospitable Andes or cordilleras to work in mines under the most excruciating conditions, where millions died. The new arrivals or colonists wanted to extract gold from any place at any cost, whether it was through human slavery or by annihilation of the Indians.

For the exploitation of resources, the early conquistadors and colonists initially used a system called *los repartimientos*, divisions, in which the Indians were divided into various work forces for agriculture, husbandry, public works, and, the largest force, mining. This system, which abused and enslaved the Indians, was not ordained by the crown. To amend this practice, the crown formed the *encomiendas*, trusts, which instead consisted of entrusting the care of a group of Indians living in a particular area to an *encomendero*, a conquistador to protect the Indians and teach them the Catholic faith. This plan was wishful thinking by the crown, for in the *encomendero* system, the Indians were even more brutally exploited, but now with the backing of the Christian faith and the Spanish monarchy. The abuses were so atrocious that the system was abolished in 1542.

Finally, to correct these systems of exploitation, Spain established the Mita in 1575, which made it obligatory for a group of Indians to work in the mines for one year. This also led to such abuses as discrimination, where the caciques and their relatives were excluded, as well as Indians who could pay their way to freedom. The Mita led to the abandonment of agricultural land and the movement to unfavorable mining areas where the Indians were forced to excavate day and night in the heart of the Andes, without safety precautions, food, clothing, and other basic necessities. Millions lost their lives in falling tunnels and avalanches of earth and rocks. Not surprisingly, the Indians had to feed and clothe themselves, paying exorbitant prices for those necessities in advance, which caused them to have to work longer than the one year stipulated by law, thus making them perpetual slaves to the mines.

The Mita system caused the annihilation of entire segments of the rural population due to sickness, fatigue, and profound grief. Added to this insult, the Indians had to leave their families, who were then left completely helpless and without protection. Thus, the true social picture of the Indians of the time (and even now) was the exploitation of men by men, the exploiters going by different names: the *encomendero* (guardian); the *corregidor* (overseer); the rural Catholic priest (cura); and finally, the Indian cacique.

In all these ways, the Indians were maltreated by all social classes, and even worse, by their own blood brothers. But the Indians were patient in all areas of work and they labored without complaining. The only thing they had was common land for common use, the Ayllu, which the conquistadors and colonists and—after independence—the republic took away from them. These actions left this race in a state of complete bewilderment, which they are still in to this day, a legacy of moral destruction and distrust that has created a special personality with its own characteristics. Perhaps, historically, the problem was already among the Indian nations of the Andes, according to chronicles like that of Pedro Cieza de Leon. At times they were hard on each other, and God knows, our indigenous subconscious is made up of centuries, if not millenniums, of despotism. Those are the forces that mold a nation, and the predominantly Indian countries have not defined themselves yet; they are in constant turmoil and continuously changing as blood and cultures intermingle and also as the world shrinks with the modern times.

The social classes that developed in the Peruvian colony of the 1500s to 1800s were the product of opposite extremes: the Inca empire where the main activity was the institutional mandate of work according to the capacity of each group; and the colony where work was mandated by powerful intruders whose only interest was to get rich. Therefore, the following classes were formed: the nobility, including conquistadors who were given noble titles for their conquering efforts; and criollos, sons of the conquistadors, who were born in Peru. The high upper class included conquistadors who got rich on their own efforts and bought noble titles; bureaucrats who came with titles of nobility (such as viceroy); industrialists who were able to buy titles; and the clergy.

The middle class of colonial Peru consisted of Spaniards and criollos without nobility or title, but who had some wealth and also included the professionals, lawyers, and doctors, even if they were mestizos. This class looked for more benefits for themselves and were the main instigators of the emancipation of Peru, concluding with independence from the Spanish yoke under such leaders as Simón Bolívar and José de San Martín.

The lower class was made up of Spaniards, criollos, and mestizos who worked at lower-level or manual jobs and who lived in poverty. The Indians, who were the true owners of Peru and its great Tahuantinsuyo lands, became the dominated and enslaved class. Although they were considered from the beginning as subjects of the crown, the Spanish kings passed laws to prevent abuse of the Indians, but these efforts were only theoretical. This lower class of Indians and mestizos was the one that suffered the most by exploitation, despotism, and inhuman treatment. To this day, there are still visible in both body and spirit remnants of the excesses that will take a long time to eradicate; and I am not certain when it is going to happen.

The lower class consisted also of blacks, called in Spanish "negros." The blacks were introduced as slaves after the Indians were almost exterminated. The few remaining Indians began to rebel against forced work. The African slaves worked mainly in the coastal areas on big farmlands, and as in the United States of days gone by, they also were servants in magnificent, pompous houses of the landowners of the big latifundios, plantations.

I would like to end this brief history with a description of the rebellion in 1780 of Tupac Amaru II, who epitomizes the state of affairs in Peru. The hero of all time, Tupac Amaru II, or José Gabriel Condorcanqui, descended from the Incas on his maternal side. As described above, the abuses in the colony were intolerable and had reached a point of no return. The rebellion led by Tupac Amaru started by asking for social justice, not only for all Indians, but also for mestizos, blacks, and even Spaniards. Thus started the first fight for independence from Spanish rule, similar to the efforts of George Washington and other great Americans, except that Tupac Amaru was a native South American who had the same ideals of freedom and justice for all.

The rebellion took place a few miles south of Cuzco on November 4, 1780. This cacique took hostage and prisoner the abusive corregidor Don Antonio de Arriaga, who was quickly executed.

After the execution, Tupac Amaru marched on, accompanied by Indians who adhered to his cause, armed with simple agricultural implements and few firearms. They won a few battles due more to their numbers than true military effectiveness. Instead of taking Cuzco when he could have, Tupac Amaru went to his place of birth, Tinta, and wrote a manifesto explaining the reasons for the uprising. Then he traveled extensively for months, explaining his cause and gaining more followers. After about a year, however, the viceroy of Peru, Don Agustín de Jauregui, sent troops to Cuzco under the command of the Visitador José Antonio de Areche, giving him extraordinary powers to end this uprising.

The Spanish reinforcements arrived and stationed themselves in Cuzco. Tupac Amaru, unfortunately, at this very disadvantageous time, decided to take the imperial city of Cuzco, but by then it was too late. The Spaniards with all their might went to Tinta looking for Tupac Amaru, where they fought, defeating the townspeople and razing the city. The would-be Inca leader, his wife, and three children escaped to the village of Langui, where they were soon taken prisoner with the help of traitors among his ranks. What happened next is worth describing to realize the cruelty of the times and to give the reader a feeling of perhaps why the Indians are what they are. The following account is translated from the classic history of this event, the martyrdom of Tupac Amaru.

Once taken prisoner, Tupac Amaru, his family, and loyal followers were immediately sent to Cuzco, where Tupac Amaru entered the imperial city in heavy chains riding on a mule. They were kept in an old Jesuit seminary. Immediately the process of "justice" began by Oidor (Judge) Matalinares. Meanwhile, El Visitador (viceroy representative) Areche humiliated the conquered rebel with lashings and torture, interrogating him about other collaborators. A true hero, Tupac Amaru kept quiet. Eventually, he broke his silence, answering Areche defiantly, "Here there are no more collaborators than you and I—you because you are an oppressor, and I because I am a liberator, and we both deserve to die." This attitude of Tupac Amaru, which was nothing less than heroic and stoic, gained him the punishment of having his arm fractured. But he still kept quiet like a true Indian who has tolerated for centuries criminal tortures in the forced labor of the mines.

By now, however, this Inca hero was weakened and feeble. The Spaniards then expedited the justice process. Finally, he was sentenced to die, and three days later on Friday, May 18, 1781, Tupac Amaru was tortured to death.

The execution was carried out in the cruelest way possible and deserves to be described, especially for those who have no notion of what happened to the Indians and why. It is imperative that stories like this be told to help the American people understand the plight of the Indians.

The execution of Tupac Amaru occurred in the center of Cuzco's main plaza. The Spaniards assembled a makeshift scaffold from which to hang many of his followers. The plaza was surrounded by soldiers with arms readied and fitted with bayonets. The prisoners were brought in, walking behind the horses of the high officers and church officials. In macabre succession they climbed to the hanging wooden plank floor and were hanged by the neck—Tupac Amaru's loyal collaborators Berdejo Castelo, Bastidas, and a black man named Oblitas. Then came the eldest son of Tupac Amaru, Hipolito, and his aging uncle, Francisco, who had the added punishment before hanging of having their tongues cut out. Meanwhile, all this was witnessed by Tupac Amaru. There were also Peruvian women, true to the cause of Tupac Amaru, whose courage was also punished by death. First came the cacica (female cacique) Conde Mayta, who was garroted on the hanging platform. Then came Doña Michaela Bastidas, the wife of Tupac Amaru, who helped her husband in all his endeavors and who fought side-by-side until their supreme sacrifice of death together. She climbed the scaffold and refused to have her tongue cut out as was planned by the ver-dugo, executioner. Instead, he had to cut out her tongue after she died. Because of her thin neck, the garroting did not immediately kill her and while still alive, the executioners put her out of her misery with horrendous kicks to the stomach and breasts, eventually killing this heroine.

After having seen all this with his own eyes, it was finally Tupac Amaru's turn to die. He had suffered perhaps the cruelest of punishments seeing his own loved ones die so violently. It was now his turn for glory, ending forever what he had seen. He was taken to the center of the plaza, his tongue was cut out, then he was placed in the center of four horses and each arm and leg was tied to one of those inno-cent, powerful animals. One can imagine the sounds and the time it took to prepare this final sacrifice! Then came a hand signal from the powerful Spaniard, pointing to the infinite sky, telling the skilled horsemen to pull Tupac Amaru apart in all four opposite directions. These apocalyptic, strong, beautiful horses were unable to break apart this fortress of a man. For a while Tupac Amaru resisted, shaking his body with the last strength in his being, hearing his youngest son Fernando, who was forced to witness his father's death, cry with an anguish that must have echoed for years to come in the ears of those people who heard him. Finally, the Visitador

Areche, perhaps with a minuscule amount of human-ity, ordered Tupac Amaru decapitated. Then the peaceful mutilated bodies of Tupac Amaru and his wife; Doña Michaela, dead but forever alive in their glory, were burned and their ashes thrown into the Huatany River (where I used to play as a child, not knowing that this river was sacred with the remains of their glory and the anguish of such a grotesque death). Added to this infamy, the heads and extrem-ities of both Tupac Amaru II and his wife were taken to different churches of Cuzco and placed on spikes to warn any rebels of the possible future conse-quences of uprisings.

Thus, with a hand painful from scribbling these passages and with tears in my eyes after reading, translating, and writ-ing about these events, I have tried to explain why this his-tory is in my veins. Although America the beautiful has been good to me, it cannot erase this pain I feel for my people; worse yet, there is little I can do to help them, but at least I can let you know that the Indians are still in chains and they will be for a long time. With the passage of the ages and gen-erations, perhaps their pain will cease, but meanwhile, let's try to understand them. But how? I do not know. They are human and have the same faults that we all have, and getting to their hardened hearts may be more than we can imagine, but let us try!

I am still young enough to do more and, I hope, to become the fifteenth Inca or, as Harry Owens used to call me, "the last Inca." We will see; maybe it will happen. You will hear from me.

Acknowledgments

I want to thank my daughter, Anja Helene Sánchez-Lasthaus, for her spiritual intuition in deciphering my doctor's prescription–like handwritten manuscript, thereby making this book possible.

I appreciate and thank my wife, Dorothy, for her understanding and support.

Finally, I want to thank the many people who gave me moral support to go on with this book and those who showed me the path into the wonderful world of writing and publishing: Mary Huntley-Kaufman, Viqi Wagner, Jeff Paris, Beverly Trainer, Deborah Mosley, Lynn Hovland, Norma Sierra and Robert Martin.

For all inquiries about this book
please refer to the publisher:

CARLOS J. SANCHEZ M.D., INC.
1635 Third Ave., #J
Chula Vista, CA 91911
Phone (619) 426-8121
Fax (619) 426-5950
E-Mail—CONDORSOUL@AOL.COM

The author is an active member of the following organizations:

- Fellow of the American Academy of Pediatrics
- Diplomate of the American Board of Pediatrics
- Assistant Clinical Professor of Pediatrics, University of California, San Diego, School of Medicine.
- American Medical Association
- California Medical Association
- San Diego County Medical Society
- Past President of the California Hispanic American Medical Association–CHAMA San Diego Chapter
- Peruvian American Medical Society–PAMS

The proceeds of this book will go toward fulfilling my dream of building a hospital boat in the Peruvian Amazon, and a clinic in Andahuaylillas.